Writing for
Design Professionals

Writing for Design Professionals

A Guide to Writing Successful Proposals, Letters, Brochures, Portfolios, Reports, Presentations, and Job Applications for Architects, Engineers, and Interior Designers

STEPHEN A. KLIMENT

W. W. NORTON & COMPANY
NEW YORK • LONDON

FOR FELICIA

Sine qua non

Copyright © 1998 by Stephen A. Kliment

Printed in the United States of America
First Edition

For information about permission to reproduce selections from this book,
write to Permissions, W. W. Norton & Company, Inc., 500 Fifth Avenue
New York, NY 10110.

The text of this book is composed in Garamond and Futura
with the display set in Bodega
Manufacturing by Hamilton Printing Company
Book design by Gilda Hannah

Library of Congress Cataloging-in-Publication Data

Kliment, Stephen A.
Writing for design professionals : a guide to writing successful proposals,
letters, brochures, portfolios, reports, presentations, and job applications for
architects, engineers, and interior designers / Stephen A. Kliment
p. cm.
Includes bibliographical references and index.

ISBN 0-393-73026-3

1. Architectural services marketing—United States. 2. Engineering services
marketing—United States. 3. Design services—United States—Marketing.
NA1996.K57 19   9898-29153
808'.0662—dc21   CIP

W. W. Norton & Company, Inc., 500 Fifth Avenue, New York, N.Y. 1011
http://www.wwnorton.com

W. W. Norton & Company Ltd., 10 Coptic Street WC1A 1PU

0 9 8 7 6 5 4 3 2 1

Contents

Acknowledgments

Many people contributed to the birth of this book, knowingly or innocently. I thank Steve Ross, who knows more about electronic hardware and software than I can ever hope to, for sharing with me over the years nuggets from his treasure house of learning, and for reviewing the chapter on on-line communications.

Dean William Mitchell at the School of Architecture and Planning at Massachusetts Institute of Technology and Dean John Meunier at the School of Architecture, Arizona State University, gave me useful insights into the arcane mores of academic writing.

Much practical wisdom about the underlying objectives of design business writing came from design professionals such as Bradford Perkins, Norman Kurtz, Charles Baskett, Gene Kohn, Roz Brandt; Rachel Towle at the Walker Group/CNI; Paul Segal, Steve Davis; Tom Zurowski and his partners at Eastlake Studio; Peter Bohlin, Will Bruder, Bill Rawn; John Kane at Architekton; and many others whose paths have crossed mine over the years.

For enlightening me on the subtleties of writing to global markets, I am indebted to Leslie Robertson, Herb McLaughlin, and two of Herb's colleagues who direct the firm's Asian work, Lena Ning Zhang and Ken Minohara.

I also thank the following individuals: Tony de Alteriis for sharing with me two mordant letters to the editor of the London Times on e-mail etiquette; Catherine Teegarden, coordinator for the New York City–based Architecture-in-the-Schools program, who arranged for me to reproduce in chapter 1 examples of clear, unspoiled writing by grade-school students; Suzanne Stephens, Robert Campbell, and Paul Goldberger for their exemplary blend of content and style when writing about architecture and design; Richard Fitzgerald and Michael Hough for their clear vision of the design professional's information needs; Richard Blowes and Marian Seamans of the Town of Southampton, New York, for making available request-for-proposal documents on the town's projected community recreation center; Pat Lambert for scrupulously photographing my artwork; and Nancy Palmquist of W. W. Norton for her superlative editing of my copy.

Special appreciation is due chairman Donald Ryder, Stephanie Smith, and professors Gordon Gebert and Judy Connorton at the School of Architecture and Environmental Studies at City College of New York for their support of my course on verbal skills. I thank Dean Cynthia Weese and Professor Jo Noero at the School of Architecture, Washington University, St. Louis, and Assistant Dean William Saunders at the Graduate School of Design, Harvard University, for encouraging me in teaching verbal skills to their students.

Indeed, I owe a special debt to my students and former students at those places, as well as to my former editorial colleagues at John Wiley & Sons, Whitney Library of Design, and Architectural Record. They contributed to my education more than they can ever realize.

I commend my daughters, Pamela and Jennifer, for helping me keep in proper perspective the once explosive issue of gender-conscious language.

Gordon Bunshaft and Pietro Belluschi separately provided the spurs for my embarking on journalism as a career.

Jean Labatut, Donald Egbert, Jean Lajarrige, and Bill Caudill were my mentors at crucial times. They instilled in me standards of clarity in design and writing for which I continue to strive.

Finally, this book would not have taken shape without the support, encouragement, and vision of excellence of my editor at W. W. Norton, Nancy Green.

Foreword
by Hugh Hardy FAIA

Here it is at last, a professional Baedeker for the written word. In this single volume you will find all forms of verbal expression appropriate to professional life. As successful design practitioners know, words and images are linked together as an intrinsic part of professional life. No matter how compelling their designs, all professionals are required to present themselves and their work using words, and all clients begin the process of design with a verbal expression of their needs. As each project passes through its several stages of development, verbal explanation is required. In fact all the steps required to make the built environment, from concept through construction, require the skillful use of words. Although some professionals use the written language to obscure their intent, believing mystery can increase their allure, such foolishness is quickly dispelled by this volume's direct admonitions: "Keep it Simple," "Be Specific," and "Shun Jargon."

Just as the sensitive designer recognizes the need to use varied visual vocabularies to solve diverse design problems, the skillful author must choose the appropriate form of written expression to suit his need. Proposals require a sensibility different from that employed by print media. All the appropriate forms can be found in these pages. In some cases examples of verbose and opaque communication are contrasted with skillful and concise prose showing how simply ideas can be directly conveyed. In other cases, sample letters and documents show how to write clearly.

Kliment's emphasis upon the audience's need to understand and the designer's need to avoid "Designer Babble" is typical of the book's calm authority. While some may delight in verbal pyrotechnics, this volume's merit lies in its insistence upon reaching the public, not showing off to fellow professionals. Clear communication and business success are interrelated, and taking these pages to heart cannot help but enhance a designer's economic prowess.

Of course a book about writing must itself be exemplary in the use of language, and this volume is a model of lucid prose. Often laced with humor, it gently challenges the reader to respect and delight in the rich and supple language we share. In the pages which follow, good writing becomes not only desirable but also obtainable for everyone. This is a splendid and lively primer, guaranteed to be a stimulating companion for any professional.

Why Writing Matters: An Introduction

"A few million years ago, man [and woman] picked [their] knuckles off the floor and began to walk upright. [They] learned to control fire, use rocks and sticks as tools, and grunt in ways that actually meant something to [their] companions. A few thousand millennia later, we've learned to control the atom, bend everything in nature to our particular use, and communicate via digitized transmissions. Now our grunts can be heard instantly around the world." This observation, which appeared in 1997 in *Asenta,* a Ghanaian newspaper published in New York City, puts in perspective how far we have come in communicating, but it says almost nothing about the quality of our communication. We have advanced from gouged rocks and tablets through quills, metal pens, and typewriters to word processors and e-mail. Too often, however, our messages come across with the clarity of grunts.

A nineteenth-century guide to writing cited in 1997 by Alan Robbins in a column in the *New York Times* offered seven ideals of good letter writing. Letters had to be clear, correct, complete, courteous, concise, conversational, and considerate. Not a bad set, when you apply them to today's great array of communication types and media. Clearly, they not only call for basic humaneness when writing to clients or professional colleagues, but also highlight the strictly practical need for writing text so the recipient gets the message straight and without having to consult a dictionary.

Writing (and speaking) well is important to all design professionals and students, and also to their clients, consultants, suppliers of building products, and contractors services. You write to cause action. You write to a client prospect because you want an interview, or to submit credentials, or to respond to a request for proposals (RfP). You write to current or past clients to be remembered when new projects arise, or to be recommended to others. You communicate with team associates and consultants to keep the current project on track. You contact the media to get your work published, or to have an editor use you as a resource. You connect with your peers or competitors for an association or a joint venture, or because they serve on selection committees.

As a student, you write well to get good grades, or to get a thesis or dissertation accepted. As a faculty member, good writing helps you with promotion or tenure. As a professional, you often must communicate with citizens' groups to get facts about a project across so that the project can proceed. You confer, in writing or verbally, with your employees because it's important to have

Many help-wanted advertisements demand some level of communication skills.

happy campers. Sometimes you communicate with the financial community if you happen to own or work for a design firm with publicly traded stock.

Take a swift look at the help-wanted pages of any newspaper or professional newsletter. Notice the high ratio of jobs that demand some level of communication skills; most of the time employers actually spell it out—e.g., "candidate must possess communication skills."

Effective writing is an unerring career advancer. Review the great range of end products that call for expertise in writing:

Article
Brochure/portfolio/fact sheets
CD-ROM
Design award submittal
E-mail
In-house memorandum
Job application/resume
Marketing correspondence
Newsletter
Press release
Promotional or advertising copy
Proposal
Report
Text on display panel or board
Speech
Student assignment
Web site

Writing categories can also be divided by objective:

Marketing: Responding to RfPs. Correspondence. Design award submittals and exhibit boards. Client newsletters. Spoken and multimedia presentations. Press releases. Brochures and portfolios. Standard Forms 254 and 255. Promotional copy. Personal job applications.

Project-related: Client, project team, and in-house correspondence. Research, feasibility, and planning reports.

Academic Advancement: Faculty—Reports. Writing for learned journals. Applications for promotion or tenure. Student—Course assignments. Theses and dissertations. Text and labels on display boards. Job applications.

Publicity: Approaching the media and getting published. Building descriptions. Design criticism. Technical or practice articles.

Product literature: Direct mail copy. Advertising copy.

Written products can also be classified by media:

Printed.
Graphic: Hand-drawn, CAD, transparency, video, animation.
Spoken: Speech (face to face, voice mail).
Electronic: e-mail, the Web, CD-ROM.

There are a number of points you should keep in mind as you read and use this book.

The medium does have an impact on the message, as the following chapters point out. I keep a quill, an ancient fountain pen, and my old Lettera 22 typewriter next to my word processor. They remind me that the character of the medium helps determine whether the message is (or can afford to be) extensive or succinct, more (or less) legible, in color, illustrated, easily saved, deliberately stored without reading, or promptly discarded.

Remember your audience. The principles I spell out in these chapters are central and necessary, and you can apply them with comfort to anything you write—provided you remember your audience. When addressing a scholarly colloquium on the finer points of stylistic iconography of late–Middle Age cathedral gargoyles, you can risk a higher level of jargon than when speaking to a school architect selection committee that may include a veterinarian, a service station manager, a company CFO, and a head of household. Even when submitting your credentials or delivering a two-inch report to the facilities chief at IBM or to a contracting officer at GSA—all people with, one assumes, a professional background—keep in mind that final decisions typically are made higher up, by top executives and administrators to whom your jargon may be so much gobbledygook.

I have known architects who claim that part of their charisma is the knack of conveying a bit of mystery about their line of work when speaking to a selection committee or at a community meeting. They are not the only professionals to use this technique. Doctors, lawyers, generals, ministers, even barbers and car salespeople, have been known to invoke this "I know best" ruse. It is not a good technique. We live in the age of the Internet, the Freedom of Information Act, and intense public curiosity. Frankness, clarity, and honesty are expected of those with special skills and responsibilities.

Remember who *you* are. This book is not designed to spawn a generation of writers whose every letter, memo, or pronouncement is identical in style to everyone else's. One of the qualities that those who hire you look for is uniqueness and personality, and you cannot project uniqueness unless you define your image and that of your organization. Personality will ultimately creep into your writing. Such attributes as hip, formal, cool, folksy, conservative, and kooky will—and certainly should—show through in what you write. I know of one architectural firm that was designing a college facility for a country the head of whose royal house was taking an active part in the project's progress. The firm, known for the informality of its contacts with the world around it, addressed all its prospects and clients with a simple salutation—"Heather:" or "Kevin:." No "Dear." How, then, to address His Majesty? No problem. "King:." The good relationship survived. Another example of such an informal approach appears in chapter 2.

This book's focus is on the written word, on-line communication, and, to some degree, speech. While multimedia presentations, including animation, are closely connected with written text, the topic's intricacy takes it beyond the scope of the book. Refer to one of the excellent works included in the Resources.

The instructional method I have used in this book consists of narrative text supplemented by examples. Examples are often in the form of scenarios, such as a marketing situation or a school writing assignment, followed by a sample response, and rounded out by comments. Names of firms used in the scenarios are fictitious, except when otherwise stated. Because the design professions are made up overwhelmingly of small firms, many of the examples are geared to modest-sized practices.

Writing should work for you and not against you. For that to happen, certain forms of style, grammar, and syntax (defined as "the due arrangement of word forms to show their mutual relations in the sentence") are known to communicate well, whereas other forms are known to fail. In my years of work with architectural and other design firms, as well as with students, I have come to recognize the difference.

Know your recipient. The nation's most successful firms got there in large part because they deliberately research their clients, then address them in ways that engage the client's personality and temperament. And the best firms carry this off without diluting their own integrity.

Always define to yourself in advance exactly the point or points you want to make, and why. This is a fail-safe method to successful communication. Do this, and the rest will flow easily through your fingers into your keyboard and out to your audience.

Finally, be aware that corporate and public facility clients are consistently appalled by the turgid quality of writing delivered by designers who want to do business with them. So are discriminating deans at the professional design schools, who worry about the level of writing they see among students and faculty. And the general public continues to wonder why designers, when they write and talk, do not make more sense.

This book is your chance to reverse course, and do yourself some good.

Principles of Writing for Impact

1

The eight principles of good writing that comprise this chapter are designed more as a guide to good writing than as a formula approach. The chapter covers hurdles and pitfalls that may obscure your meaning, trespass on the grounds of political correctness, or yield to the temptation to be clever or elegant but not clear.

Every age has its values and its standards. This is as true for writing as it is for sports, nutrition, ethics, and design. The nineteenth-century guide to letter writing cited in the Introduction stated that letters had to be clear, correct, complete, courteous, concise, conversational, and considerate. These are still excellent guides and, given the evolution of writing technology, far-sighted. You can apply them today not only to letters but also to all the other end products of a designer's and student's day-to-day output. Especially "courteous." Courtesy, in the old-fashioned sense of elaborate greeting and sumptuous valediction—the French until recently favored the delectable ending "please accept the assurance of my most distinguished sentiments"—is today more restrained, especially in the case of e-mail, as we shall see in chapter 11.

The aim of the eight principles is to serve as an alert for bad sentence forms that obscure your meaning, for word choices that don't fit the level of understanding of your receiver, for human touches that will enhance understanding, and, last but not least, to highlight the advantage of writers who know precisely what they want to say. Beware of the albatross carried by anyone who is ready to write but isn't clear as to the message.

1. Write as You Would Talk

Many people talk with comfort but freeze when compelled to write. There's an odd but widely held perception that writing is different from speech, that a certain formality is required that differentiates writing from speech. As an editor, I had a letter from an author some years ago who, having told me in one-syllable phrases by phone that his article would be late, followed it up with a letter that included this: "the eventuality of [the article] getting to you in time is problematical." Another writer, urging architects to aspire to greater public respect, wrote that "architects must increase their upward migration capabilities." The perception that writing is somehow different from talking is more at the root of pompous, hard-to-grasp language than nearly any other cause.

Read this example from actual project correspondence.

> Implementation of the construction program's first phase will be initiated as soon as proper authorization is received.

No professional would talk this way to another professional. You have to read it twice before the sun of meaning pokes through the clouds. The project manager is merely writing—after perhaps having raised the subject verbally—to say that work will go ahead as soon as a written okay arrives.

Try fixing the sentence, then compare it with a suggested solution. Don't, however, go to the lengths that the brilliant verbal stylist, the late architect William Caudill, might have gone ("Say 'frog'; we'll jump").

> We'll start construction as soon as authorized.

2. Keep Sentences Short

Great eighteenth-century writers often rolled out page-long sentences. It was an era when readers had time to plow through such prose. It was hard to write and authors honed it to a fine skill. Nor are today's design professionals in the business of emulating the multipage literary stream-of-consciousness excursions of a James Joyce. The goal today is to keep sentences short. It's easier to make a point clearly if you try not to exceed eighteen words per sentence (this sentence has seventeen words). Avoid cramming in too many ideas—one idea per sentence is plenty.

Read the following example from a proposal.

> Our multi-disciplinary team offers not only capabilities in space programming, site planning, architectural design, structural, mechanical, and electrical engineering, but also provides services in the areas of financial feasibility studies and environmental assessment, as well as in the administration of the construction contract and in the development of post-occupancy monitoring systems, all of which are critical elements in the successful implementation of a viable construction program.

Here the meaning is hidden in a jungle of verbiage. Try to pinpoint the several ideas, and make each one into a separate sentence. One solution:

> Our multi-disciplinary team offers these services:
> - Space programming, site planning, architectural design including construction contract administration, as well as structural, mechanical, and electrical engineering.
> - Financial feasibility studies and environmental assessments.
> - Development of post-occupancy monitoring systems.
>
> These services are critical to a viable construction program.

3. Shun Jargon or "Designer-Babble"

Do not confuse jargon with technical terminology. Every profession has its terminology, a kind of shorthand that allows its members to talk with one another without defining every word. Designer-babble is different. Not only does it use technical terms with audiences that do not understand them; it invents words and phrases that confuse the public and may cause even hip professionals to run to the lexicon or throw up their hands in despair. As David Chappell said, jargon "tends to be the last resort of those with nothing much to say."

Acceptable are technical terms such as "decibel," "BTU," "lumens," or "pediment." Each describes an object, standard, or condition that could not be stated differently without a long description.

On the other hand, terms such as "space modality," projects that are "either investigative or accommodative," "iconicity," and "contrapuntal juxtaposition" are at best a pernicious effort to invent new terms in hope that they will enter the common language, or are at worst a futile self-indulgence on the part of their inventor.

For examples of unavoidable technical or design terms, see the following list:

ashlar	honeycombing	plenum
brownfield	Howe truss	purlin
BTU	hypocaust	quoin
caisson	impluvium	rafter
camber	isometric,	register (as an hvac
capital	axonometric	component)
CFC	joist	repoussé
chlorosulphonated	King post truss	reverberation time
polyethylene	layer (as in CAD)	seismic code
CMU	linenfold	shear
corbel	lintel	shim
decibel	lumens	slump
egg-and-dart	mimbar	spandrel (historical,
elevation	mitigation	contemporary
emission	module	meanings)
emissivity	narthex	torchère
English, Flemish, Dutch	oculus	Vierendeel truss
bond	overmantel	VOC
entourage	parging	voussoir, keystone
glulam	parti	web, flange
hacking	pediment	withe

Now read the following sentence from a building review.

> Colliding volumes provided a convincing contemporary interpretation of spatial transparency, as extrapolated by an axiomatic juxtaposition of superficial tension.

A thought appears to be fighting to break through, but the rest is conjecture. Perhaps the author had in mind the notion that two intersecting building parts were glass-faced so you could see through them (that's the first part of the sentence). The second part is anyone's guess, but it possibly carried the idea that when next to each other, the same two buildings had a bigger impact than when alone. But who can tell?

Here are some other examples of designer-babble. Chapter 7 contains suggested solutions to three examples.

They are articulating their experiential experience. *(refers to a house client)*
Justifying [the result] by their contrapuntal juxtaposition. *(description of a design)*
Formal strategies are consistent. . . . The detailing ethic is the same—it's for ever. *(description of a design)*
Projects are either investigative or accommodative. *(profile of a firm)*
To maintain its cultural, social and moral value in the face of the media, architecture can no longer rely on its imagery, iconicity alone . . . *(excerpt from text accompanying an architect's submittal to a major international competition)*
Activating axiomatic topologies of non-nomadic tribal elements . . . have been interpreted within the archaeological context of the site . . . *(comment by design award judge)*

4. Be Specific

On-line communication and the precision of the computer have little tolerance for the loose and the imprecise. An on-line search can be prolonged indefinitely by not being specific enough. But the need for precision isn't limited to the on-line message; it is a key ingredient of clear communication in any medium. Don't write "bring to reality" when you mean "build"; say "partition," not "divider element"; when discussing a building's security system, someone who might break in is an "intruder," not an "unauthorized level of access person." Avoid inexact space wasters such as "interesting," "impressive," "basically," and "situation"—as in "interview situation." They are filler words and, unless defined, add nothing to your message. Note that use of a vague term where a specific one would work better often stems from vagueness of thought, and in such cases if the thought can be sharpened the words will come. As Nicolas Boileau-Despréaux wrote, "It is easy to state clearly that which is clearly understood."

Consider the following sentence from a proposal introduction.

> The self-contained instructional space—a splendid teaching medium for a specific objective—is simply inadequate for other tasks.

Work on the term "self-contained instructional space," then compare your answer with a solution, below.

> The enclosed classroom, superb for some types of instruction, simply won't work for other tasks.

5. Keep It Simple

Along with being specific you need to keep your writing simple. Today's client has neither the time nor the patience to wade through seas of murky prose. Whenever construction carries on after strikes by the electrician and sheet metal trades, don't write the client that "circumstances now allow for an effectuation of a resumption of construction." Or why take up space with "optimum" when "best" will do? Here are some other dos and don'ts.

Don't use: optimum, initiate, implement, aspirations, maximum, utilize.
Do use: best, start, carry out, hopes, most, use.

> Reluctance to engage expert consultants is often considered under contemporary management practices to be an inefficient utilization of resources.

Fix the above example from a marketing letter. See how your own wording compares with this solution.

> It pays to use consultants.

Or, in a lighter vein,

> "If you have a dog, why bark?"

On occasion, local groups of design professionals agree to write and circulate to clients—especially inexperienced clients—guides to various aspects of the design and construction process. In 1996 the Boston Society of Architects and DPIC, a liability insurance group, prepared a lucid series of such booklets. Topics included fast-track scheduling, value engineering, and the handling of Requests for Information (RFIs) during construction. See the following good excerpt from these documents.

WHAT EVERY OWNER NEEDS TO KNOW ABOUT RFIs

When a contractor has a question about the plans or specifications for a project, a request for information (RFI) is submitted to the architect or engineer who created the document. The design professional reviews the RFI and responds to the contractor with the requested additional information or a clarification. The RFI process is a normal and necessary element of the construction phase of a project. It allows the design professional to fine-tune the construction documents by providing answers to reasonable questions from the contractor. When used by competent and well-meaning parties for its intended purpose, the procedure works very well.

Abuse of the Process

The abuse or excessive use of RFIs is another story. Increasingly, some contractors generate unnecessary RFIs at the drop of a hard hat, often when a simple review of the construction documents and other available data would reveal the required information. A contractor who uses the RFI process in this manner is really attempting to unfairly shift its responsibility for thorough document review to the architect or engineer.

Unnecessary RFIs can result from a variety of factors. By far, the most ominous is the contractor who intentionally abuses the RFI process in order to pave the way for claims for extras and delays.

If the contractor is in a severe time or money squeeze, he or she may look to the RFI process for financial salvation. The desperate contractor may attempt to build a case for extras and delays by issuing urgent RFIs for every reason he or she can invent. By the end of the project, the total number of RFIs (legitimate and otherwise) may reach into the hundreds or even thousands.

In so doing, the contractor buries the design professional in paper and forces him or her into "unacceptably" long response times. (The infamous Denver Airport project, for instance, reportedly had over 12,000 RFIs filed—many of which were later deemed unnecessary.) This then gives the contractor the pretext to later sue the owner for delays and extras, citing the designer as the cause of the problem. The Germans have a word for it: papierkrieg. It means "paper war' or the art of obfuscation by bureaucracy. That's exactly what happens when the use of RFIs is allowed to get out of hand.

I often look back at material written by myself and members of my family in grade school and wonder at the frank, uncomplicated expression of thoughts. So, when in the spring of 1997 I was invited to view an exhibit of written work and sketches by a group of third-grade children, I hurried over. The show was put on under New York City's architecture-in-the-schools program, sponsored by the New York Chapter of the American Institute of Architects and the New York Foundation for Architecture. I looked to see whether perhaps the next generation knows something that we have managed to unlearn.

I wasn't disappointed. Look at the illustration opposite, sample result of an assignment in which the teacher asked the children to describe a building and what architects do. Note the student's simplicity of language and ability to convey a flood of meaning in very few words.

6. Use the Active Sentence Form

The men and women who teach creative writing in our colleges dwell heavily on the need to use active verb forms to grab and retain the reader's interest. "Jack loves Jane" sparkles; the passive form "Jane is loved by Jack" is dull. The same good advice holds true when design professionals and students write. Apply this advice consistently, and you'll greatly sharpen your impact, as you can see in these before and after examples.

> It is intended that AutoCAD Release 14 will be utilized and files plotted to devices using Windows NT Print Manager drivers.
> *(from a proposal letter)*

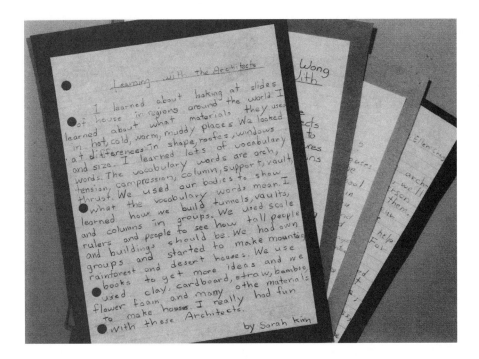

Try turning this sentence around, then check your result with the new version.

> We intend to use AutoCAD Release 14 and to plot files to devices using Windows NT Print Manager drivers.

7. Don't Forget People

We are a people-focused culture. The general media have boosted sales for years by casting their stories around an individual. *People* magazine made an instant hit by focusing its entire contents on people. The professional design media are now taking their cue from this universal trait of human nature, and more and more of their articles, even cover stories, dwell on the personality and performance of designers and their colleagues.

If you intend to capture the interest of a selection committee or a powerful patron, you need to mix in with your writing a generous dusting of human references. Clients are more likely to identify with a message if it is styled with people involved, rather than as a dry-as-dust task by an anonymous presence. Avoid this example from a firm's quarterly newsletter.

> Past costs and schedules on similar projects are analyzed in order to achieve viable final cost estimates and realistic completion dates.

Try the following instead.

> Our firm's cost estimators under Jane Vega analyze past projects to arrive at realistic final cost estimates for your project. Oscar Choudhury and his project managers review previous job schedules to come up with a feasible schedule for our clients.

8. Know What You Want to Say

A virtually foolproof technique for clear writing is to decide first what you want to say. What is your basic message? Write it down in a single sentence (see some examples below). Test the sentence on colleagues. Break it into its several parts. Show these as a bulleted list—a progression of points. Is the progression logical? Will the link from one bulleted item to the next be clear to the reader or listener? Then start to write.

TYPICAL BASIC SENTENCES

Town's fitness center is designed as community magnet for citizens and visitors.

4000-student high school is made friendlier by division into eight "houses."

Partner's long-term musical experience enhances firm's qualifications to design drama school.

Computerized animation lets you judge the landscape design at various phases of plant growth.

Some designers stretch the stylistic envelope; others follow trends.

Gender-Neutral Language

Thirty years ago, anyone who read a report or a pile of project correspondence would have been forgiven for thinking that the design professions consisted entirely of men. The truth was quite different. More and more women were graduating from the professional design schools, working as designers and, in due course, principals in firms and as teachers and deans in the schools, staffing private-sector and public agency facilities organizations, working on construction in the field, and serving as members of selection committees.

Yet the written record shows little evidence of this. The language was still peppered with references to *he, his, him, draftsman, workman.* Designers, partners, school board members, hospital administrators, construction workers, and contractors still were referred to as though such jobs were solely in the province of men.

In the late 1960s—a turbulent era in this country in many ways—the consciousness finally broke through that language has to reflect reality, and the reality was that women in growing numbers were working in the design and building industry as active players.

The path to gender-neutral language was anything but smooth. Some of the media rapidly established writing guidelines that reflected the new reality; others ignored the problem. Three directions emerged:

Ignore the situation and cover yourself with a statement along the lines that "for simplicity's sake we will use male terminology, with the understanding that this also encompasses females." That is clearly a cop-out and has virtually disappeared over the years.

Every time you are faced with a situation where the possessive form *he/his/him* arises, write *he/she, his/her, him/her* (or even *s/he, her/him,* etc.). This shows good intention, but it is clumsy. Some writers (and speakers) to this day try to compensate for past sins by using the term *she* on all occasions, but this is no better than using *he.* This problem wasn't always so. Some years ago, then Princeton University provost and now Harvard president Dr. Neil Rudenstine, an English scholar, told me that in Saxon days there was a word that meant *he or she*—an all-gender singular form of the personal pronoun. It atrophied and died. What a pity!

Work around the problem in ways shown below. Opt for a vocabulary that does away with gender-specific references: for instance, make a list of words that through long usage have acquired a male-only or female-only implication, then replace them with words that are gender-neutral.

manpower	*use* workers, human resources
mankind	*use* humanity
manmade	*use* built, synthetic, manufactured
man-sized	*use* large, husky
man-hours	*use* staff hours, hours
manhole	*use* access hole
councilman	*use* council member
fireman	*use* firefighter
eight-man board	*use* eight-member board
salesman	*use* sales representative
cameraman	*use* camera operator
workman	*use* laborer, carpenter, etc.
draftsman	*use* drafting staff (less good: drafter)

(A common point of contention is use of the word "chair" to describe a chairman or chairwoman. I am always embarrassed to hear a person introduced or referred to as a piece of furniture. One is either a chairman or a chairwoman. If you don't know, use "chairperson.")

Often, gender language carries with it a note of condescension, which you should avoid or rephrase when writing.

career girl	*use* architect, designer, engineer
male nurse	*use* nurse
policewoman	*use* police officer
the fair sex	*use* women
lady of the house	*use* head of household

At times, when use of the singular throws up hurdles, you can draw on a virtue of English grammar that allows you to use the plural. Look at these examples:

The designer sometimes takes his work home with him.
Try: Designers sometimes take their work home with them.

The designer should then turn on her computer.
Try: Designers should then turn on their computers.

Every employee must turn in his time-card.
Try: All employees must turn in their time-cards.

Avoid becoming paranoid over the issue of gender. Indications are that writers in the new generation aren't as skittish as those who grew up a generation or more ago. Potentially elegant sentences have been butchered on the altar of gender-neutral prose. We read of congresspersons (better: "members of Congress"). Twenty years ago a judge reportedly denied a change of name to a Ms. Cooperman (to Cooperperson) on the grounds that it set a precedent that might lead to a Jackson changing the name to Jackchild, Manning to Peopling, and Carmen to Carpersons.

Partners in design firms and agencies should set a clear policy in the matter of gender-neutral writing. Check first if there is a problem by reviewing samples of recent correspondence, project reports, and brochures. If revisions are in order, develop, circulate, and enforce a simple document based on some of the foregoing suggestions.

When to Break the Rules

A well-traveled anecdote involves Marcel Breuer, who was asked by a residential client couple to work out even minute details, to the point of selecting and placing every lamp and ashtray. A year later, while visiting the town, he called and was asked to dinner. Looking around, he was flabbergasted to find everything—table lamps, ashtrays, pencil racks, magazine stacks—in precisely the spots where he had placed them. All spontaneity had been lost. Lesson: Breuer had placed the items as suggestions; the owners were meant to feel free to change or move them around.

Similarly, when writing, do not let rules or guidelines get in the way of spontaneous expression. If a snappy word, turn of phrase, or rearrangement of material strikes your fancy and in your view adds to the strength or sparkle of your message, trust your intuition and go for it. Mozart was able to rise above the restrictions of classical form; why shouldn't you?

For an example of this, see the marketing letter, pages 44–46.

Think of the principles and suggestions in this chapter as guidelines, not as rules. The intent is to trigger in your mind an attitude, rather than to think of suggested practices as dogma. With practice, these guidelines will become second nature.

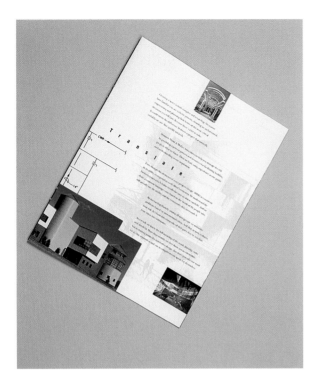

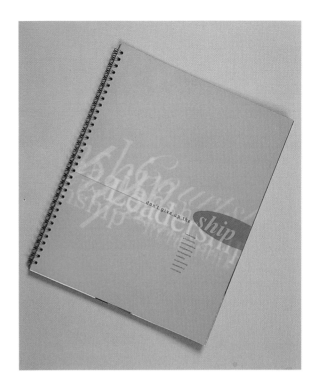

Page from 8-page brochure by Symmes Maini & McKee Associates (above left) expounds theme of listening to owners, then translating program into design. Half of the 26 pages in Walker Group/CNI's spiral-bound brochure (above right) include foldouts. Cut-out pocket in back is for single project fact sheets.

Pages from Walker brochure (below left and right) zero in on two of the attributes the environmental design firm wishes to impress upon clients—marksmanship (instinct, skill, patience, courage) and leadership. Illustrations are small, in line with current usage.

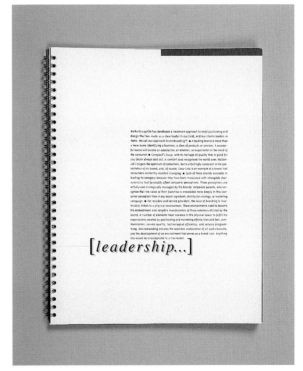

Insert page (above left) from Walker Group/CNI brochure is one of several that describe individual projects. Newsletter by the firm (above right) is an 8-page publication depicting new work by the firm and including a detailed update on trends in retail architecture. Project and services facts sheets (below) portray the work of consulting engineers Flack+Kurtz. Sheets are assembled in a red folder.

Moore/Andersson Architects mailed an engaging foldout piece (above) to clients, prospects, and the media. The 5½-inch-high item has slots for inserting photos of buildings. Shown is an art museum in Manhattan, Kansas. Picture postcard mailings, with minimum text (below) are a low-cost, high-impact way to keep clients updated on newly completed projects. Clockwise: double post card with four academic buildings by William Rawn Associates; retail interior by Buttrick White & Burtis; house by Bohlin Cywinski Jackson; theater restoration by Hardy Holzman Pfeiffer Associates.

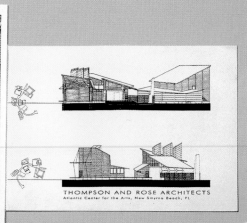

Covers of two proposals by Venturi, Scott Brown and Associates, Inc. (below) are direct and easy to read.

WITCHBROOK MEADOW HOUSE
MARTHA'S VINEYARD, MASSACHUSETTS
THOMPSON AND ROSE ARCHITECTS

THOMPSON AND ROSE ARCHITECTS
Atlantic Center for the Arts, New Smyrna Beach, FL

Postcards (above) show a house at left and sketches of an arts center, both by Thompson and Rose Architects. Cards (below) are, clockwise from top, an office tower, a retail/office building, an athletic center, and law offices, all by CBT (additional smaller projects are shown on the cards' reverse sides). The white-framed card shows an interior by Ronnette Riley Architect.

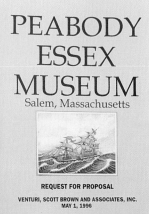

A Bucket of Oil *(below) was researched and written by the CRS Group to point up solutions to the oil crises of the 1970s.*

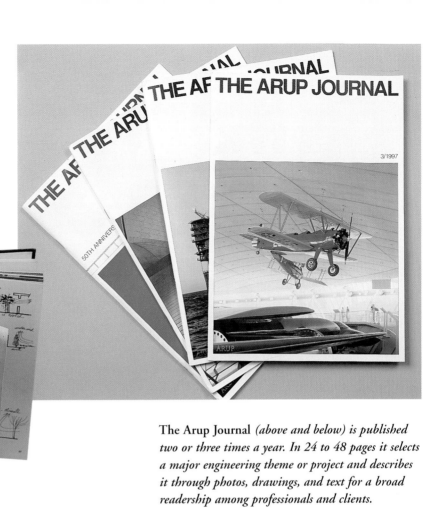

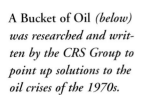

The Arup Journal *(above and below) is published two or three times a year. In 24 to 48 pages it selects a major engineering theme or project and describes it through photos, drawings, and text for a broad readership among professionals and clients.*

Spread from @issue: *magazine (above) shows a range of aids to the reader, including a bright headline, a five-line deck, and headshots of the article's subjects. The article opener in* Engineering News-Record *magazine (below left) offers a clear headline, informative two-line deck, and on top a small "kicker" flagging this as a story about materials. On the page in* Architecture *magazine (below right) note the graphic device used to highlight special sections of text.*

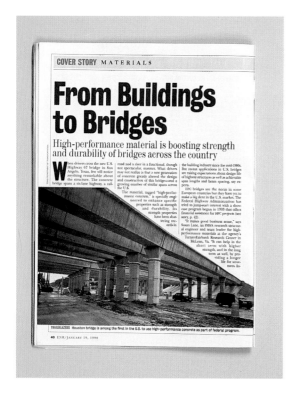

Thirty years FOSTER AND PARTNERS

Foster and Partners have produced this CD-ROM which shows more than 90 projects that illustrate the progress and diversity of the vastly innovative practice's work over the three decades of its existence. The AR is delighted to be associated with the enterprise, which is a remarkable breakthrough in publishing contemporary architectural work. It offers new ways of examining buildings and projects complementary to ones given by magazines and books, and it allows you to make your own preliminary exploration of information far more easily than is possible with large masses of paper. The symbiotic nature of paper and electronic looking at the coverage of the Duxford American Air Museum on the disk and p52 of this issue.

System requirements
Before playing this CD-ROM please note that the minimum computer and CD-ROM specification required to run the CD satisfactorily is: *PowerMacs* PPC 601 processor, 60MHZ, 8MB RAM free, System 7.1, 640x480 16 bit colour monitor, Double-speed CD-ROM drive. The CD is optimized for Windows 95/NT. *PCs* 486SX66, 8MB RAM free, Windows 95 or NT, 640x480 High colour (16 bit) monitor, sound card, Double-speed CD-ROM drive and Quicktime VR. (Qt32 can be loaded from the disk.) For best performance, copy the contents of the disk on to a local hard drive. If you do not have the minimum system requirements the CD is unlikely to function properly.

For Windows 95, go to Start and Run, type in D:\Foster.exe (or the correct letter of your CD drive), then press OK. Macs should boot up automatically. Double click on the Foster icon.

Searching
The screen offers different ways of approaching the practice's work. You can choose the list of projects and look at it either alphabetically or chronologically: clicking the cursor on any name will bring up the relevant material. Also, under the simple 'search' rubric the system will find what you want (or the nearest to what you have entered it can deduce). Location: clicking the cursor on the relevant flag causes a map to appear, showing the location of Foster work in each country; click again to call up the project shown by a yellow dot. You can search out the issues of the AR in which particular works were published and find more information on each than is possible to publish on the disk.

Looking: *Example* DUXFORD
Click on projects, then click on search and type 'ameri'. Click on either the text American Air

the mate
ages is
ented by
d building

ex
at th
In pa
available. T
the building in us
themselves, but the big
IPIX 360 degree immersive imaging technology
(see more at www.ipix.co.uk). These images give the impression that you are actually in the building controlling your navigation round it. From the plan choose a blue dot on which to stand, turn round, look up and down and use binoculars to examine the space (the aeroplane icon shows where you are moving; the + and – icons allow you to zoom in and out of the image).

The two linked circles icon connects to all other animations. The yellow circle icon will close any window or close the disk.

Other copies
The disk is free with subscriber copies of The Architectural Review. Additional copies of the disk can be obtained (priced at £30 postage inclusive) from CRC. Tel: +44 171 505 6622, Fax: +44 171 505 6606. E-mail: crc@construct.emap.co.uk. Credit cards accepted.

The Architectural Review and Foster and Partners have checked the CD-ROM for known viruses at all stages of production, but cannot accept liability for damage caused to your data or your computer system which may occur while using either the disk or any software contained on it. If you do not agree with these conditions, you should not use the disk.

ADDITIONAL COPIES OF THE DISK CAN BE OBTAINED (PRICED AT £30 POSTAGE INCLUSIVE) FROM CRC. TEL: +44 171 505 6622, FAX: +44 171 505 6606

THE ARCHITECTURAL REVIEW

thirty years
foster and partners
CD-Rom Mac and PC
Foster and Partners

Foster and Partners developed a CD-ROM about the firm (above). It was attached to a descriptive page (shown here) and included free in subscriber issues of Architectural Review *magazine. The disk includes video "walkabout" clips of key projects, a clear, simple statement of philosophy, partner information, the Foster firm's web site URL, and an e-mail address for inquiries.*

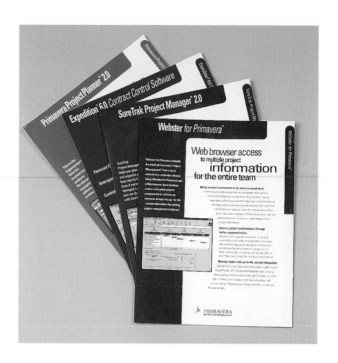

Series of brochures by Primavera Systems, Inc. (right) describe individual project management software packages produced by the company. The type is large, the layout direct; the text is informative and shuns jargon and hype. Postcard mailings by vendors of products and services (below) are a form of direct mail that demands efficient use of a very small area available for text, artwork, and ordering boxes.

Marketing Correspondence

2

The two principal types of writing—marketing and project—have much in common but also differ in major respects. Both seek to influence an audience; each does it differently. Project writing transmits useful information or instructions; marketing writing sells something—a personal service, a firm's services, a request for a meeting or for data.

Marketing writing follows its own drummer. The next four chapters examine the range of marketing communication most likely to come up in the design firm's day-to-day practice. This chapter tackles marketing correspondence. Chapter 3 covers the brochure and the portfolio. The focus of chapter 4 is on the request for proposals (RfP) and how to respond appropriately. Chapter 5 deals with newsletters and other marketing tools.

Marketing correspondence is most commonly triggered by the carrot of a commission. Either you are the prime design professional or you are looking to be a consultant to a prime design professional. There are other scenarios. You work in Charlotte and you write to a firm in Chicago suggesting an association on a pending job where you have the home connections and Chicago has the specialized expertise. Or you hear of a project that is to be design-build, and you propose to the designated general contractor and/or owner that you be on the team. Or you want to approach a developer of office buildings with your space planning and interior design services.

The marketing arena, even in a thriving economy, is not designer-friendly. Long lists and short lists of designers are becoming increasingly crowded; designers are being asked to provide more information and pre-agreement services than in anyone's living memory. Firms have to invest growing sums in marketing (the average today is 7.8 percent of net billings, according to the 1997 AIA Firm Survey Report), and marketing staffs as a percentage of total staff are rising. Yet downward pressures on fees do not always guarantee that these up-front dollars are recouped as profits. Hence, the marketing strategy that precedes the actual writing of the marketing materials is critical.

What actually happens? Your firm, informed of a prospective commission, typically goes through an internal process. The partners meet. A tentative project team is identified, and past firm work, friends in the marketplace, the Web, and other sources are enlisted to size up client and prospects. Is it a real project? Is it funded or likely to be funded in time for design and construction to happen? What is the client's track record in honoring commitments and paying bills? Are competitors out there with an unbeatable lead in the type of work; are they "wired"?

Smaller firms go through this planning process faster than larger firms. On the other hand, smaller firms also tend to spend time and money chasing projects with slim prospects, when they could be massing their efforts on work with more promise or more in line with their experience.

You decide to go for the project. The first item on the agenda is to compose a terrific letter that will bowl over the owner with your skills as a designer, manager, and personality. How do you compose such a letter?

The Marketing Letter

The marketing letter is your first contact. It should not be confused with a cover letter to a proposal. There usually isn't space to cite your qualifications in much detail. The proposal comes later and is the vehicle for a message in greater depth.

The marketing letter that gets results is best organized in the following parts.

Prospect's name, address: Formerly everything was spelled out, and conservative firms still do so. But in the interest of saving time and space, cool firms abbreviate Street (St.), Boulevard (Blvd.), Suite (Ste.). But always use the two-letter state designation (TN, OR).

Salutation: A few firms omit this, but the current usage is still to use Dear, followed by Mr., Mrs., or Ms., or first name if appropriate. The practice, now dwindling, has been to differentiate between women who are married (Mrs.) and those who either are married or single (Ms). Follow the recipient's preferences—if in doubt, use Ms. (The French have solved this puzzle with their usual elegance, using Me. to replace Mme. and Mlle.) If you don't know, use "Dear Heather Wade"—an excellent choice, especially when you're not sure of the gender (Chris, Alex, Leslie, etc.). When writing not to an individual but to a group of mixed gender, ladies and gentlemen will do—it's surely an improvement over the standoffish To whom it may concern. Even better is to use a collective address term such as Members of the selection board. Those with a taste for the homespun have been known to use "Folks." This term is best saved for clients with whom you already have an informal relationship, or cases where you know that the personality of the client fits with such an informal term.

Opening: In your first sentence, get to the point. Why are you writing? What are you asking for? Avoid an interminable lead-in. Today's prospects have neither the time nor the inclination to wade through streams of verbal ore before hitting pay dirt.

Core content: Your audience is looking for evidence that you are the right firm to do the work. This evidence typically consists of the seventeen factors, often called hot buttons, listed on the following pages. Not all the points mentioned may be germane to your marketing letter, but be prepared because on all of them the client will need answers, if not now, then later. The order shown is a suggestion; let your appraisal of the client determine the sequence of points, and which ones to include.

Questions: You will no doubt have questions as to size, budget, and timing of the project, the nature and schedule of the selection process, and the names of competing firms. Decide to strike a good balance between seeming too nosy too soon and a legitimate need to know.

Your objective: Make it clear what you want out of this exchange—an invitation to follow up with more detailed credentials, an appearance before the selection committee, or more information. Be frank and clear. What you have written will not do you much good if the reader can't grasp the aim of your letter.

Conclusion: Keep it short and upbeat. Leave the impression that you're a good firm to do business with. Be cheerful without being exuberant—spirited, respectful but not ingratiating, enthusiastic but this side of wild-eyed.

Name and signature: Don't type your name if it's printed on the letterhead. You may indicate a file name, but in very small type.

As you review a draft, ask yourself these questions.

Is the lead paragraph too long before you get to the point? Is the point buried in the paragraph?

Is the style out of character—yours or the client's? Beware turns of phrase that are either too glib ("Hey man—we dig this gig") or too formal ("We beg to respond to your invitation to state our interest in being considered for the design").

Is the letter too long (or too short) for your message? The initial marketing letter should fit on one page or at most two. If you run out of things to say after half a page, you're probably not telling the clients what they want to know. If you're still at full steam at the end of page two, you risk overburdening the reader with more information than is wanted. If in doubt, get an opinion from an associate.

Is the material arranged in an illogical flow?

Is the ending too drawn out?

Does the ending lack a clear request?

Common Pitfalls

Use "hot buttons." The client will need to know whether your firm:

1. has an understanding of the client's goals and needs? Of all the hot buttons, this is perhaps the most critical. If your research has been on target, you'll know what's right.

2. offers experience in the client's project type? Most clients will require that you have handled their type of project before, whether it's a shopping center or a middle school. This places you on the defensive if the project is your first shopping center or middle school or seismic consultation or public park, but it challenges you to cite similar experience at a previous firm—if you have had it—or to make a strong case for original thinking unjaded by too much prior experience. Think of Eero Saarinen or Jørn Utzon, some of whose best work—airport terminals, concert halls, skating rinks—was done on never-before-tried project types. Impart your problem-solving ability by citing other work, not necessarily in the client's building type, showing how you tackled certain challenges and resolved them.

Hot Buttons: What the Client Wants to Know about Your Firm

3. possesses a record of good relations with prior clients? Offer—but do not at this point enclose—testimonial letters from past clients and/or the readiness of those clients to answer questions about the caliber of your performance. This information can make or break your chances, so make a habit of obtaining such references soon after each job.

4. benefits from a high ratio of repeat business? For prospective clients, the ratio matters and can work in your favor. Some firms point with pride to a repeat business ratio of 80 percent (out of every 100 jobs on the boards, 80 are for previous clients; or stated another way, of every $1,000,000 in annual fees, $800,000 comes from previous clients). Few firms do that well. Many firms are happy to reach 50 percent. Clients won't expect young firms to have built up a high ratio, so you need to pinpoint excellence in other areas, such as experience in the building type.

5. retains a high caliber of staff? Point to the education and experience of your workforce, citing project managers who may be assigned to the job who have experience on similar projects, and what you look for in staff people before you hire them. You probably won't cite names at this stage, unless asked. That comes later.

6. has received professional recognition? Cite awards, honors, and major publications where your work has been published. Stick to the most impressive ones; there will be time later to send full listings. If you are a young firm, list awards from previous firms' projects on which you had a role.

7. has an effective working procedure? Summarize your process—how you assemble your team, who is the point of contact with the client, and any special procedures that have worked for you in moving projects forward, such as intensive on-site fact-finding sessions.

8. has good working contacts with consultants, contractors, suppliers, and public agencies? The client isn't buying just your services; your range of contacts that will make up the project team is also in demand.

9. can control project costs? The best way to prove this lies in your record. Avoid glib statements that you believe in accurate estimates and thorough cost management (who doesn't?), and that you have always managed costs. Instead, provide figures—simple in your letter, more detailed as the job-getting process unfolds. In the marketing letter, try a short affirmation that "on the past 28 projects bids came in to within plus or minus 3 percent of estimates, and those projects where scope didn't change were built to within plus or minus 4 percent of bids." (The latter is of course as much a feather in the contractor's cap as in the architect's.) Younger firms too can boast good track records, albeit based on a slimmer volume of completed work.

10. can control project schedules? Relay your track record of having met design and production deadlines. Indicate that you operate on state-of-the-art project management software.

11. can manage environmental concerns? Cite experience, when appropriate, in such areas as specification of sustainable materials, products, and processes, and in energy-conscious design. Many emerging firms have excellent track records in dealing with these challenges.

12. can manage remotely located projects? A remote site, a remote client, or both, puts extra stress on managing the project. Point to past experience in handling this kind of work, especially on overseas projects. One Midwestern firm with a regional rather than a local practice owned a small aircraft, allowing the partners to tell prospects that no project for which they were hired would ever be more than an hour's distance away from their office. If a private plane is immoderate, one alternative, often required by clients in such conditions, is to associate with a local firm. Indicate your readiness to do so.

13. owns and applies state-of-the-art production and office systems? Clients expect their design professionals to run their shops at a level of sophistication at least equal to their own. That requires at a minimum a late version of CAD software, plus project and financial management systems and project Web sites. Since client prospects on occasion visit their main consultants' offices, attention to the efficiency, congeniality, and style of your workplace can win you points. In a marketing letter, an invitation to visit will suffice.

14. is adequately capitalized? No client wants a consultant who will have trouble meeting a payroll. Such cases have been known to occur and do not sit well with clients (the reverse is also true; as noted, check out your client before you go for the job). You are not expected to attach an income statement and balance sheet here, but an indication that your office is solid is welcome. If you are invited later to submit a proposal, a bank reference, if not requested, is certainly in order.

15. has a preferred method of compensation? If not in the marketing letter, certainly at later stages of developing the project the client will want to know your wishes as to the fee arrangement—percentage of construction cost, multiple of labor cost, unit cost, lump sum, or whatever. Chances are the client will have a preference.

16. is available? Does your firm have the capacity to take on this project? A few years ago an architect with a moderate practice of mainly single-family houses was invited to take on the commission for designing a main house, a guest house, and assorted collateral buildings for the wealthy head of a major corporation. The architect had always had a strong conviction for limiting his firm to about twelve people, so rather than staff up for this commission, he decided to risk putting several other client prospects on hold while he took on and completed the new job. Not every designer is sanguine to this degree, but the case highlights an issue owners want to know about.

17. is firmly interested in the job? There's nothing a client—or, for that matter, any buyer of a product or service—likes more than a vigorous appetite for the job. It's a good way to end your letter.

Scenario

You are an eight-person, five-year-old firm located in the Soho district of New York City. You have a mixed practice consisting mainly of institutional work and comprising small to midsize projects such as schools, community facilities, neighborhood clinics, and an occasional fire station and residential remodeling. You have learned that the Bryan Soames Foundation has agreed to underwrite the costs of a 20,000 sq. ft., $3.5 million community center on an infill site on

Sample Letters

East 20th Street. The architects are to be chosen by a selection committee appointed jointly by Community Board #13 and Elizabeth Sanchez, executive director of the foundation. The center will house day care, senior citizen recreation, community social functions, limited food facilities, offices for social services staff, and an apartment for a full-time custodial person. You have made phone calls to the board and the foundation and were told, as the first step, to write a letter of interest to the selection committee. The letter needs to indicate your interest in designing the project and spell out the reasons why you should be considered. You may send two enclosures. The selection committee will review all letters and invite a short list of architects to respond to a more detailed request for proposals (RfP) at a later date.

Letter

Ms. Elizabeth Sanchez
Executive Director
The Bryan Soames Foundation
13A Fromm Street
New York, NY 10013

Dear Ms. Sanchez:

I write because my firm, Johnson and Roe, would like to be your architect for designing your new community center.

We understand you will want to include, in the center, space for day care, senior citizen recreation, community social functions, limited food facilities, offices for social services staff, and an apartment for a full-time custodial person, totaling about 20,000 square feet.

The site is to be an infill location on East 20th Street. We have examined the site and believe it is suitable for containing your space requirements, with a unique opportunity for a cheerful, well-functioning building that is inexpensive to operate. We also learned that while many in the local community are excited about the project, others have questions about the added traffic it will bring to the area, along with the possibility of an increase in crime. Be assured that we found a similar situation on the Wilson Community Center, which we designed in 1996 on Broome Street. We were able to meet regularly with the community and, jointly with the sponsor, share with everyone all details of the plan. The community in the end came to recognize the value the center would bring. We are convinced a similar approach will work in your case. We will be happy to send you press reports on this and similar projects.

Ours is a mixed practice consisting mainly of institutional work and including small to midsize projects such as schools, community facilities, neighborhood clinics, and an occasional fire station. Our firm has a record of excellent relations with current and past clients. This is attested to by the fact that two out of three projects on our boards are for previous clients.

Our work has been recognized by local as well as national professional societies, including a 1995 national honor award from the American Institute of Architects for the Wilson Center, which also received the Medal of Honor from the AIA's New York chapter, along with a citation of merit from the mayor of New York. Our work has been published in several noted publications, including the *Architectural Chronicle*, the *New York Times, and* the *Village Voice.*

We choose our new staff from the top twenty percent of the nation's outstanding professional schools, and subject all members of our firm, including partners, to rigorous standards of performance in matters of design, cost and schedule management, and evaluation of construction materials and products. In working with you, we'll assemble a team of members best adapted for your building, and appoint a manager who will be your chief contact and available to you at all times.

Our track record in controlling clients' budgets and schedules is outstanding. On the past 18 projects, all have been bid within a range of plus/minus 3 percent of final estimates. On the same 18 projects, 17 have been completed and occupied on or ahead of schedule; one was delayed two months due to an unforeseen strike by locals of the sheetmetal worker and electrician unions.

We make a point of carefully screening materials, products, and construction methods for their ability to support and protect the environment. We specify only replaceable species and cut your utility costs using heating, cooling, and ventilating systems that conserve energy.

We invite you to visit our offices. We are proud of a workplace that is congenial and efficient. Members have independent workstations with individual controls over lighting and climate. We operate with up-to-date design, production, project management, and financial computer software, including AutoCAD's version 14.

Although we are blessed with a solid backlog of work, our capacity is flexible, and we are able to take on new work such as your building with a very short lead time.

We are pleased to have had this opportunity to tell you about ourselves and our work. We are eager to be selected to work with you in designing your new building, and hope to be appointed to the short list of architects to receive your request for proposals.

Sincerely,
Mary Davies Roe
Partner
Johnson and Roe, architects and planners

P.S. I enclose a list of similar projects we have completed in the past five years, and a reprint of an article published on the Wilson Community Center and the Thomas Carry Recreation Center published in *Architectural Chronicle.*

Scenario:

You are Chen Associates, a consulting engineering firm specializing in high-tech structural engineering. The San Diego architectural firm of Lloyd, Oswaldsen and Associates is interviewing structural engineers for a new terminal for Alpha Airlines as it readies its qualification package for submittal to the airline and to the San Diego County Administration. Your practice includes the design of large-span structures using tensile or thin-concrete technologies. Lloyd, Oswaldsen is at this stage undecided as to the structural system for the building, as the program for it is still incomplete. You have worked with the firm auspiciously on previous projects, but so have many of your competitors. Write a letter to Henry Lloyd, partner-in-charge, stating your eagerness to be part of the design team.

Letter

Henry Lloyd, Partner
Lloyd, Oswaldsen and Associates, Architects
12860 Coronado Blvd.
San Diego, CA 92118

Dear Henry:

I am told that Alpha Airlines is planning to replace its present terminal building at San Diego International Airport with a new terminal. We at Chen Associates are eager to be part of your design team, and this letter is to highlight the benefits Chen will bring to such an association.

As you know, we have worked together on other projects, such as the La Jolla Stadium. The experience was a gratifying one for both our firms as well as for the client: the work was completed on time and on budget, and yielded excellent publicity in local and national media.

Chen Associates has made a point of laboring at the cutting edge of long-span technologies, and I'm convinced the Alpha Airlines project is a splendid and logical opportunity to break new ground in providing large, uninterrupted, uplifting, and secure space for the tired or jaded traveler.

Despite the "first-time" quality of much innovative large-span work, we have never encountered problems of safety, budget, or schedule, during either construction or occupancy. That's due in large part, we feel, to the high quality of our engineering design and project management staff and the currency of our computer design software, which includes the state-of-the-art Primavera version 12. Our financial management software has allowed us to pinpoint costs related to structure up to the last moment before projects are sent to bid; on the past 20 projects we have been within an average of 4 percent above/below bids. Our computerized production system is, if you recall, compatible with yours, thereby cutting the risk of errors to a minimum.

If selected, we would assign our most experienced designers to the project, including, as I believe she will be available, Fawn Carvalho, who worked with you on the La Jolla Stadium.

Please tell me what additional credentials I can send you to strengthen your submittal. We have a wide selection of color transparencies, printed four-color descriptive sheets, a 20-minute video of the La Jolla and Las Vegas projects, and an animated CD-ROM on our firm.

I'm excited at the unique opportunities contained in this work, and hope we may resume our previous fine relationship.

Kind regards,

Louis Chen

Principal

Comment

Note that this letter is more concise than the Roe letter, because the writer knows the receiver and has worked with him before, and he can assume the receiver is likely to be familiar with the writer's more recent work.

Scenario

Unlike the Chen letter, from a structural engineer to an architect involving a specific project, the following letter is from a consulting mechanical and electrical engineering firm sending a letter to architects with no special project in mind. Note the differences and similarities between the two letters. This is an actual letter and does a laudable job in pinpointing the firm's strengths. (The recipient's name and address have been changed.)

Letter

George Porter, AIA
3500 Fifth Avenue
New York, N.Y. 10000
Re: Mechanical & Electrical Engineering Services

Dear Mr. Porter:

We are a consulting engineering firm and would like to enlarge the circle of our clientele. This letter is intended to introduce us to you.

Our office has practiced consulting engineering for more than forty years; we have designed over three thousand mechanical/electrical systems and installations for office buildings, office tenants, shopping centers, department stores, apartment houses, hospitals and schools.

There are approximately 40 people on our staff in the New York headquarters; we have maintained for the past 30 years a European branch, operating out of Paris, and also a branch in Parsippany, New Jersey. Our offices are divided into four departments: Heating and Air Conditioning, Electrical, Plumbing, and Computer. These departments comprise an integrated engineering office capable of handling all phases of mechanical and electrical design, as well as material quantity forecasts, economic feasibility studies, engineering-oriented sections of landlord-tenant leases and developing energy conservation criteria.

Presently most of our drawings are done on AutoCAD Release 14. We also have computer systems that permit us to analyze the economy of operations, available energy sources and maximum-investment returns. We have developed a method that permits proceeding with the tenant space design before the tenant layouts are finalized. The computer keeps track of the construction phase too: documents, quantity of material used and percentage completion.

Our forte is most economical design, in terms of initial investment and operating cost. Furthermore, thanks to the integrated and computer-assisted design operation, we can produce the work most speedily, while maintaining the highest quality.

We would like an opportunity to meet with you at your convenience to present our expertise in more detail.

Very truly yours,

Sidney W. Barbanel, P.E.

Scenario

Albinoni Contractors, Inc., has invited four architectural firms to submit credentials for a design-build project. Albinoni will select one of these firms as part of its team to promote the new 200,000 sq. ft. central public library for the city of Indianapolis. The award hinges on a bond issue to be voted on nine months hence, but the city wishes to sign up the design-construction team earlier so it can play a part in promoting the project. Albinoni has used design-build on medium- to large-sized building projects over the past eight years, mostly institutional work such as educational and healthcare facilities. Its record for delivering on time and budget has been good, but sporadic cases have been reported where design members of the team have been unduly pressured to change design concepts and product specifications to save money. Your firm, O'Shaughnessy & Cohen, has previously designed libraries, and you have worked in the public sector but not on any design-build projects. You feel winning this project will open up new opportunities for you, both in the library facilities market and as a profit-making participant in future design-build ventures. Write a marketing letter to John Albinoni, CEO, whom you have met briefly at various civic lunches but with whom you have not had a professional relationship, requesting to be his architect and head of the design team. Now read the following.

Letter

John Albinoni
President, Albinoni Contractors, Inc.
4 Elm Street
Indianapolis, IN 46206

Dear Jack:

My firm would like to join yours to form an effective design-build team that will win the contract for the new central public library for the city of Indianapolis.

We understand the city intends to select a design-build team to carry out the work, and plans to do so by April 30 in order to give voters a chance to scrutinize the various teams' proposals before they vote on the bond issue in November.

Therefore, we see it as critical to develop a design package, cost estimates, project delivery schedule, and accompanying marketing materials that will impress the voters with the benefits they will receive through construction of the new library.

Our firm is well equipped to help you reach this objective:

- We have designed in the past eight years four public libraries of over 150,000 sq. ft. each, for Louisville, Sacramento, Gary, Indiana, and Youngstown, Ohio, as well as smaller but technically advanced libraries for school districts in those cities, and for the Kincaid School in Houston. These libraries were built on budget, and all were delivered on time except for the high-school library in Youngstown, which was delayed four months due to bankruptcy of a major supplier.

- The four public libraries attained instant acceptance in those cities, yielding several favorable reports in the local press and TV media, as well a write-up in the annual library issue of *Architectural Chronicle* magazine. We can send you photographs and other visual materials, including videotapes and 3-D animation CDs, to demonstrate the kind of materials we are able to develop to place before the voters.

- Over the years we have often appeared at public meetings to make successful presentations to community groups. We have videotapes of such sessions should you wish to see them.

- We have worked steadily over the past ten years with a small group of highly skilled, dependable professional consultants in structural, mechanical, electrical, and civil engineering, with landscape architects, as well as with two of the nation's most eminent lighting designers and an acoustical consultant in wide demand. These consultants know our procedures for delivering contract documents, and we know theirs. The result will be a smoothly operating team that will mesh well with your own staff.

- We have a record of cordial relationships with general contractors, and will be glad to send you a list. They will tell you that we always combine fresh design thinking with a realistic eye to its cost implications. Indeed, we respect value engineering and believe that it is possible to combine quality design with rigorous management of costs and schedules.

- Our in-house computerized CAD and project and financial management software will allow us to link with your systems to maintain a high level of communication with members of the design team as well as with your staff. I invite you to visit our offices so you can see the advanced state of our design and production systems.

We welcome your suggestions as to the best type of contractual arrangement between you and our firm.

We look forward to being part of your team. This is a splendid opportunity for both our firms.

Very sincerely,
Maurice O'Shaughnessy
Partner

Enclosures
List of clients (past five years)
Fact sheet of completed libraries

Comment

Note that this letter extracts from the list of hot buttons certain ones that differ in focus from a more traditional contract with a traditional client, especially a concern for value engineering, costs related to scope, management of the design team, and ability to produce on a fast schedule.

Scenario

The following was an actual project and letter (the recipient's name and address have been changed). The writer's firm was one of two still in the running for the commission to tackle the planning and construction needs of a county school system in south Florida. It is clearly not the first correspondence between writer and receiver, but it packs a wealth of marketing savvy and a unique arrangement into a tight space. The superintendent of schools had asked the two finalists to submit a convincing document to accompany his recommendation for an architect to the county school board. The writer, the late William Caudill of the firm then called CRS Associates, had known the superintendent for years and was able to adopt a decidedly informal tone. The letter recaps the firm's understanding of the issues in a fast-growing school district that already had an inventory of not-adequate existing schools.

Letter

John Brown
Superintendent of Schools
Broward County
1 Coconut Avenue
Fort Lauderdale, FL 33302

Jack, I've done my homework:

A. WHAT YOU HAVE:

1. The Board of Public Instruction of Broward County, Florida, is operating on the advanced edge of primary and secondary education—individualized instruction, team teaching, and ITV being the major educational methods used.

2. Recently constructed elementary and middle schools most vividly show in no uncertain terms manifestation of the team concept, which appears to be synonymous with the "open plan" idea.

3. Broward County schoolhouses make up a 3-D history of education in this country, ranging from the 40+-year-old two-story mission-type schools through the self-contained finger-plan multilateral lighted schools, to the compacted open-plan EFL-inspired plant. Broward busted the box.

4. There are not enough schools to go around, even by busing. Double sessions are inevitable unless drastic management and technological changes are made to deliver schools at a faster rate.

5. The new schools are going up too slowly to take care of rapidly increasing enrollment, and, in some cases, rather wastefully—overhangs that protect neither people nor windows, unnecessary geometry for small auditoriums, false structural expressions, and mansard "roofs" that are not roofs. Unfortunately, the new schools lack the amenities—those human values which the 1926 Northside Elementary School possesses.

6. The old schools need both air-conditioning and functional conversion. For example, the self-contained classroom—a splendid teaching tool for a specific job—simply will not do for another task (team teaching), like a cotton-picking machine is no good for threshing wheat.

B. WHAT YOU SHOULD HAVE:

1. For one thing you need better schoolhouses to match your fine curriculum. The school—the most important and expensive machine for learning—either helps the teacher teach or gets in the way. The old schools deter. Broward County's commitment to high-quality education is a commitment to high-quality facilities.

2. You need faster ways to plan and construct schools, such as fast-track, critical-path, and system building.

3. You need more economical ways to beat rising construction costs and inflation, making use of techniques mentioned above, plus sophisticated programming that separates "wants" from "needs," pares the "fat," and sets up early computerized cost controls. You need to work fast with effective teams of many specialists.

4. You need to supplement local talent/experience with outside expertise that can help the school board, the superintendent, and his staff initiate these new ways—better, quicker, and more economically—to provide those urgently needed high-quality facilities.

5. Overriding any one of the methods suggested is the need for a high-level centralized team to motivate and manage the school planning/construction program that brings into full play the coordinated efforts of users, designers, manufacturers, and builders. Such a management team must be

systems-oriented, must have the sensitivity to human values as related to the physical environment, and at all decision-making times must have empathy for the child and the teachers.

C. HOW YOU CAN HAVE WHAT YOU SHOULD HAVE:

1. You need outside talent/experience—a team of experts whose members are highly competent in both system building and management of planning/construction programs.

2. You asked if our team is qualified and available. We are on both counts.

3. Availability? Say "frog," we'll jump.

4. Qualified? We are 24 years old, a team of highly competent specialists. Baltimore (public schools), Hartford (public schools), New York (higher education); each can vouch for high professional performance of our team concerning the aspects of management. Texas (mental health), Merrick, Long Island, and SCSD [School Construction Systems Development] substantiate our experience in system building.

5. People? Consider these members of our team [there follows a listing of seven individuals with experience in school building systems development, school design, project management, research, fast-track construction, and building technology].

If you want to take quick action (you need to), pick up the phone anytime and call [lists phone number]. Talk with either me or [my assistant] Jan Smith, and be assured we will schedule two or three key staffers (specialists in management and system building) to fly immediately (on us) to discuss our services—scope and cost—with you, your staff, and your board.

You wanted action. You got it.

Bill

(William W. Caudill)

Comment

Some of the references to then state-of-the-art school education concepts are dated, but the letter is a fine example of sparkling yet spartan, staccato writing, effective salesmanship, and an upbeat ending. Note the generous and effective use of "you" compared to the more self-serving "we"—this letter contains only six "we's" but a convincing sixteen "you's"!

Marketing Letter for Firms Just Starting Out

As a recently organized firm, you cannot fall back on a long list of completed projects, honors, awards, and clients. Instead, you need to focus on work in which you took an active part as an employee of another firm; highlight outstanding school work; mention travel and foreign languages where appropriate; show a solid grasp of CAD-based design, animation, and production; and vaunt the fresh look and enthusiasm brought to a job by designers with modest experience but a solid mastery of the design process.

Scenario

You have learned that the Washington County school district is looking for architects and interior designers to convert a 500-pupil, thirty-year-old open-plan elementary school into enclosed classrooms, and to rejuvenate an obsolete wiring and communication complex into a modern, wide-bandwidth system that will accommodate emerging electronic instruction techniques. Here is one way to write your letter:

Letter

Ms. Nefertiti Jones
Superintendent of Schools
Washington County
1 Elm Street
Middletown, AR 70000

Dear Ms. Jones:

I recently visited Polk Street Elementary School, and entirely agree that the facility needs urgently to be modernized to make way for the progressive teaching techniques you have planned for your school district. This includes above all the enclosure of classrooms and a wiring and communications network and capacity that will allow you access to the wealth of resources available on the Internet and through other on-line means.

I believe that my firm, Izumi Associates, can make this happen.

Before starting my own firm in 1996, I worked for six years as a designer and project manager at Perkins & Will in Chicago. While there I was lead designer or project manager on four elementary and two middle schools, all with educational demands similar to yours. Half the schools were new, the other half renovated. Of these schools, two were published in the *Architectural Chronicle,* and received honor awards from the American Association of School Administrators, the Chicago Chapter of the American Society of Interior Designers, and the Midwest region of the American Institute of Architects. Those client references are yours for the asking.

My firm offers both interior design and architectural services. You need excellence in both fields to achieve your goals.

As you select architects and interior designers for your three-firm short list, be aware that Izumi Associates, while not a large or old-line firm, offers you several advantages. You secure the solid professional background of its staff, our firm's close physical presence twenty minutes from the site of Polk Street School, and a state-of-the-art computer-aided design and production system that includes an animation program. This will allow you and your colleagues to preview the various design schemes in three dimensions.

We are also ready, if selected, to present, at your request, the design schemes to parents and teachers in the community.

Whether you select Izumi or not, we wish you success in your endeavor.

Sincerely,

Donald Izumi, Partner

Enclosures [six project fact sheets]

For the special challenges found in communicating with overseas clients, see chapter 16.

Following Up the Marketing Letter

When and how to follow up on a marketing letter can be a puzzle. Contacting a nonresponsive prospect calls for firmness and tact. Chances are the client's silence is for reasons out of the client's control; or the decision has not been made or has been postponed; or a decision has been made but is not to be disclosed at this time. It makes sense to initiate the follow-up sequence with a mild phone call on the lines of "I'm calling to follow up on our letter (or presentation) of June 12. Is there more information you require?" This commonly triggers intelligence as to the status of the decision. When testing the lay of the land this way, begin no less than two and no more than three weeks from the time you mailed the original letter or made the presentation.

If voice-mail messages begin to pile up unanswered at the client's end, send a letter or e-mail on the lines of "We are still interested and look forward to your decision." If that doesn't work, a more outspoken letter may be in order, such as the one following.

Scenario

Five weeks after your firm, Feng and Ivanov, made a proposal for the Pontefract Laboratories' new clean laboratory building, and after two follow-up phone calls and no response, you resolve to write a letter.

Letter A

Dear Dr. Pontefract:

I'm sorry we have not succeeded in reaching you by phone to discover when Pontefract Laboratories may be expected to reach a decision in the matter of the proposed clean laboratory building.

We are anxious to hear from you as we have pending commitments to which we must assign staff and resources we had planned to reserve for your project.

We were glad to have had the chance to share our qualifications with you, and we continue to hope for your response. We'll be happy to deliver any added information you may need.

Sincerely,

Feng Wan-Seung

Comment

If this doesn't work, save your hounds for a more promising fox.

Whenever the answer is that you haven't made the cut or that the work has been assigned to another firm, a gracious response is vital and can serve as a pretext for ferreting out the reason the client went to another firm. Some firms include a mild pat on the back for the successful competitor.

Letter B

Dear Ms. Kenworthy:

We were disappointed not to have been chosen to design your new sculpture museum. We believe that Gómez and Partners whom you selected will do a fine job for you.

We enjoyed the chance to show you our work, and we look forward to another opportunity of working with you.

Sincerely,

George Oban

Partner

Never burn your bridges.

3

Marketing Brochures and Portfolios

The brochure and the portfolio are your ambassadors. Whether each is printed, on a CD-ROM or videocassette, or appears on your Web site, it represents you when you cannot appear in person, when the client prospect doesn't find it convenient to meet you face to face, or, in case of the portfolio, when the client is looking at your work and not at you, even though you may be sitting across the desk.

Let's first define terms. The brochure is a text-and-illustration aggregate of your firm's qualifications in design, project management, and technological know-how. It is used as a pre-interview submittal or as a post-interview leave-behind. It also may be posted on your Web site. The portfolio is an illustrated album of an individual's work, usually intended to advance an applicant's cause for competition, admission to graduate school, or hiring.

The Brochure

The brochure conveys to an audience your firm's vision and professional record. How you build your brochure depends to a large degree on how you respond to certain key questions.

Marketing intent. Is the immediate purpose of the brochure an initial overture to a client prospect? supplementary matter to a proposal? a leave-behind after a verbal presentation to a client? a device to entice the media? a tool to attract gifted job applicants?

Shelf-life. What shelf-life is reasonable before changes in projects, services, and people make it obsolete?

Tactics. Will a fat and complex brochure place you at a disadvantage compared to a leaner but more sparkling and less formidable package by your competitors? Or vice versa?

Focus. If your current marketing target is a college dormitory, why clutter up a brochure—and the client's time—with pictures of mid-rise office buildings, hi-tech manufacturing facilities, and children's science museums?

Best medium. Do your chief prospects prefer to soak up their information from the printed page or through another medium, such as the Web?

Budget. How large is your budget?

Inventory of completed projects. If you are an emerging firm, how large is your inventory of completed projects?

The days are gone when a single, bound brochure had to satisfy every need. In this fast-paced age, the single, printed brochure is obsolete the day it leaves the press. A brochure—and from now on I use the term to mean any system of prepared promotional materials about your firm—has to be tailored to the conditions of your marketing plan.

To obtain a solid framework for writing the brochure, it helps to look at its principal components or modules, and to pinpoint those sections where the quality of writing is critical to the promise of success.

These days, to construct a brochure, develop a series of modules for assembling into a package targeted at a specific selling situation. The modules should be brief enough that they can be updated simply and cheaply; this beats updating and reissuing an entire brochure. A "brochure" posted on a Web site, as many design professionals now do, avoids most of these updating and reissuing concerns nicely. (On the minus side, many clients are not yet organized to look for and/or absorb Web-posted brochure information. Heavy graphics, such as photographs, take too long to load if you have a low-powered modem. Following is a listing of key brochure modules.

Firm description and vision
Project fact sheets
Services fact sheets
Staff resumes
Client liaison
Client listings
Past project listings
Publications and honors listings
Article reprints
Container or binder

Firm Description and Vision

This is the place to state your firm's vision, describe your outlook on the world of design and construction and the firm's place in it, point to eminent accomplishments in the past, identify specialties, name key players on the team and their attainments, and provide an upbeat picture of the firm without reading like a press agent's handout. Perhaps add material on how you organize projects for good client liaison, or you can place this in a separate module (see below).

Keep this piece to four pages or less. Illustrate it with a few good project shots—for atmosphere only—and perhaps a view of your offices with staff at work. Showing headshots of principals is two-edged: it risks making the piece instantly obsolete if the partner leaves; and if a member of the selection committee has a thing against men with beards, say, you may have one strike against you.

For examples of pages from firms' descriptive modules, see page 25, top left and bottom right.

Project Fact Sheets

One fact sheet per project makes it simple to assemble only those projects needed to impress a selection committee. Select significant projects (completed where possible)—buildings, furniture, interiors, master plans, landscape designs, graphic design and wayfinding systems, exhibits, product designs. Charge someone in the firm with the task of assembling the key data about each project as soon as it's completed; it will smooth the effort of writing the fact sheet if project data are recorded before the project manager starts on a new project and lets the facts slip into oblivion. In the project folder, include photography and the simplest, clearest drawings available.

If your firm specializes in certain building types or consulting services—sports facilities, for instance, or tensile structures—develop a one-page cover sheet with two or three paragraphs describing your specialty, or develop an independent brochure on sports facilities or tensile structures.

Whether printed or slated for your Web site, the fact sheet should contain the following parts:

Headline.

Description, as brief as the size of the project allows, stating the problem and your design solution.

Endorsement (excerpt from a flattering letter from a client, or a published media comment) (optional).

Statistical box score (area, cost, major materials, structural, mechanical, electrical, and communications systems). Make concise, as this type of information may not make exciting reading for the client (optional).

Credit box (names of clients—obtain approval before going any further—architects, engineers, interiors and landscape architects, other consultants, photographers, your firm's project team leaders).

Photographs (interior, exterior) with one-line captions and photograph credits.

Drawings (site plans, floor plans, landscaping plan, axonometrics if not so intricate as to be unintelligible.)

Firm's contact person or telephone/fax/e-mail (T/F/e) data.

See the following examples of headlines and project descriptions.

Project Fact Sheet A

New Canaan Country School
New Canaan, CT

In 1994, the school asked us to find a way to convert the 1955 auditorium—outmoded and inadequate to contemporary standards—into a space that would meet fully the needs for assembly and performance. Even as we were discovering the building's severe limitations as an auditorium, we embarked upon a campus-wide master plan that brought the old gymnasium, built in 1906 as a chapel, under scrutiny.

We saw that the gymnasium would make a wonderful auditorium and, with the surprised but enthusiastic approval of the school, we set about trading places. If the auditorium now serves doubly as a recreational gym, the gymnasium's essential architecture makes a nearly ideal auditorium. The 1,200-square-foot flat area serves for performances or for additional seating, while the steeply raked fixed seats ensure excellent sightlines.

Caption accompanying illustration: Cherry veneer wall panels and matching wood theater seats give the space a warm feeling as well as acoustical vibrancy. To accommodate the requirements of musical performances, an acoustical shell is created from tracked panels stored in the stage wings.

Oak Knoll School of the Holy Child
Summit, NJ

Oak Knoll's 1950s "gymatorium"—a multipurpose space for assembly and liturgical functions, drama and music performance, and physical education—was suffering from problems typical of such facilities: it lacked the appropriate configuration and ambiance of a first-rate auditorium, was too small to be a good gymnasium, and created scheduling nightmares. In implementing our ongoing master plan of the campus, we first created a new freestanding gymnasium for physical education, freeing up the old gymnasium for fewer and more coherent uses. The new steeply raked seating yielded a significant bonus for the school: enough space beneath the sloped seating to allow us to create a large formal conference room.

Caption accompanying illustration: Carpeted floors, fabric-wrapped acoustic wall panels, painted sheetrock walls, and ceiling panels all help control and focus the acoustics, making the auditorium as functionally flexible as it is attractive.

From a fact sheet depicting recently completed schools by
Butler Rogers Baskett. Reproduced by permission.

Project Fact Sheet B

MIT School of Architecture

The School of Architecture and Planning is located within MIT's prominent "main group" of monumental neo-classical structures built in the early 1900's. Over the years, the main space—three corridors off a central rotunda—had been virtually abandoned and the facilities of the academic departments were scattered in twelve different buildings. The goal of the renovation is to reunite the academic departments, studio and review spaces and to create a coherent identity for the School on the three floors within this main group.

By reconfiguring the space around the dome, the Renovation unifies the critical mass of studio and review areas, creating a symbolic new "heart" for the school. The new plan creates an ambulatory around the dome, where exhibitions, a cafe and design reviews enliven the space with views to dome coffers. In addition, the relocation of two of the corridors to a position adjacent to a windowless attic wall creates large, windowed studios and one continuous orienting view through exhibit and studio display areas.

Between the gallery and studio, new roll-up doors offer flexibility for students to expand either the studio space or the review space. The new studio spaces are fully wired for computers and sophisticated telecommunications, with power supply and network connections at every student desk, and provision to upgrade the network as more advanced technology becomes available.

A new exhibit, thesis and conference space is developed in the departmental office wing around a huge volume containing Frank Stella's 1994 mural Loohooloo. The 97-foot long, three dimensional, acrylic-on-molded-fiberglass painting completely encompasses a new conference room from floor to ceiling, creating an exciting visual environment.

From a fact sheet by Leers, Weinzapfel Associates. Reproduced by permission.

Project Fact Sheet C

Puget Sound Air Pollution Control Authority

The new offices for this Seattle environmental agency are in the two top floors of a turn-of-the-century office building that has been newly renovated. A skylit atrium was created to provide an organizing central element. Open work areas, library and conference rooms surround the atrium, and get natural light from it. A new connecting stair is located in this space, reinforcing the sense of community in the work place. The kites provide a Northwest air motif. The materials and design are direct, bold and clear, reflecting the agency's desire for a high level of design within the parameters of a public agency budget.

From a fact sheet by Paul Segal Associates Architects. Reproduced by permission.

Services Fact Sheets

If your firm's output is not a tangible product such as a building or landscape, but a service (see list below), consider developing a series of fact sheets that describe each service. Do this only if these services generate enough billings, or are projected to do so in your marketing plan, to justify creating sheets.

Examples of services may include: research, reasibility studies, client facilities inventory and database development, building systems development, environmental studies, energy conservation investigations, programming, construction management, software development.

In your text, cover these points:

Describe the service.
Tell the client why it's significant (helps the environment, reduces operating costs, speeds construction, enhances quality, improves community participation).
Describe briefly major accomplishments in this service.
Name the partner who directs this service; list major personal qualifications.
Give "how-to-contact" information.
Include endorsement or excerpted quote from a happy client.

For examples of project and services fact sheets, see page 26, top left and bottom.

For examples of project and services fact sheets, see page 26, top left and bottom.

Staff Resumes

Whether you enclose staff resumes with your brochure or with a proposal depends on the circumstances. Typically, brochure resumes comprise one sheet per significant person. For proposals, transcribe each prospective team member's biodata from your database into a narrative that shows how this person's talents will enhance the job.

Opinions vary on how to organize a person's brochure resume—listing or narrative? chronological order? most recent effort first or last? include a photograph or avoid it? On the whole, the most useful arrangement is:

Name and title.
Snappy sentence or two summarizing person's role and chief contributions in the recent past.
More detailed narrative of person's contributions (start with most recent, and work backward).
Education and licensing (weave into a narrative or list).
Personal information (marital status, children, place of residence, age) (optional).
Photograph (optional).

For a staff resume write-up, see the following example. (See also organization for proposals in chapter 4 and job applications in chapter 9.) Be sure to treat names equally for men and women. Use either first names or last names consistently for both sexes.

Elena Karageorgiu, Partner

Elena heads the firm's school planning and design services. Since joining the firm in 1990, she has contributed as a designer, and later as an associate and partner, to the planning and design of six suburban and inner-city high schools, three schools for grades K–8, and two facilities for special education. As partner in charge of Powell High School, St. Louis, she devised innovative, economic ways of building flexibility into the school, giving educators the option to apply new teaching methods with minimum need for renovation. On Thomas Middle School in Hannibal, Missouri, she incorporated into the design a simple but effective system for computer access in all classrooms and the resource center. All projects in which she had management input met clients' budgets and schedules.

Before joining Smith, Karageorgiu and Smith, Elena worked for six years at HOK in St. Louis, where she was project manager on several institutional buildings, including schools and small health facilities.

Elena has bachelor's and master's degrees in architecture from the School of Architecture at Washington University, St. Louis, and a master's degree in education from Columbia Teachers College, New York City. She is registered in the states of Missouri, Kansas, Colorado, California, and Ohio, and has the NCARB certificate.

In 1996 she received a special citation from the American Association of School Administrators for her contributions to school planning. School projects in which she took a role have been published in the *St. Louis Post-Dispatch, Architectural Chronicle,* and the *School Board Journal.* She is the author of *Schools and Education: Design Matters,* published in 1995 by Plato Press.

Client Liaison

Few items cause clients, new and seasoned, more anxiety than wondering how they will get along with their architect or other design professional. For example, what process does the consultant intend to establish to get the design started, and the work completed on time, on budget, at the specified quality, and with minimum friction all around?

Therefore, a page that depicts how your firm sets up the job, who will coordinate it and connect with the client, and what sorts of controls you have in place to manage costs, schedules, and quality are very useful in pursuing a job. (You can also incorporate this information into the initial firm description page of your brochure.)

As you write the page, avoid peppering it with vapid generalizations about your pledges to place the client first in all things, and vague pronouncements about your commitment to see that the project is built as designed, on budget, and on the money. If you do this, your page will resemble the page of every competitor who hasn't bothered to define the firm's strengths and has fallen back on clichés.

Try writing a 400-word statement about your firm's process, then compare it with the following client liaison statement.

As soon as a new client signs our agreement, Callay Associates appoints an associate of the firm who manages the project from beginning to end, under the overall guidance of a Callay partner. The project manager stays in constant touch with the individual assigned to the project by the client. The partner in charge is also on call to the client at all times.

The project manager establishes a schedule for delivering the project, including an estimated completion date, and develops daily schedules with each activity identified with a start and estimated completion date. By monitoring this schedule daily and relating it to key milestones and final completion, the project manager is able to adjust activities and bring added staff and other resources to bear to keep the client's project on schedule.

Callay also helps in organizing the client's staff for making the most effective decisions. Where appropriate, we bring our design team to the client's site for highly focused planning sessions in which the client's staff and user representatives play active parts in reaching design decisions.

The client's budget is a critical factor in our thinking. Like the client, we abhor surprises. From the start Callay makes sure that the scope of the client's project matches the client's budget. If there is a lack of fit, we propose alternative choices that bring the budget in line. Callay selects products, materials, and construction methods that offer the best performance for the cost, both to buy and to operate. We conduct frequent cost estimates at all phases, using our in-house estimating staff; we also retain outside estimators to check on our work. As a result, on our 30 most recent projects, final estimates have averaged within plus or minus 3.5 percent of final bids.

Callay operates with a sophisticated computerized management system using state-of-the-art project management and estimating software. Contract documents are produced on late-version CAD software (AutoCAD 14), and project documentation is routinely shared with consultants at the various phases—and with the client's representative as necessary—thereby reducing the risk of error. The system is run by designers and managers who are all computer-conversant. On complex projects, we recommend a project Web site.

The project manager consults with the client to schedule presentations and to obtain approvals at key phases of the work. After the project is completed, Callay helps clients resolve any post-occupancy issues.

Client Listings

Past clients intrigue future clients. List clients for whom you have done work in the past fifteen years, organized by type of project. In the case of very large firms with vast numbers of clients, make up separate sheets for each building type or project category. Choose clients who are likely to give you a good endorsement, but to add a note of realism do not omit clients with whom there were honest differences and who will be fair if contacted. Provide each client's city, state, and/or country, but avoid names and telephone numbers so as to keep some control over who is being contacted. As a courtesy, inform past clients they are to be on your list.

Past Project Listings

As with client listings, project listings give the client a flavor of the firm. Divide projects into categories. Include the name, location, area in square feet and metric, completion date, and a one-sentence description (such as "first coed dormitory on the St. Paul's campus"). Avoid cost figures—inflation may make older projects seem cheaper than they were; also, does the figure include site costs, fees, fixtures, furnishings, equipment—who knows? Best omit.

If you have a Web site, where space is not, relatively, a limitation, you can include more facts and crosslink to project fact sheets and added illustrations.

Publications and Honors Listings

Clients may or may not be interested in books and articles written by members of the firm. Include them if the client committee is heavily academic or the project involves government-sponsored research, where technical review panels are impressed by published works.

On the other hand, every client wants to know what honor awards your firm's projects and its staff have gained, and who has published articles about your work. That kind of third-party endorsement is gold.

Introduce the list sheet with a short statement, such as the following.

> The following listings reflect the views of others about our work and our people. The listing is divided into three parts: works written by our members; design honors awarded to our firm (personal awards are listed under each member's resume in another part of this brochure); and articles in the press about our projects or staff. Note that since 1976 Callay Associates has received 49 national or regional honor awards for design, and our work has been published at least once in each of the 11 professional journals listed in *The Architectural Index*.

Article Reprints

Have the graphic designer of your brochure develop a simple holder for article reprints. Unlike a dozen years ago, when magazines came in all sizes, today's magazine formats vary little. This makes it simpler to fit all reprints into one holder. Arrange with the journal's reprint department to fix typos or errors of fact. Most journals recommend waiting until the article appears before ordering reprints (ordering a press overrun ahead of time saves on some costs but creates others). Check too if the journal is able to forward an electronic image of the article directly to your Web site.

Containers and Binders

You can develop three sorts of binders for your brochure.
 • A folder made of stiff paper and die-cut pockets. The folder should be big enough to accommodate reprints from standard-format magazines. Some firms

cut small diagonal slots into the pocket flaps for slipping in a business card. Typically, you put inserts in the right-hand pocket and your transmittal letter in the left. Large or multidiscipline firms may develop a folder for each specialty, and print the name of the firm and the specialty on the cover. Decide how many pages you are likely to insert, so the folder is neither too stuffed nor too empty. Assume that the client won't reassemble the inserts in the order you planned, so mark the order of each insert with a numeral.

• A mechanical binder with a transparent acetate cover sheet and a plastic or metal spiral or ring binding. You can bind in the transmittal letter, and not have to worry about the inserted items getting lost or wrongly reassembled.

• A permanent binding. You keep insert items in inventory, then select appropriate items for a specific client or project and bind them permanently between preordered hard covers imprinted with your firm's name. The process is expensive. It may impress some clients with its extravagance, but it may alienate others for the same reason.

For an example of a binder, see page 25, top right.

For an example of a binder, see page 25, top right.

Smaller or emerging firms, with fewer projects to show, fewer articles and awards to their credit, and fewer dollars to invest, have other ways to bring their experience to the eyes of client prospects. As a partner in a young firm with a limited marketing budget, you should decide whether your dollars are better spent elsewhere, such as increased travel and "sales calls." This means more frequent travel to remotely located interviews, stepped-up bird-dogging, and investment in first-class photography, while reducing the role of printed brochures and similar "indirect" marketing products.

Brochure for the Emerging Firm

Here are suggestions I give smaller firms for reducing the size of your brochure while still communicating your credentials:

Combine in a single, four-page piece a description of your firm and its vision; how you work internally and connect with clients to keep projects on track; photographic images of two or three significant completed projects with short captions; listings of clients and of previous and current projects (if the list is short, give it more details); and a listing of published articles. Don't hesitate to include work and activities from prior firms, so long as you acknowledge the fact.

Include one-page resumes of key firm members.

Use top-quality prints of selected projects, with short attached descriptions and box score (area, cost, year completed, principal consultant credits, photo credits), or a sleeve of 35mm slides (slides can be awkward if the receiver does not have a light table, loupe, or projector).

Add article reprints to the brochure. These can be expensive for the small quantities you need; some firms order extra copies of the magazine and enclose a copy, with the article marked.

Review sample texts in the larger-firm brochure discussion above, and use them as guides to develop more concise versions for your own use. Simple brochures can be very effective even for larger firms. I once judged a marketing materials award contest; after looking at a great number of expensively produced brochures, my colleagues and I gave first prize to a clearly low-budget entry consisting of a brilliant, two-page, typed statement printed on the firm's fine letterhead, along with top-quality prints of four recently completed projects, with caption material attached to the backs. It isn't always the dollars that matter, but the insight that puts them to work. See the examples of low-cost projects with impact shown simply through good photographs, with brief captions attached, on page 27 and 28, top and bottom. Often these images with captions are mailed independently to lists of clients and prospects.

The Portfolio

The portfolio differs from the firm's brochure because it is a personal document. Whether you are applying for a grant or scholarship, for admission to graduate school, or for a job in a firm, you develop a portfolio to strut your talents. The portfolio is essentially a one-person brochure.

A design portfolio tends to be heavy on images and light on writing. That doesn't mean that you can ignore the written parts. These may include:

Transmittal letter
Statement of purpose
Descriptions and captions for design images
Resume

The mechanics of designing and producing a portfolio are covered in Harold Linton's work *Portfolio Design* (see Resources).

Student Portfolios

As a student, you will need a convincing portfolio to impress a granting agency or foundation and, above all, the interviewer at what may be your first employer. The core of your portfolio is examples of school work, especially drawings. Unless you elect to drag around full-size examples in a large portfolio carrying case, your drawings will need to be reduced to folder size. This risks losing a lot of detail, so you may have to simplify your full-size presentation drawings so they can be read at a reduced size.

Observe the top design magazines. They undertake this simplification process routinely; often designers edit out any complexities (such as toilet fixtures; window lines; sometimes even door swings) before sending drawings to the journals. You should go through the same editing process. Be sure to select only your best projects. No employer or foundation grants committee has the time or patience to look at every line you ever drew. Make sure your drawings are clearly identified—you may need to write short captions.

Then attend to your written material. Even if you present the portfolio in person, include a leave-behind customized letter of transmittal that dwells on your enthusiasm in being chosen, and summarizing (no more than that) your qualifications. Include in this letter presumably what you will be telling the interviewer in person—namely, your purpose in looking for work with the firm or in soliciting a grant from the foundation. Avoid pat generalities; be frank and open. Finally, include your resume (check chapter 8 for ways to write a strong one). Also review chapter 2 for good letter-writing technique.

Proposals

4

Proposals are marketing tools of the first importance. Clients issue requests for proposals (RfPs) to qualify vendors of design and other services on large or complex projects, and to look for specific qualifications as they seek the right firm to do the work. Clients do not, as a rule, select their design professionals only from proposals, but also do follow-up interviews. Since clients may expect a high number of responses to their RfP, the proposals allow them and their staffs to review qualifications at leisure. The far more time-consuming mode of face-to-face interviews follows once a short list of firms is established.

Writing the winning proposal therefore requires a blend of marketing savvy and effective packaging, made up of focused writing and catchy visuals.

A typical RfP for design services includes a statement of the desired result, a description of the circumstances of the project, the delivery schedule, the budget (not always included at this stage), a detailed description of services required, and instructions to proposers as to the form or format for submitting the response. If there is a point system for the evaluation, it is described here. Some RfPs request a prescribed or "closed" form of response. Closed forms include the so-called federal SF 254 and SF 255 forms described later in this chapter. The format for "open" forms is left to the responding design firm. An example of an actual RfP is shown later in this chapter.

Whether or not to respond to an RfP is a business decision. Factors to consider include the size of your backlog, your proficiency in the design type being solicited, the odds on the work being "wired" to another designer, the reputation of the client, and the size of the fee. (Being "wired" occurs when designers who help the client develop the RfP—because of special expertise—are sometimes rewarded by receiving an inside track in the competition.) The message—in this case the marketing message—must shape the writing. Said another way, the written message must be closely linked to its marketing purpose. The parts of a proposal ordinarily included in the response to an RfP (listed on page 62) comprise a framework. From it we will focus on certain proposal components where the quality of writing is critical and can make the difference between a winner and an also-ran.

A typical proposal comprises the following parts. You may consolidate some parts if the proposal is modest in scope, but be sure all the subject is covered.

Cover
Letter of transmittal (sometimes attached to the cover, sometimes bound into the proposal, sometimes both)
Executive summary (or abstract)
Table of contents (for long proposals only)
Statement of your understanding of the problem
Scope of offered services
Organization of the team, and reporting relationships
Resumes of key team members, including recognition
Proposed schedule for completing the work
Record of experience on like projects, including Uniform Resource Locator (URL) of your firm's Web site
Firm honors, awards, and publications
References
Requested fee (if asked; usually sealed)
Other supporting materials (project description sheets, slide sleeves, reprints, CD-ROMs, diskettes)

All parts of the proposal are critical. Lists of projects and clients and personnel resumes need to be rewritten from a master and adapted to each project proposal. Other parts are written from scratch and are extremely important. These include the letter of transmittal, the executive summary, the statement of understanding of the problem, the scope of services, and the personal qualifications of key proposed team members.

As noted, proposals are often evaluated on a point system, with a total of attainable points ranging from several hundred up to thousands. Points are awarded for responses to such criteria as clarity of concept, the proposer's credentials and experience, cost effectiveness of the proposal (unless this is a design-build project, this is usually deferred to a later stage), and readiness to meet a delivery schedule.

In addition, there are always special hot buttons that your shrewd reading of the RfP will uncover, even though the RfP may not list them specifically.

Check out the following selection of potential hot buttons:

Concern for environmental features, such as wetlands
An ironclad budget
Proposer's skill in helping promote project to voters, when a public project is not yet funded
Concern over operating costs, including energy conservation
A desire for breaking the mold in design, technical innovation, urban planning
Concern for minority participation
An inflexible schedule (start of school or academic year; space leasing agreements; scheduling of major concert or art show)
Ability to handle overseas language and practices
Concern for security

There may be additional hot buttons you discover as you scan the RfP. Your response to these must be clearly stated in the executive summary, and kept in the forefront as you write the other parts of the proposal.

The following is an actual RfP. It has been adapted to the format of this book, but its salient points have been retained. I have eliminated the part of the request asking proposers also to build and operate the facility and help finance its construction. Read the text and note on a pad any hot buttons that emerge.

Southampton, a prosperous township on the south shore of Long Island, New York, resolved to build a new indoor recreational, health, and fitness facility within the town limits. Following are key selected sections of the town's RfP. A suggested executive summary in response to the RfP appears on pages 70-71.

Examining a Request for Proposal (RfP)

TOWN OF SOUTHAMPTON
Department of Parks, Recreation & Human Services
Community Recreation, Health & Fitness Complex

Introduction
The purpose of this Request for Proposal (hereinafter referred to as "RfP") is to solicit proposals for the design [construction and management] of a new indoor recreational, health, and fitness facility located in the Town of Southampton (hereinafter referred to as "the Town"). The Town envisions a centrally located, family-oriented facility featuring an indoor pool and other amenities.

Backgrounds
The Town of Southampton is uniquely blessed with an attractive physical setting that has fostered a rich and intriguing history of events dating back to the colonial period. Still largely unspoiled by urbanizing influences, Southampton draws its vitality from a unique interdependence of farming, fishing, tourism, and the second-home industry. The community is particularly noted for the varied mix of its people, which includes artists, intellectuals, sports enthusiasts, nationally recognized entertainers, and captains of industry, as well as people who support the above sectors of the community's economy. It is this unique balance between all sector interests that we are striving to retain and enhance.

The Town lies 68 miles east of New York City. It is approximately 145 square miles in land size and is the largest of Suffolk County's five east-end towns in land area.

The Town has a population of approximately 45,000 year-round and 85,000 peak seasonal, or a grand total of 130,000 seasonal plus year-round population. Projections are that the population of the Town will continue to increase to over 47,000 year-round residents by the year 2000. Further, it is believed that as lifestyles change during the remainder of the century and beyond, many seasonal homes will be occupied year-round or for most seasons (e.g., all but winter).

Municipally sponsored recreational, health, and fitness programs are administered by the Town's Department of Parks, Recreation & Human Services. Town programs cover a wide range of topics, including funding of human services projects, art instruction, nutrition programs, senior clubs, exercise classes, senior adult day care, and educational events. The majority of these programs take place in Town buildings.

The Town also sponsors swimming lessons. Although the Town's waterways are its greatest natural resource, Southampton currently lacks adequate aquatic municipal year-round recreational facilities for its residents and visitors. The Town provides swimming lessons to only about 500 of its youth on an annual basis, the Town being limited in this regard to giving these lessons in its natural waterways during the summer season. Of the more than a dozen elementary schools, at least four high schools, and one college located within the Town, not one has a swimming pool.

The Town now seeks to create a complex of size and diversity that encourages interaction, involvement, and vitality among all its people. The continued success of Southampton as a resort depends on a successful planning project that will continue to protect these intrinsic qualities of the Town that create a magnet for regional tourism.

Priorities

The Town invites proposals to provide adequate year-round recreational facilities for its residents. The centerpiece for the proposed complex would be an indoor swimming pool to accommodate swimming lessons, fitness classes, leisurely swimming, and competition. It is important to the Town that the pool be readily accessible at all times to members of the public.

The Town is seeking to establish a complex in size and diversity that encourages interaction and involvement of all the Town's residents. The Town believes that a recreational complex that includes, but is not limited to, an indoor pool, weight training room, gymnasium, and aerobic classroom will accomplish this objective.

[There follows a listing of key spaces, with areas.] Spaces include an entrance lobby suitable for exhibitions and other educational and public activities; a pool to be used for competitive, instructional, and recreational swimming; a weight training room; an aerobics room; a gymnasium; men's and women's locker rooms; and a storage area of approximately 500 square feet to hold equipment, supplies, and miscellaneous items.

Also required is an on-site child-care room. Added later may be an outdoor pool and other facilities adjacent to the recreation complex. The facility will also house the Town's Department of Parks, Recreation & Human Services administrative personnel.

The design of a coordinated community-based services delivery system rests with the community, including the active participation of the community advisory network. This advisory network is composed of agency and individual representatives from across the socioeconomic spectrum of the community.

Proposals will be evaluated on a point system (total 350 points) described below.

Goals and Objectives

The Town has the following objectives for the Community Recreation, Health & Fitness Complex with an overall goal of providing integrated services directed towards youth, seniors, and families:

- To work with families, agencies, schools, citizens, and governmental leaders to ensure effective local community planning, development, and use of resources.
- To facilitate the design of specific integrated services for youth, seniors, and families.
- To facilitate the delivery of integrated services responsive to community needs, in a more cost-effective manner.
- To encourage community health and fitness through the use of recreational facilities in a therapeutic environment.
- To make the facility and its programs available to visitors in order to create a magnet for regional tourism.
- To achieve accessibility to the greatest number of residents and visitors.

Basis of Award

Proposal Content
- Cover letter. The letter must contain a statement of intent, indicating the proposer's understanding of the project.
- Proposer information.
- Abstract [executive summary]. Please provide an abstract of no more than three hundred words about your project. It should address, at a minimum, the items listed below. You may also include other information relevant to the project:
    who will be served by the project and what is their need;
    the approach you will take to meet that need;
    the results you anticipate from the project;
    the project location.
- Scope of work.
- Estimating ultimate results. Based on the needs of the community your project will serve and the service(s) your

project will offer, estimate, in measurable terms, the performance targets you aim to achieve.
• Project management. Provide a statement of qualifications and resume of each member of the project management team.
• Budget.

Evaluation Criteria
Proposals will be evaluated on a point system, with a total of 350 points available. Criteria include qualifications, experience, past performance of proposer and staff, budget, and overall quality of the proposed approach to the program.

A rapid scan of the above RfP immediately suggests certain hot buttons. These include:

A desire to attract families to the township by offering an attractive recreation facility
A desire to develop town-owned land
The goal for the complex to serve as a community focus for the town's diverse constituencies, such as well-to-do business people, artists, and sports partisans, thereby boosting their loyalty to the town that is part of their lives
Preparation for increased year-round living in this historically summer resort township
Serving the athletic needs of local schools
Desire to hike municipal revenues through heightened tourism.

Planning Your Proposal

You have gone into a huddle with your partners, decided that according to criteria noted in this chapter the job is worth going after, identified your project team, composed your statement of the understanding of the client's problem, forged your take on the scope of services you will offer, determined the delivery schedule, adapted the resumes of the team leader and team members to the job, and gathered related project lists and reprints.

When responding to an RfP, avoid the kind of writing that has come to be known as "proposalese." Writing a proposal is no different from writing a letter. Yet some proposals read like a cross between a specification for a space station and an insurance policy. Avoid such clunkers as "the undersigned shall initiate, implement, and finalize the contract documents within a time frame of thirteen calendar months" when you can just as well write "we will complete all contract documents in thirteen months." Good English, as noted in chapter 1, can be made to appeal to many client levels—the level of a General Electric Company technical staffer ("influencer") reviewing a proposal to build a fiber-optic cable manufacturing facility, or the level of the vice president for facilities or CEO ("decision makers"), whose votes help select the winner.

A proposal is not commonly a contract document. If accepted, the lawyers will enter to convert its provisions into a legally tight contract. This does not, however, excuse loose language in the proposal, any more than it does a surfeit of designer-babble.

Finally, in your concern for style, don't neglect the whole. There is always the risk, with many staff people in your firm tapped to write and assemble the proposal package, for consistency to be lost in the shuffle. Most firms with an active RfP response program appoint a manager to shepherd the process. It's too easy, in the pressure to complete the whole, to lose sight of the written quality of the parts. Every sentence, diagram, and supporting item must bolster the theme of the proposal. Just as a fine building, park, bridge, or interior has its artistic unity, so a skillfully prepared proposal hangs together as a single, cohesive example of good writing (and good marketing).

Organizing the Proposal

In your preliminary huddle, canvass your firm for unique types of contributions. For example, if your proposal deals with renovating a large, outdated exterior theater in a big city, make the most of a partner with a lifelong interest in the theater who worked as a production stage manager, has a degree in theater and lighting design, and may even own a stagehand union card.

Appoint a proposal-writing shepherd at the start; this person makes assignments for writing text, assembling illustrations, and making sure that RfP requirements are strictly adhered to. The shepherd should develop a simple critical path pinpointing which activities are pressing. Arrange for fact checking, editing, printing, and binding (some clients, especially public clients, may demand up to 50 copies).

Even if you are a very small firm, the process for organizing the proposal is much the same. It is like cooking a meal—some items have longer lead times and need to be caught, bought, processed, and cooked earlier than others. A simple bar chart, with days marked across the top and activities listed down the side, is useful to keep work on target.

Finally, do not try to save pennies on the delivery. I know of a firm that shipped an important proposal due in Washington, D.C., at 5 P.M. on a particular Wednesday, and thought it would save money by sending it first-class mail. The proposal failed to arrive, and all the effort was wasted. I have known firms to send a staff member by plane to deliver a proposal personally. When you consider that a proposal may be worth $80,000 in fees, it seems absurd to try to save the difference between a $300 plane fare and $4.75 in first-class postage. Yet it happens more often than you would think.

Above all, focus on how to make your proposal stand out from your competitors'. First, offer a clear sense of understanding the client's wants and needs (note the difference—what the client wants may not be entirely what the client needs. It's your job as a design professional to point this out). Second, come through with a clear direction as to how you would go about solving the client's problem. Check and recheck the applicable hot buttons. Third, keep your writing simple; avoid throwing a lot of complex terminology at a client. Why waste effort on a brilliant content if the message is lost on the client?

Letter of Transmittal

The transmittal letter is as a rule a short note (no more than one page) to the designated client official. The purpose of the transmittal letter is to provide a personal touch to the proposal package, to highlight in a simple paragraph what you expect to bring to the table, and in general to set an upbeat tone for your proposal.

Scenario

Write a transmittal letter for your proposal prepared in response to an RfP calling for preserving and recycling a historic courthouse as a step in reviving a decaying neighborhood. Compare it with the following example.

Letter

Ms. Maria Overton
Contracting Officer
State Facilities Administration
2000 K Street NE
Chicago, IL 60690

Dear Ms. Overton:

Attached is our firm's proposal for services in response to your RfP #98-415 for architectural and engineering services for restoring and renovating the historic Van Buren Building on F Street.

We are very excited about what this project will do to revive a once eminent city neighborhood while adding valuable office space.

Our proposal presents our firm's ability to make good your goal. George Links, our award-winning preservation architect, will be assigned to the project, backed by a team of experienced specialists, with a single project manager responsible to your designated contact person. You will see from their resumes that they are a creative and experienced group.

You will also find a detailed description of the scope of services we propose. We understand you must move into the renovated building by September 2000, and the proposal specifies how we plan to meet your schedule. We also include an illustrated portfolio of similar projects designed by our firm, including the Hay County Courthouse, winner of an Illinois state design honor award, and a CD-ROM with a profile of our 18-year-old firm.

We hope this submittal gives you the information you requested, and that it conveys our enthusiasm for the project. We look forward to introducing our entire team as you proceed with your selection process.

Sincerely,
George Grant
Partner
Grant, Grant and Smithfield

Proposal-writing architects sometimes use the cover letter as a letter of introduction to summarize their take on the project. Here is an actual excerpt from a short-listed proposal for the new San Diego Main Library by the association of William P. Bruder-Architect, Ltd., McGraw/Baldwin Architects, and Manuel Oncina, Architect.

The new San Diego Main Library will be the last large American library to be completed before the start of the new millennium. It must acknowledge the finest traditions of the past in which librarians were the recognized caretakers of knowledge. As the concept of the library is transformed into a space-age platform of technology in 1999, librarians will be the navigators of knowledge. Their computers will instantly make the collection available to the entire globe. We will no longer define libraries according to number of volumes, but by megabytes! . . .

While some may see the site covered by a building edge to edge, we see a great landscaped public piazza, an energized entry forecourt over which a library of the future magically hovers as it kinetically reaches out to its citizens. Creating a place of sensual power and public pride will be as important as creating a place which seeks functional perfection . . .

The Library must reach to greet the light of the sun as a distinctive sculptural form of timeless civic presence. The opportunity to create a garden in the sky adjacent to reading rooms and collections is an idea that has much more power than creating a mere roof.

A city's main library is where children come to meet their first books. A main library is a place where a city defines its respect for knowledge. A main library is where young adults discover where their lives will take them. A main library is a place where people go for free entertainment and cultural growth. A main library is a building where everyone wins and memories of life begin.

To conceive a library whose architecture inspires the soul and thrills the senses must be the goal. To build a place of pride, pragmatism and poetry must be the charge of us all.

This text contains a poetic quality unusual in typical proposal writing.

Executive Summary (or Abstract)

The executive summary is one of the most critical elements of a proposal. It is read by two categories of people—influencers and decision makers. The influencers—the client's technical staff—go through the entire proposal with a fine-tooth comb and make a recommendation. The top official—the decision maker—is usually a nontechnical person, and is certain to be pressed for time. So keep technical verbiage to a minimum, eliminate jargon, and limit the executive summary to three pages at most.

Write your executive summary last, after the rest of the proposal has been written and assembled. The executive summary is for those decision makers without the time to scrutinize the whole proposal, and often without a technical grasp of the design profession's terminology. Use the summary to give those readers a capsule version of the proposal's content, highlighting the main direction of your approach to the problem. The summary should rarely exceed three pages, or it loses its value.

Thus the executive summary for the Southampton recreation, health, and fitness center on pages 63–66 could read as follows in this excerpt:

We understand the Southampton citizens' resolve to attract families by offering an attractive facility for recreation, fitness, and health. Given Southampton's special standing in the Long Island region and its broadly diverse community-oriented citizenry, this project will be another valuable asset in a town already rich in built and natural resources.

Because the population of Southampton varies widely, from a constant base to summer peak population, we believe it is in your best interest for the project to be designed to expand as necessary. Conversely, whenever the population diminishes, the complex must be flexible enough so that portions may be dismantled until the need reappears.

The idea for an indoor pool to accommodate multiple uses is practical, but we suggest that two smaller support pools be added. Very small children, pregnant mothers, elderly people, and the infirm can choose these pools instead of having to swim in the heavily used main pool.

Your budget as it looks now seems to us low for what you hope to obtain. To build 35,000 sq. ft. at $150 per sq. ft. requires $5,250,000, which is considerably higher than your stated budget of $3.5 million. We recommend that you approach sources of added funding at the state and federal levels and in the private sector (we are ready to suggest an array of such sources); you may also phase the scope of the work by building certain facilities—such as the pool complex—first, and others as funding becomes available.

Your projected occupancy date is May 1999. We feel this date is feasible provided you select the design team before March 1997 and you authorize design to get under way immediately thereafter. To further ensure that your dates are adhered to, we propose that project delivery be done on a fast-track or phased basis. This may make for earlier occupancy of the buildings and reduce the interest and carrying charges on construction financing.

Added sections of the executive summary would introduce the key prospective team members, describe project management and leadership, and briefly list your firm's main qualifications.

Statement of the Problem

The statement of the problem is a sign from you to the client that you have captured the essence of the client's purpose in issuing the RfP. But rather than merely throwing back at the client what is in the RfP, you need to convey your understanding of the client's underlying needs, not only the listing of spaces and connections.

Using the Southampton example, consider this wording (excerpts):

- Despite the abundant waterways around Southampton, which are also the town's greatest resource, there is no adequate year-round municipal recreational swimming facility. Of the more than dozen elementary, secondary, and college facilities located within the town, none has a swimming pool.
- The proposed complex would encourage greater and better contacts throughout the community, and provide a focus for such contacts.
- The complex will also become a source for additional revenue as tourists and summer families take advantage of its facilities.
- The town boasts a diverse community of artists, artisans, show business and media people, academics, and sports enthusiasts. The complex will encourage useful interplay among these groups.
- The main indoor pool is the central component and focus of the facility. It will be used for competitive, recreational, and instructional swimming. To encourage active interest, bleachers should be provided to seat up to 750 people.
- The weight room, aerobic room, and gymnasium are to serve all segments of the community, from infants to the elderly. A child-care room will allow parents or guardians to drop off children so they may use the pool and other amenities.

Other sections of the statement deal with integration of various age groups in the town, the need to run the sports facility under professional guidance, charging modest fees for use, and seeking additional financing through direct investment or fundraising.

Covers

Proposal covers should be simple, lucid, legible, devoid of cute graphics, and should clearly list the name and location of the project and the name of your firm (see page 28, right).

Standard Forms 254 and 255

Standard Form (SF) 254 is required by the federal government when it is procuring architectural, engineering, and related services from firms. The 11-page, 8½-by-11-inch form is kept on file at any federal agency with which a design professional wants to do business.

The 11-page SF 255 is submitted to supplement SF 254 and covers a specific construction project for which the government has just issued an RfP. The two forms are also popular, as is or amended, with state, county, and municipal agencies and in the private sector.

Instructions for filing are included on the first two pages of each form. (Forms may be ordered singly, in pads, or as formatted software from the U.S. Government Printing Office, North Capitol and H Streets, NW, Washington, DC 20540. Telephone 202/512-0000, or the Federal Office Building bookstore in your area.)

In SF 254, there is little leeway on the form itself for writing, beyond the need to make lists and references precise. The form discourages enclosures such as brochures, added lists, and photography. The time required, according to the government, to assemble material for this form is one hour. Be sure to replace SF 254s you have on file at agencies with updated ones from time to time.

In SF 255, for a specific project, the best opportunity for creative writing occurs in section 10. This is the last section, and it consists of a blank page in which to insert "any additional information or description of resources (including any computer design capabilities) supporting your firm's qualifications for the proposed project." In other words, you have about 350 words in roughly 12-point type to convey a strong message of competence, suitability, and depth. Because in earlier sections of SF 255 you have listed past projects and resumes of the principal players, here's your chance to shine with an elevating, spirited declaration of your understanding of the problem, citing the main hot buttons, describing in more detail one or two key past projects and why they are important, and listing any added resources. These may include your state-of-the-art CAD system or the plane you own to service a remotely located project.

Newsletters and Other Marketing Tools

5

This chapter takes up writing newsletters, news or press releases, and text for design award submittals and exhibit panels.

Firms use newsletters either as a marketing tool or, internally, to inform and motivate their staff. The client newsletter is taken up in this chapter. The in-house newsletter is discussed in chapter 6.

The external, or client, newsletter is a helpful marketing tool so long as its content provides value. Avoid the common habit of focusing so much on the firm's in-house activities of little or no interest to outsiders that it reads less like a newsletter and more like a house organ.

The newsletter as a modern medium is a way of reaching people who are strapped for time. It can be fast and economical to produce, is versatile, and lends itself to simple but telling graphics. In an era of Web sites it is easily posted, thereby avoiding the cost of printing and mailing—although for years to come there will always be a demand for a printed version. State-of-the-art desktop publishing, equipped with chart-making and page-making software and a good scanner, can make the entire writing, design, and production process fast, cheap, accurate, and, depending on the graphic design, attractive.

What matters is the content. Select topics you can link closely with your firm's objectives but, at the same time, spark the interest of prospects in your marketplace. For example, an architect or consulting engineer active in environmentally conscious design can feature completed "green" projects, along with a brief article by an in-house specialist. A graphic designer whose focus is on signing (wayfinding) can show a recent directional system for an acute-care hospital or airport terminal, two building types in which it's seldom easy to find your bearings.

Do not confine newsletter content to featuring projects. Your firm's expertise most likely extends to other areas such as technical innovation, urban design experience and construction in deteriorated neighborhoods, or unusual performance in managing projects.

Before selecting client newsletter topics, consider the following criteria.

Performance. Does the story show clear evidence of good performance, measured by such factors as user satisfaction, productivity (if a workplace or factory), and design recognition?

The Newsletter

Budget, schedule. Did the project meet the owner's construction budget and delivery schedule? What about the maintenance and operating budgets?

Good will. Was there evidence of good rapport with the owner during design and construction?

Special issues. Can the project be viewed as a symbol of your progressive attitude on such matters as the new workplace, social concerns for the sick and the elderly, the special challenges of international practice, the adoption of a state-of-the-art lighting or acoustical technique?

Topics for a Client Newsletter

The following list suggests candidate topics for a newsletter. Note that every article doesn't have to be about a project. Don't be modest about your firm's other accomplishments, such as public or professional recognition of one of your projects or people, or a senior promotion. At the same time, don't try to make a newsletter do the job of the news release. The news release covers a single event, and there is immediacy. The newsletter deals with many happenings and a three-month-old event is okay.

Projects
Recently completed facility or design (photographs)
Significant commissioned new work (models, plans)
Progress images of a difficult preservation job
Completed intelligent-building investigation
Recent feasibility report for a major district school renovation plan

Practice
Example of effective completion of problem-ridden (through no fault of yours) project in time and on the money
Innovative use of CAD software to produce complex project involving a large team of consultants and a many-headed client
Innovative teamwork on a design-build enterprise

Business
Merger (this story has been preceded by a news release)
New joint venture

Recognition (for a project)
Design award from a client association such as the American Association of School Administrators, the Building Owners and Managers Association International, the American Hospital Association
Design award from a society of fellow professionals and its national, regional, state, and local organizations
Design award from a journal published by the above, or by independent journals with reputable award programs
Significant story about a firm's project published in a design publication or the general media

Recognition (for staff or the firm)
Personal honor accorded the firm or individual members. Limit these to professional activities, such as election to fellowship in your society, and civic activities such as appointments to local or federal panels that deal with the built environment
Major speech to a client organization

Illustrations
Projects (completed, if possible)
People

Be sure not to let the newsletter tail wag your firm's dog. Four to eight pages is a good length. Limit the newsletter to three or four issues a year, or you'll end up an unwelcome presence in the client's mailbox. A rule of thumb is to send out a newsletter often enough so the client is aware of you, but not so much as to be a bore. Supply boxes (❏) next to individual items, so the client can check off items of interest and return that page to you for more information; you never know when a client is on the verge of launching a new project.

When putting together a newsletter, consider these steps:

Planning. A newsletter should be fresh, spontaneous, and informal. Its editor should assemble items that have accumulated since the last issue, rank them according to the criteria discussed earlier, and consult the firm's project backlog for newcomer candidates for the next issue.

Writing. Keep the style simple and informal (observe the guideposts of chapter 1). Eschew material that smacks of chest-thumping and does little to boost the client's curiosity about your firm. If you have to work with a submitted text, say from a colleague, edit it rigorously to conform to guidelines for good writing (see chapter 17 for tips on how to edit a text effectively). Headlines should be "active" and specific, and should tell a story—e.g., "$100 million teaching hospital uses innovative design of patient and visitor spaces."

Illustrations. Photographs need captions—avoid forcing the reader, in the interest of a clean-looking page, to dig for photo descriptions in the text or deduce them from a minimal caption.

Design. While writing is extremely important, your newsletter is no better than the quality of its design. Your in-house or retained graphic designer will know how to express your firm's personality with a fresh, eye-catching, and readable design. Basic standards exist about what colors and what saturation percentage allow you to read type and which do not, and how small the type can be before you need to haul out a magnifying glass. Do not allow graphic quirks to get in the way of a readable newsletter.

See the sample newsletters on page 76 and page 26, top right.

The News Release

The news release, while quite an inexpensive way to get the word out to clients and prospects—especially if you use e-mail and/or post it on your Web site—still tends to cost money and time. (It makes sense to retain a professional pub-

KCGA Fact Sheet

November 1997   Snow Loads

Snow loading conditions greatly affect building roof system designs.

General Description of Loading

When designing the roof of a structure, the two primary loading conditions are snow load and live load. Snow loads will often control roof designs in the northern half of the country. Along with the weight of a uniformly distributed snow layer on the structure, other factors such as roof shape, roof projection and location relative to other buildings will contribute to the accumulation of snow drifts and areas of increased loading.

Drift Considerations

A roof's shape is a factor in the loading of the roof. The shape affects how the snow will drift and slide. Thus, the shape can create conditions of concentrated loading above the uniformly distributed snow loading. Single gable roofs, for example, may require an unbalanced load case where one side of the roof is fully loaded and the other side is partially loaded. A tangible example of this loading is a gable facing east. Here, the south side of the roof, which receives a great deal of sun, will allow partial melting while the north side, which does not benefit from sunshine, will maintain a full snow load. Other roof areas that require special design criteria are valleys and eaves. These areas are natural locations where snow slides, accumulates and can remain for extended periods of time.

Roof projections and parapets are also locations where snow can easily gather. Examples of these include mechanical screens, large mechanical equipment and changes in roof elevation. The magnitude of the drift load at such locations depends on the height of the obstruction - the higher the obstruction the larger the drift can become. Thus, the greater the roof's snow load will become in this area.

Effects of Other Structures on Drift Design

Other factors which affect snow load design concern the location of the roof relative to other roofs and buildings. A drift load can occur if a low roof is adjacent to higher roof of the same structure or even a neighboring structure which is taller. This particular situation commonly occurs when designing an addition to an existing structure. If the addition is taller than the original facility, the existing structure must be checked for the drift loads which did not exist for its original design. Consequently, this may require reinforcement of the original roof structure should the additional loading be beyond the strength of the existing system.

Drift Calculations

Calculations for snow drifting involve several factors: the ground snow load for that area of the country, the horizontal length of roof projections or roof offsets and the height of the adjacent obstruction or offset causing the drift. The ground snow load value varies from 0 (in places like Florida) to 100 psf (in upper Maine). This ground snow load, P_g, which is used for the drift load calculation, is also used to determine the uniformly distributed roof snow load and snow density. The horizontal length of adjacent roofs, W_b, has a code determined minimum value of 50 feet. With all of the variables known, the height of the drift, h_d, is calculated through an equation: $h_d = 0.43 (W_b)^{1/3}(P_g + 10)^{1/4} - 1.5$. The drift height obviously cannot exceed the height of obstruction or offset and therefore is the upper limitation of the value h_d.

Conclusion

The code-required analysis and design criteria for snow loading is critical for the structural integrity of a building's roof framing. It can be readily seen during the winter months that snow drifting is a very real occurrence and must be factored as a part of a building's design. Not only is this design criteria important in the Midwest; but, it becomes increasingly critical in more northern areas as heavier snowfalls occur and longer periods of cold weather exist.

Marcia Bolton, E.I.T.

KERR CONRAD GRAHAM ASSOCIATES
8008 Floyd   Overland Park, Kansas 66204
913-341-5833   Fax: 913-341-9222
e.mail Address: info@kcgassoc.com

Specializing in Civil and Structural Engineering
801 Walnut, #301   Kansas City, Missouri 64106
816-474-5833   Fax: 816-474-9221
Home Page: http://www.kcgassoc.com

The Kerr Conrad Graham Associates newsletter is a simple, readable, one-page fact sheet useful to clients and published monthly. Reproduced by permission.

lic relations firm whenever the desired audience involves the mass media, where you are less likely to have good contacts than among the professional media.) To do a news release, the topic must be worthwhile. It may be the appointment of a new top principal in the firm, the award of a significant research grant, the completion of a high-profile project that fulfilled contract requirements despite arduous circumstances, the award of a weighty commission that had every competitor's mouth watering, a merger, or a new product or service—in other words, a single momentous event. Clients and editors receiving your release are already overloaded with messages, so choose your topic with care.

The date of the release depends on the event. For nonmedia recipients, such as your client database, timing is less critical than it is for a release sent to the media, which have publication dates and, therefore, deadlines. Consult one of the media directories listed in the Appendix for deadlines. Monthly magazines commonly write their news columns at least four to six weeks before their publication dates. It makes more sense to issue the release when the content is ready to be spilled. Some releases still include an embargo date ("Do not publish before May 8"), but few media observe this and the attempt is usually futile.

Finally, don't do a news release if your project client has resources and contacts far superior to yours. (Some owner-designer agreement clauses actually give the client the sole right to issue a release. At all events an okay from the client is advisable).

Most firms maintain a mailing database broken up into one or more of the categories shown here:

Past clients
Current clients
Client prospects
　　(The above three groups can be further subdivided by building type. If
　　your firm has a major concentration, such as residential, the list may be
　　further divided by single family, multifamily, assisted living, etc.)
Media
　　(Media can be further subdivided by various classes of print media,
　　broadcast media, and cable media. For details, see chapter 10.)
Web sites
　　(Your database presumably contains Web site addresses, also known as
　　Uniform Resource Locators—URLs—for the target list.)
Employees
Friends of the firm
Your clipping bureau

The news release consists of six parts:

Headline
Contact information
Release date (but see above)
Dateline
Text
Supplements

Headline. This should be informative, active, specific, and dramatic. It should not be coy, cute, or corny. Be wary of humor: everybody loves it, but it is a dangerous medium and usually ends up offending someone. Here are a few examples of poor and good headlines.

Poor:

LARGE OVERSEAS COMMISSION

Good:

CHICAGO'S LAMB ASSOCIATES WINS 20-FIRM CONTEST TO DESIGN $200 MILLION MIXED-USE CENTER IN MALAYSIA

Poor:

MAJOR PARK GREENING IS ANNOUNCED

Good:

NEW YORK CITY TAPS ELM & PARTNERS TO RENOVATE OLMSTED'S PROSPECT PARK BY 2001

Contact information. List at the top one or two persons prepared to answer questions. Provide their telephone and fax numbers and e-mail addresses. Since business is done globally these days, make sure these numbers are good twenty-four hours a day.

Release date. Optional. Avoid including data in the release that would cause harm if someone jumps the date.

Dateline. This appears at the head of the first paragraph—e.g., "New Orleans, 27 July 1998." It helps to put the event in the context of place and time.

Text. Place the beef up front. Editors begin to cut long press releases starting from the back. Other recipients, such as clients, often lack the patience to read a release to the end. The five Ws are still excellent guides. In the first paragraph or two try to tell the reader the what, who, where, when, and why of the event. As you proceed, keep adding details until you get to the two-page limit, then stop. Once you have described the event, the release is a good vehicle for piggy-backing some stirring background on your firm, especially relevant projects and other accomplishments. Work in a quote or two by key players—avoid the kind of stiff statement that was obviously written by someone else. On the printed version, double-space the text and leave one-inch margins for use by the client reader or editor.

Supplements. The news release is to whet the appetite with basic relevant facts, not to cover every angle. Supplements can include a couple of headshots, a 3-D simulation of the proposed project, a site plan of a development, or a page of statistics. Failing that, state in a final line that such material is available and give a contact number. Avoid loading up the release with supplements—the reader, instead of acting on the release, may just set it aside for further study.

Scenario

Your thirty-person firm, Brown & Madison, is about to reach its twenty-fifth anniversary, and you and your partner have picked this occasion to announce the handing over of the firm's reins to a younger group of colleagues. Over the years, your firm has designed and had built a large volume of architectural projects, especially residential work of all types and at all market levels. This has earned you numerous design and firm awards, and you now have a substantial backlog. You, your partner, and several of the designers have received honors, professional and public. You wish to spread the word on the changeover to those audiences the firm must continue to depend on for its prosperity.

Write a two-page (maximum) news release, including headline, contact information, dateline, text, list of supplements, and distribution list.

Note: The hard news is the change in ownership of a well-established firm. Collateral news lies in the firm's goals for the future. You can enhance the bare announcements with relevant facts about the new partners/owners, the firm's reputation, and a quote or two from an outgoing and an incoming partner.

Compare your news release with the version below.

News Release

BROWN & MADISON TO RETIRE, JOHNSON AND KIM TO HEAD FIRM; HOUSING ARCHITECTS PLAN TO GO GLOBAL, PUSH DESIGN-BUILD

Contact: Emily Woods, Tel: 994/345-9876, Fax: 994/345-9955, e-mail: ewoods@ola.com
Release at will

Denver, 30 April 1998. Dale Johnson and Andrea Kim will be the new principals of the architectural firm known since 1973 as Brown & Madison, partner Harrison Brown announced today. The firm will keep its present name until 1 July 1999; after that it will be known as Johnson, Kim and Associates.

"Skip Madison and I started the firm and built it into a respected residential design firm. I now feel it's time for us to move on to interests we've postponed for years, and let a new generation of architects run the firm," said Brown.

Johnson and Kim said they would expand the firm's scope to pursue overseas work. They felt confident about this due to their own overseas contacts and the presence there of several major clients. They also plan to establish a design-build development arm to capture a share of the growing design-build building construction market.

Dale Johnson, 38, is a graduate of Tulane University and Yale University, and has been with the firm for 12 years. He was the designer for Douglas Houses, a 74-unit assisted-housing development in Colorado Springs. Douglas Houses won an AIA Honor Award in 1996 and several local awards for the appropriateness of the units to a range of family groupings and the attractive development of the site.

Andrea Kim, 36, has degrees from Colby College and Yale University. She joined the firm 10 years ago. Since then she has devoted herself to forging the firm into an expert design and production machine using a highly efficient network of CAD design, presentation, and project management software. The firm now boasts one of the highest billings-per-technical-employee ratios in the country, according to a survey by BXQZ Research Associates.

"We welcome the challenge," Kim told a gathering of employees last week. "We intend, in association with private sponsors and municipalities throughout this region, to make added inroads into the dismal housing picture. We have plans to establish a separate design-build outfit. We also aim to exploit a number of bright chances to work overseas."

Since its founding, Brown & Madison has completed some 75,000 units of housing, from custom-designed to below-market-rate to multi-unit. These total over $7.5 billion in construction value. The firm has won 46 national and local design awards, and in 1994 was the subject of a major profile in the Wall Street Journal. It has also designed public schools, primary-care health facilities, and several courthouses.

Attached: Photographs of Brown, Madison, Johnson, and Kim
Photographs of three completed projects

For more information, including a listing of all past projects, contact Emily Woods or visit Brown & Madison's Web site at http://www.bandm.com/transition.

Make a record of the news release distribution.

1. Past and current client lists (attach brief, informal notes signed by the partners)

2. Selected design firms, especially those who need to be reminded of your specialty for a possible association.

3. Media lists (professional design, educational, health care, home building, general news media in Denver and 20 selected cities)

4. "Friends of the firm"

5. Local broadcast outlets (radio, TV)

Keep this in your files.

For an elegantly executed news release, see the Kohn Pedersen Fox example opposite.

N E W S I N B R I E F

The Wharton School of Business

Kohn Pedersen Fox Associates PC has been awarded the design of a new facility for the Wharton School of Business, one of the top business schools in the world.

The new 300,000 gsf building will be situated at the intersections of Walnut Street, 38th Street and Locust Walk, on the University of Pennsylvania Campus.

KPF will bring its experience in educational and institutional projects to create a flexible, technologically advanced complex of classrooms, labs and offices for Wharton's MBA programs well as its undergraduate programs.

Hong Kong Electric Company

Rising 13 stories above Kennedy road in Central, Hong Kong, will be the new corporate headquarters for The Hong Kong Electric Company.

Currently under construction, the 29,000 square meter design by KPF is situated in a wooded landscape and has a double faced composition, indicative of an earth and sky relationship.

Grown from the inspirational seed of traditional Chinese garden architecture, a civic plaza and garden will draw the surrounding landscape across the front of the building and lock the building to the site.

Telecom - Buenos Aires, Argentina

Just completed in downtown Buenos Aires, is the new office building for one of two phone companies in Argentina. The Telecom facility which reaches approximately 31,000 m² is situated within the newly created development district of Puerto Madero

Singapore Esplanade Mall

KPF continues its successful relationship with Honk Kong Land Property Company Ltd. with the Esplanade Mall project in Singapore. This development which had its groundbreaking on July 29th will be comprised of retail and office components and is slated for completion in 2000. The 50,000 gsf office component which will inhabit 5 1/2 floors is being designed for maximum energy efficiency as well as a high technology building which will be a signature for the next century.

The retail area which is 365,000 gsf (7 floors above grade) will include subterranean space for a mall and will also connect to the adjacent sites of Marina Square and Suntec City, with connections to the MRT and Raffles City.

Atlanta Federal Center, Atlanta Georgia

The newly completed 1.8 million gsf mixed-use federal facility in downtown Atlanta, situated adjacent to the Richard B. Russel federal Building and the MARTA Five Points station, houses office space, a conference center, day care center, cafeteria, and health and fitness facilities.

KPF designed an efficient and economically effective space, a building massing that enhances the character of the urban context, and rehabilitation of the historically significant Rich's Department Store.

The campus-like organization of distinct buildings encloses a vast green urban space with a 24 story tower along the Spring Street Viaduct, and a 10 story building along Broad Street, adjacent to the 1924 Rich's Department Store. The tower and lower building are connected by a 6 story building over Forsyth Street, reminiscent in its articulation of the original International Style building which previously occupied the site.

Kohn Pedersen Fox Associates PC
111 West 57th Street
New York, NY 10019
Tel: 212.977.6500   www.kpf.com   Fax: 212.956.2526

The news release by Kohn Pedersen Fox is compact and informative. Combining several developments, it has some of the characteristics of a newsletter. Consider the technique when there are no time constraints on publication. Reproduced by permission.

On the following pages is another example of an actual news release. Note the crisp, fact-filled style of the release, and the clever tie-in to A/E/C Systems, a major trade show serving the design professions.

Industry Alliance for Interoperability;
Enabling Interoperability in the A.E.C.FM Industry

Editorial Contact: Julie Brown, 415-824-1795
News Release
At A/E/C Systems '96

IAI SHOWS NOTABLE GROWTH, ADDS BOARD SEATS AND INTERNATIONAL CHAPTERS; DRAMATIC EXPANSION FUELS GLOBAL ACCEPTANCE OF THE IFC STANDARD

Anaheim, Calif., June 18, 1996—Citing global membership expansion and support for its developing Industry Foundation Classes (IFC), the Industry Alliance for Interoperability (IAI) today announced six international chapters, the addition of three new seats on the North American chapter board of directors and a membership milestone of more than 250 companies worldwide.

The three new directors on the IAI board are: Bentley Systems–Rebecca Ward; IBM Scott Sherwood; and Turner Construction Company–David Furth. This brings the number of seats on the board to 13, including officers. Other companies holding board director or officer seats are: Autodesk, Inc.; Carrier Corporation; HOK; Honeywell Inc.; Jaros Baum & Bolles; Lawrence Berkeley National Laboratory; Lucent Technologies; Primavera Systems, Inc.; Softdesk, Inc. and Timberline Software Corp.

Global Expansion
The TAI was incorporated as an independent, not-for-profit organization in September 1995, with nine member companies in North America. Since then, chapters have been formed in Germany (German-speaking), the United Kingdom, Japan, France (French-speaking) and Singapore. Other chapters are now being formed in the Nordic region, the Benelux, Australia, Italy and other countries.

Each chapter is managed locally, sponsored by a local company and holds two seats on the International Coordinating Council. The North American chapter is sponsored by Hellmuth, Obata & Kassabaum (HOK), Inc. The German chapter sponsor company is Obermeyer Planen + Beraten; the UK chapter is sponsored by John Laing plc.; Kajima Corp. sponsors the Japan chapter; SAA Partnership Pte. Ltd. sponsors the Singapore chapter; and Ingerop Systems sponsors the French.

Membership Milestone
The global acceptance and support of the IAI "has been tremendous," said Patrick MacLeamy, Chairman of the IAI North America chapter board of directors. "Since the IAI was incorporated last September, our international presence has grown from just nine members to more than 250 member companies. This demonstrates that the idea of projects defined using

Industry Foundation Classes is truly an international concept that meets a universal need."

In addition to the board members mentioned above, a few of the most recent IAI members in North America are: AIA, AT&T, Johnson Controls, MKS-20/20, Naoki Systems, Trane, Turner Construction and the US General Services Administration. A complete list of all members of the IAI is included in the press kit.

Twenty IAI members are exhibiting at the A/E/C SYSTEMS '96 show, They are:

Member	Booth #	Member	Booth #
AECS Solutions	# 457/2103	Nemetschek	#409
AIA (Masterspec)	# 701	Primavera	#419
APEC	# 2144	Quickpen	#800
Autodesk	# 741	R.S.Means	#300
Bentley	# 1189/1803/2303	Rebis	#657/2203
IBM	# 182	Softdesk	#781
Intergraph	# 609	Timberline	#541
KETIV	# 560	Trane	#381
MC2	# 2151	U.S.Cost	#500
Naoki	# 741	Visio	#349

The Industry Alliance for Interoperability (IAI) was formed to define, promote and publish specifications for Industry Foundation Classes (IFC) as a basis for sharing AEC project information globally, across disciplines and technical applications, throughout a project life cycle. It is an independent, not-for-profit organization, open to all companies in the building industry.

# # #

For more information about membership, the IAI, and the IFC, contact: Executive Director Ken Herold, 1-800-798-3375; fax to 1-314-432-3130; send e-mail to iaiexec@interoperability.com; or, visit the Web site at http://www.interoperability. com.

News Releases and Newsletters for Small Firms

News releases are inexpensive to write, produce, and disseminate. Newsletters can be as elaborate or simple as you wish (see the example of the KCGA newsletter earlier in the chapter, which is not costly but is very effective). Therefore, developing these two marketing tools is not a matter of firm size so much as intent. A young firm with a local clientele can keep its prospects informed of new developments in ways other than the sometimes daunting-looking news release—for example, through postcards and similar methods illustrated in chapter 3. Avoid news releases if the subject matter isn't up to it. Always ask yourself: if I were a client or prospect, why should I bother to read this?

Client newsletters, on the other hand, are an efficient way of keeping past and present clients and prospects abreast every quarter or so as to activities in your firm. Make sure what you tell them is useful—whether it deals with wetlands or the new workplace or complying with ADA regulations—and not just a vehicle for sharing trivial internal activity. Since newsletters can be brief, even limited to a single page, and are moreover easily disseminated on-line, even small firms can take advantage of this vehicle. For ways to compose a newsletter, refer to earlier parts of this chapter.

Design Award Submittal

A direct route to fame for professional design firms, faculty, students, and award sponsors is the design award. Awards trigger publicity of all kinds—magazine articles, newspaper profiles, TV interviews—publicity that has been known to snowball into an avalanche of national recognition.

This is especially true since awardomania, or the uncontrolled expansion of award programs, has come to reign as a cultural icon of our society. There are few creative efforts today for which there is not some form of award recognition. Typical sponsors are:

National, regional, and local committees of the architecture, engineering, landscape, planning, industrial, and interior design societies—at professional and student levels
Federal, state, county, and municipal departments and agencies
Civic groups
Professional, business, and general magazines
User associations such as school and healthcare facility administrators, housing officials, and developers
Building product manufacturers, individually and as trade associations
Corporations or individuals seeking to recognize excellence in architecture or another design field (examples: the Aga Khan Award for Architecture; the Pritzker Prize; the Carlsberg Prize)

These groups sponsor award programs of varying quality and distinction. If you resolve to enter your projects in an awards program, it pays to do it right.

Plan one year ahead to identify award programs you want to enter. This will help you budget the effort and meet early deadlines. Assess the prestige factor of the award, the prize money, and the caliber of publicity the donor is likely to generate (for example, the Federal design award program is highly publicized and is likely to get you into the White House to meet the president).

Are you prepared? Choose projects with a good chance of success, because readying a winning submittal takes staff time and money. Who are the judges (names are usually published), and what type of work is likely to captivate them? Compare with your staff the innovative features of, say, three candidate projects. Note the "selling points" and incorporate them into your submittal.

Keep it simple. Judges or jurors—"assessors," as they are known in some English-speaking countries—are pressed for time, having other business besides serving on juries. They may have to review 100 entries in a day. Hence they like to have their submittal presentations short, graphically attractive, and focused on the issues.

As a young or emerging firm, watch for special award programs, magazine features, and exhibits geared to you.

Each contest's rules are set by the sponsor, so you have no choice but to follow inconsistent sets of rules. All, however, demand some sort of statement—strictly limited as to number of words—that lets you put the best face on your project. *The best way to structure the statement is to start with the problem and follow with your design solution.* Avoid generalized statements such as "due to the school district's rising enrollment," in favor of the more specific "the district's enrollment has climbed 22 percent in five years and is expected to rise another 19 percent by the year 2003." As noted in chapter 1, avoid designer-babble, especially if the jury includes laypeople who will rightly resent having to read statements they cannot decipher. Consider these criteria:

What is the central essence of the design object or article and how does it reflect the values of the sponsor agency?

If it is a design or graphic product, what are its superior aesthetic, technical, and functional qualities; its success in its physical and historical context; and its preeminence in environmental, social, or operational terms?

If it is a printed product, how should you describe its intent and the degree to which the intent was realized through public or professional demand or other type of response?

How has the article's graphic design contributed to its impact?

Organize your statement into easy sections, preceded by numerals or bullets, for example:

- the problem
- the design solution
- benefits to the owner/user
- user response (if available)

Edit brutally; make sure every word pulls its weight. Then proof with care: typos are not in themselves mortal sins, but they betray a lack of attention to detail that may color jurors' perception of your firm's professionalism. Throughout the submittal, worry about credits—are all included? are they correctly phrased and spelled? are they to be sealed or left open? are square feet and dollars correct?

When nominating a completed project for an award or prize—whether a design project or a design-related piece of published writing—on behalf of another candidate, you need to touch certain bases in your statement to capture the review committee's good will. (See the criteria listing, above.)

Some sponsors, such as the Pulitzer Prizes, ask you for a one- or two-page summary of the submittal's contents. This makes sense especially for pieces such as a thick report or a long article series that would take a reviewer too long to read in its entirety.

The following sample design award submission uses the bulleted organization of sections.

Scenario

After reviewing candidate projects for a design award, you and your partners have decided to submit your design for an inner-city mosque for resident and visiting Moslems located at a busy intersection on the East Side of Manhattan. The program is sponsored by the City Club and is aimed at recognizing excellence in architecture, interior design, and landscaping.

- The problem was to create a building that combines religious and educational functions, that uses modern materials and systems, and that retains dignity within the hustle and bustle of a busy New York street. It also had to fulfill the architectural demands of Islamic scripture.
- The design solution was to bring together modern building techniques and materials under an umbrella that carefully arranges the building's mass, enclosure, and finishes. The mosque is placed at 29 degrees to the Manhattan street grid so as to face Mecca, the only physical demand in Islamic scripture. The interior is a majestic 90-foot clear span, with a grid of four trusses supporting a steel-and-concrete copper-clad dome. A modern adaptation of Arabic calligraphy is used in lieu of animal ornament, which is forbidden. The space is lit by a circle of steel wire-supported lamps, which were derived from traditional circles of oil lamps. To fulfill its cultural purpose, the mosque is flanked by classrooms, a library, and social spaces.
- The center is a popular magnet for Moslems visiting and living in the city, not only on Friday holy days but throughout the week. It supplements the network of storefront mosques that dot New York's outlying boroughs.

Note: This example is based loosely on the Islamic Cultural Center of New York, designed by Skidmore, Owings & Merrill and Swanke Hayden Connell.

Exhibit Panels

Developing text for exhibit panels is rigorous because the viewer is usually even more strapped for time than design award judges. Therefore, as the late Jean Labatut used to tell his Princeton architecture students, "you must achieve the maximum with the minimum."

Panels are of two types: those showing projects that are already award winners and end up as elements in an exhibit; and boards and panels showing schemes and concepts, such as at a school review.

Completed project exhibit panels are commonly displayed through invitation to award winners by professional architectural, engineering, landscape, and interior design societies. These allocate space to exhibits at their national and regional conventions. So do associations of school, college, and healthcare facilities administrators, and other client associations that have trade shows. In addition, community gathering places, including local schools and colleges, suburban shopping malls, and museums, are known as venues for exhibits showing design work.

The challenge is to grab the attention of the walking viewer. The viewer may well be on the way from lunch to a seminar, or heading for the car after a burst of shopping, and must be lured by a beguiling panel. You are also competing for attention with perhaps three dozen other panels. Go for uniqueness without vulgarity. Make it broad-brush, large, and simple. Select one striking image and make it big. (The core of a panel is the illustrations. Drawings should be simplified, not cluttered with lines that don't add to understanding. Poché walls in black or dark; possibly differentiate circulation from programmed space using tones.)

Now concentrate on text. Write a powerful, active-word headline—tabloid newspapers such as the *New York Post* or the *Daily News* have much to teach as they pack a maximum message into the fewest words. A dull, static title and long-winded, jargon-filled text drives the viewer to your rival's boards.

Write a succinct, perhaps bulleted, text. Use large type (to decide how large, test different fonts and sizes and see how close you have to stand to the panel in order to read the type). State, as with award submittals, the problem, its solution, its benefits, and (if you have it) its reception by the users. Use photograph and drawing captions to reinforce the message of the headline and the main statement. But keep captions brief—three to four short lines maximum.

Review the following example of an exhibit board headline and descriptive statement.

Scenario

Your energy services center has been selected for exhibit at the next convention of the Council of Educational Facilities Planners. You are to develop a headline and descriptive text.

COOL CHILLER: UCLA ENERGY SERVICES CENTER GRACES CAMPUS AND PLEASES WELL-HEELED BEL AIR NEIGHBORS

• Aging, dispersed, inefficient, pollution-causing network of boilers and chiller units supplied campus hospitals, food services, labs, other functions.

• UCLA decides to build single central plant applying cogeneration, using waste heat to produce steam and added electricity.

• Plant is to supply steam, chilled water, electricity to entire campus, and demands very large single-story site.

• No large site available, so plant had to be split into three stories; also must present friendly front due to central campus location and adjacent wealthy neighborhood.

• Design solution features two heat-recovery generator stacks, resembling

old ocean liners. Mid-level screens partially reveal high-tech equipment behind.
- Two shades of brick wall in irregular pattern create lively street rhythm.
- Benefits: site is conserved; air quality maintained; money saved.
- Reaction from campus and adjacent high-income communities of Bel Air, Beverly Hills, Westwood: thumbs up.

Sometimes exhibit panels are required to display planning or research results that cannot rely for effect on striking photography or elegant drawings. The panels instead depict a process or system of organization that can only be conveyed through text and a few charts and diagrams. Examples could include the outcome of an investigation into energy-conserving building systems, or an innovative management process designed to control schedules on complex engineering projects.

Attract and hold the panel viewer with bold activity boxes linked to a process path, accented by color and clear type. Avoid cramming in too detailed an analysis—viewers are here to be stimulated, not to take a course of study. If intrigued, they will want more; help them by including a name and phone number.

Looking ahead, exhibit panels and boards may well become an endangered species. Some architecture schools separated by continents already band together to solve an identical problem, linked on-line, with results viewed and judged through modem-transmitted images projected on screens. The time will come when convention exhibits, often at the bottom of show-goers' tight agendas, are replaced by on-line exhibits. Viewers can access them in their hotel rooms, at terminals on the convention floor, or at the office before or after the show.

Project Writing

6

Marketing writing seeks to persuade the recipient to grant you a wish. Project-related writing, the subject of this chapter, has a very different purpose. Also known as informational writing, it is designed to give information or to unravel a situation connected with a project or your firm. It is the most common form of writing by design professionals.

Project writing consists of the following types:

Correspondence
Planning, feasibility, research, and other reports for clients
Investigative reports sponsored by your firm
Internal newsletters or house organs
Obituaries

Clear project correspondence is the grease that runs the machinery of professional projects, smoothly functioning teams, and happy clients.

Some examples and themes of correspondence writing are:

Correspondence

Letters
Project manager to client (notify concerning change in choice of facing material; schedule a meeting; schedule site visit by client's CEO; review impact of strike by electricians' union; introduce punch list; notify concerning changorder requiring budget adjustment; advise on options for ordering and installing high-school educational computer system)
Partner to residential client (discuss living room furniture options)
Consultant to prime professional (review impact of floods on landscaping plan; identify discrepancies between structural and mechanical systems' space requirements; list problems encountered by acoustical, lighting consultants)
Partner to head of citizen review committee (schedule public informational meeting of citizens)
Project manager to consultant (discuss lateness of drawings; explain pending changes in seismic code; demand environmental impact statement)
Office business partner to vendor (letter to legal counsel, accountant, insurance representative, rental agent; order computer software, hardware, office supplies)

Specification writer to supplier (request to send rep with stone samples; request for added performance data on new product)

Project manager to general contractor (alert over community complaints about site noise; ask why delay in preordering steel frame; confirm schedule adjustments)

Project manager to team (meeting minutes)

In-house memoranda

Managing partner to staff (vacation schedule; significant new commission; new bonus plan; opening of new branch office; promotion)

Project manager to partner (send cover note accompanying weekly status report; forward, with comment, letter received from client)

Social correspondence

Partner to client (invite to share box at Camden Yards stadium; send "thank you" note for successful fishing excursion or dinner invitation)

For letter writing to be effective, it must be geared to the recipient's need to know; adjusted to the recipient's ability to understand it; of a length consistent with the nature of the message; clear; and able to get to the point quickly, then stop.

The informational letter has some things in common with the marketing letter (chapter 2), especially in the matter of formatting the name, address, and salutation, and getting to the point. It differs in the matter of intent, which is to convey information, often followed by a recommendation; in contrast, the marketing letter is a solicitation for work, or a request.

To shape the informational letter, use this format:

Recipient's name and address (see chapter 2).

Salutation (see chapter 2).

Opening. State what you are writing about and why it's important.

Core content. Describe the issue—whether you are dealing with latent community opposition to a neighborhood construction project; a consultant's lateness in supplying drawings; a need to review brick samples due to a change in design; or attaching your comments to minutes of the last job meeting with the client's facilities manager. To make this material jump smartly off the page, consider bulleting your key points.

Decision and marching orders. End by pinpointing what the recipient has to do as a result of the situation you have just described, and by when; what you and your firm must do; what is up to third parties, and who is to notify them.

Brief summary.

Closing. End on an upbeat note, with a cordial greeting or a cool adiós (as warranted); propose the next contact date; and sign off.

cc/bcc. Whom to favor with copies of your message can be a subtle game of politics. It's a way of enlisting a person's support, for instance, without actually requesting it. Indeed, the identity of those on the copied lists may be more significant than the original recipient. Shrewd, politically savvy writers play this game with great aplomb. Some take it a step further: in addition to typing "cc" at the end of the letter and listing the names of those copied, they send so-called blind copies, or "bcc." A bcc goes to individuals you want to see the letter *without the knowledge* of the original receiver.

Scenario

You are one of two partners in Gómez and Abernathy, a ten-person architecture and town design firm. You have been hired to renovate a two-block deteriorating area at the eastern edge of downtown Cleveland. Your plan calls for tearing down some dilapidated five-story walk-ups that are still 50 percent occupied and replacing some of the units with infill housing, building a small clinic, and using some of the new and existing vacant lot space for an outdoor neighborhood gathering area to include benches, plantings, a small playground, and a fountain. The project is now in design development. Due to faulty communications, the community has not been kept abreast of the plan. While most of the area's citizens hope the project will improve the quality of life, there is much uneasiness about the final outcome of the scheme, and a strong anti-faction is emerging.

You decide to approach William Patterson, chairman of a local citizens' group, about convening a town meeting at which you will present the plan and answer questions. You write a letter to Mr. Patterson explaining your idea for such a meeting, and suggesting a site, format, agenda, and proposed participation. You plan to follow up with a phone call.

Letter

Mr. William Patterson
Chairman
East Downtown Cleveland Citizens Committee
800D Euclid Avenue
Cleveland, OH 44100

Dear Mr. Patterson:

The Cleveland 2000 project for which our firm is the architect and town designer is now in design development. We are confident that, when completed 18 months from now, it will make for a happier, prouder community, preserving what is fine, removing what is crumbling, and adding much that is good, including new housing.

We sense that most of the citizens hope the plan will be for the best. Our project manager and staff have, however, noted a good deal of doubt and uneasiness about the final outcome of the scheme, and a strong anti-faction is emerging.

I am writing to enlist your help. I know that much of the apprehension arose because the community doesn't know enough about the project and the impact on its people. I accordingly suggest, with your support, that we convene a town meeting at which to describe the plan. Citizens will be encouraged to ask questions and share their concerns.

To recap the salient features of the plan, the community gains a net of 48 housing units, a small clinic, and an informal gathering place including benches, plantings, a small playground, and a fountain. It will lose 8 dilapidated five-story walk-ups and two trash-filled empty lots. The mayor has approved safe, clean, affordable temporary housing for the families displaced by the construction.

We will be very grateful if you could contact the community's leaders and discuss a place and time for the meeting, avoiding weekday daytime so working people can attend without missing work. Meanwhile, we will begin to prepare a visual display and demonstration that will clearly explain the scheme. We'll also alert those of our consultants who should be present. I will follow up with you this coming Tuesday.

This is a worthy project that will benefit all concerned. We hope that with your help and the right communications, we will reverse the current anxiety, and the community will give the plan the support it deserves.

With best regards,
Henry Gómez, Partner
Gómez and Abernathy
Architects and town designers

cc: J. J. Smith, chairwoman, Cleveland Housing Agency
     Amelia DeFiore, president, Ohio Community Foundation
     Herb Green, landscape architect
bcc: Thornton Lee, mayor of Cleveland

Scenario

On another project, your firm, Gómez and Abernathy, is in the awkward position of watching, as it proceeds with design development on a new elementary school, the estimates rising uncomfortably above the client's budget. You had warned the client earlier that the scope was too ambitious for the budget, but the client insisted on moving forward. You have now reached the point where you feel you must share the brutal truth with the client.

Letter

Ms. Ivana Kopecky
Facilities Officer
Sandusky School District
1 Acacia Street
Sandusky, OH 44870
Subject: Garfield Elementary School

Dear Ms. Kopecky:

I must tell you that estimates for Garfield Elementary School continue to come in well above your budget for the school. We have worked hard to find ways to bring the costs down. We have explored alternative materials for the exterior wall facing, for the lighting system, for the classroom furnishings, for the cafeteria and gymnasium finishes, along with additional avenues to save on costs. This effort was successful in reducing construction costs to a degree, but we have now pared those costs to a point where any added substitutions would bring the school's quality below the standard you would want.

The only option that remains to us now is to reduce the scope of the project, a condition we alerted you to in our earliest discussions. We now recommend that you agree to revise the scope of the work as follows:

- eliminate two classrooms and one administrative office
- reduce the areas of the remaining offices by 15 percent
- erect only the shell of the fitness center, for eventual completion as funds become available
- eliminate all but basic food preparation; instead, bring in meals from outside
- postpone landscaping except for paving and seeding

While not an ideal solution, we feel that these measures will bring your school in on budget. More, it will bestow on your district a school that provides a stimulating setting for learning as well as a notable new landmark in its neighborhood.

To review this situation in greater detail, I suggest that Jerry Smith and I meet with you at your office as soon as convenient. Please call me about a date and time.

With kind regards,
Victor Abernathy, Partner
Gómez and Abernathy

cc: J. Smith, project manager

This letter is courteous, detached, and raises the issue of an earlier warning over the scope-versus-cost issue, without rubbing it in. It shows effort on the architect's part to reduce costs, but holds out for quality.

In-House Memoranda

The in-house memorandum, or memo, differs from standard correspondence mainly in the compactness of its content and form. It is the vehicle commonly used for managing projects in-house and for conducting the firm's internal business such as business planning, accounts, human resources management, marketing preparation, and links with branch offices.

The memo should include the heading box and the substance. Include names of the receiver, sender, and those to be copied; the date; the topic; and a file name or number. Many firms arrange these data in a standard electronic format with preset tabs. You merely fill in the information. When developing the substance of the memo, largely follow the format for letters: what the issue is; why it's important; who is being tapped to deal with it, and when. Organize this material in short paragraphs, identified by numerals or bullets.

This type of memorandum is also suited for dissemination on the intranet, if your firm has one (see discussion of the intranet in "Not on Paper Alone," below). For an example of a concise internal memo, read the following.

Scenario
Your firm, Knudsen, Carlson, and Knudsen has just learned of a new commission won after strenuous effort. As the managing partner, you decide to let the staff know, hand out the bouquets, and make assignments.

Memo

DATE: 9 June 1997
TO: All staff
FROM: Bob Knudsen
SUBJECT: New project
FILE: KCK-RLK200

FOLKS:

Good news! I just learned that the Magruder Art Foundation has chosen Knudsen, Carlson, and Knudsen to design the building, interiors, signing graphics, and landscaping for MAF's 80,000 sq. ft. art museum near Little Rock, Arkansas. Congratulations to Marilyn DiPaglia and her business development team for this success.

•We have designated the team to shepherd this project. John Coelho will be project manager, Priscilla Davies will be architectural design leader, Capability Jones is landscape designer, and Kevin Leung will take the tectonics and computer support lead, with myself as partner-in-charge. We'll meet in conference room 2 this Monday at 9 A.M. to kick off the process.

•Our consultants will be: Tension Associates (structural); Bernouilli Engineers (mechanical, electrical, plumbing); Matt Sabin & Associates (acoustical); and Lumen Associates (lighting). We'll meet at a time to be determined at our Monday meeting.

•As is our practice, the team will establish itself as a working group, this time at the northern corner of the main drafting room. Willie Kelly [office manager] will have workstations rearranged in the next two weeks.

•Marilyn DiPaglia will arrange ASAP to issue a one-page news release to notify local and national media, as well as the C1 section of the client list.

Bob

Meeting minutes can be short or long, depending on whether you include only actions taken or discussion too. Minutes of society chapter or committee meetings are best kept concise and limited to actions taken. Job minutes need to include discussion, to keep absentees posted and to inform those who don't participate but need to be kept au courant. The record of discussion should be kept also for legal reasons.

Give each major topic a number, the first subordinate topic a number with a decimal, each second subordinate topic a number with two decimals, etc. See the following example.

Scenario

As project manager you have just completed the Monday meeting of the design team working on renovation of the old Vedette vaudeville theater on Maple Street. You need to let all know what was discussed and what was decided. Arrange the material either in the order in which it was discussed, or according to priority.

Minutes

Vedette Theater Renovation
Minutes, 27 October 1997

Present: Jane Talavera, Jane Chang, Charles Mann, William Hord
Absent: Herbert Smith, Sonny Chavez

1.0 Team member reports
    1.1 Jane Talavera
    1.2 Jane Chang
    1.3 Charles Mann
    1.4 William Hord
2.0 Cost estimates
    2.1 Overruns
        2.1.1 Foundations
        2.1.2 Framing
    2.2 Report on labor prices
3.0 Schedule
    3.1 Report and discussion on fast-track bid packages
        3.1.1 Steel
        3.1.2 Curtain wall
        3.1.3 HVAC
4.0 Future meetings

Your writing style should be tight, with unnecessary words omitted; for example:

    1.2 J. Chang reported that desired glazing system may need substitution due to cost and unreliable delivery. She will explore options and report in two weeks.

Alternative Media

Both the form and content of your message are affected by the medium you use to transmit it. Until recently, paper was the chief carrier. Even the quality of voice mail had far to go to reach today's levels: you can now convey information without ever speaking to a live person (you know the routine—it's grist to the mill of every standup comic in the country).

It's not that bad. Communicating by voice mail has the virtue of simplicity; it's suitable for short messages, not long rambling disquisitions—remember that the ear is an inefficient medium for taking in information: it takes about ten times longer to hear than to read the same number of words, according to consultant Roslyn Brandt (although the ears can hear three times faster than the maximum speech rate). Software is on the market that allows you to dictate messages of any length into the computer, which converts it into e-mail and transmits it. This way you get the best of both worlds; but the technique is still imperfect and has restrictions that don't yet make it an ideal technique. Voice mail is good for short messages involving simple questions or answers; it is less good for long opinions or instructions, which the hearer must somehow record, or take notes on, before responding.

This is not to belittle the standard two-or-more party telephone conversation, which is efficient for hammering out decisions between people who cannot meet face to face.

An infinitely more promising medium for intra-office messages is a form of e-mail transmission known as the intranet. The intranet, which emerged from a group of proprietary closed network services such as Lotus Notes, connects all eligible employees in a company. It allows them to communicate by e-mail, but provides in addition such features as controlled access, security, confidentiality, simple insertion of recipient's address and any added receivers, and the ability on some networks to transmit graphic materials and attachments.

The principles for writing intra- or inter-office messages over the intranet do not differ greatly from sending memos on paper. If anything, brevity, getting to the point quickly, and determining what action is required are even more critical than when using paper. This is in part because too much time spent in front of a monitor is bad for your eyes, hands, and posture, and in part because the format and generating system of the computer encourage speed, precision, brevity, and candor. I have noted in my years of computer experience a tangibly greater succinctness in received messages compared to the days when most correspondence went out on paper.

The etiquette of writing has changed in the process. Salutations are more Spartan, or gone altogether; there are fewer verbs and adjectives, greater use of the imperative, and less grace in giving instructions. The result is choppier text, and the etiquette of responses is often limited to monosyllables. It's a throwback to the military-style terseness of General McNaughton as he responded to the German call for surrender in the Battle of the Bulge with a simple "Nuts!" and to the pithy brevity of old Western Union telegrams, where each additional word cost you money. Do not let this style cause your messages to be brief to the point of curtness or hostility. That may cost you. Also, many more typos and errors occur in e-mail messages than on paper. If these messages are important, proof them minutely. For a more in-depth treatment of on-line "writing," see chapter 11.

Whereas e-mail's impact on writing styles has been highly reductive, facsimile (or fax) transmission has hardly affected writing styles, because the decision to send a message by fax commonly happens only after a letter already exists on paper. Software now exists that allows you to create and transmit faxes completely electronically.

If there is a rush to get your message out, the route of choice is increasingly to go e-mail and not bother with fax. Chances are that by the end of 1998 all businesses, even modestly sized ones, will be "wired."

On occasion you will be called upon to write on matters that, while linked to business, are so clearly social as to call for a departure from the detached, impersonal tone of most correspondence. Consider the following situation, and the called-for response.

Social Correspondence from All Over

Scenario

Your travels as a partner in the eight-person, Atlanta-based office of Heron & Heron take you to Sacramento. This also happens to be the home town of Gene Gerahty, a junior designer who recently joined your firm. Gene gave you an introduction to Mr. Reginald James, a prominent Sacramento businessman and philanthropist. The Jameses ask you to dinner at their impressive mansion situated not far from the California governor's new house. The dinner is sumptuous—Gene is obviously a James favorite. Just before the dessert, it transpires that Mrs. James chairs the Sacramento Symphony Foundation, a largely fundraising society that is looking critically at the size and condition of the city orchestra's cramped current quarters. No direct, but a few indirect, overtures were floated as to a future role for Heron & Heron in the matter.

The encounter clearly calls for a thank-you note. The borderline between a marketing and a social occasion is fine, as in this case. Probably the best approach is to dwell on the social occasion, to mention favorably but not gush about the work of the symphony foundation, to mention that both Mr. and Mrs. James had revealed a polite interest in architecture and in your firm, and that you would send them for their amusement a profile article the *Atlanta Constitution* had done about four young Atlanta firms the previous month— yours among them. Keep it brief. Then sign off. And avoid presents. If you have personal office stationery, now is the time to use it. Omit your title in the sign-off; it smacks of business.

Letter

Mr. and Mrs. Reginald James
8 Elm Drive
Sacramento, CA 95801

Dear Mr. and Mrs. James [or Dear Mary and Reginald—it's your call]:

Thank you for having me over to your house last week. It had been a strenuous day, and I was grateful for this chance to unwind in such an pleasant setting and friendly company. It was kind of Gene to suggest the idea.

The challenges facing the Sacramento Symphony Foundation seem rather awesome. I admire the vigor you bring to the task.

You kindly encouraged me to talk about our firm. I'm proud of it, as you gathered, and enclose a nice story our hometown paper did recently on emerging Atlanta firms, including ours.

I look forward to showing you our offices should you ever head this way, and your joining us for dinner.

Sincerely,

Charles Heron, Jr.

cc: Gene Gerahty

Research, Feasibility, and Planning Reports

The work product of a designer's commission often ends up not as a building or a landscape design, but as a report. A wag once remarked that thick reports are required to justify the fee. As the final product of your work, the report is one of the most challenging projects for the writer. Reports are often an excuse for pompous, jargon-packed language, which has given them a bad name over the years and the fate of being consigned to gather dust on remote shelves.

The report is especially significant, as it is generally the end product of a designer's services. No building, no landscape, no interior, no restoration, nothing in 3-D exists. Instead, the report is a monument to the designer's skill in doing research or investigating a topic, assembling the material in an arrangement that makes sense to the client, and writing it in a style that encourages reading.

Beyond its role as the end product of your services, the report has wide-ranging marketing value: a copy of the report can be a powerful attachment or supplement to a proposal or to your brochure or portfolio. As a leave-behind resting on your client's desk or forwarded to the client's associates and friends, it's an eloquent emissary for your firm.

Reports can cover a wide array of topics:

Feasibility study
Campus master plan
Health facilities merger analysis
Energy use analysis
Environmental impact study
Wetlands mitigation report
Building operations and maintenance manual
Company workplace reorganization report
Programming study for a primary healthcare unit
School district facilities retrofit plan

Neighborhood housing development plan
Central business district parking study
Integrated product systems development

The purpose of the report and the way it is to be used set the pattern for its organization and style. A research report on energy conservation guidelines prepared for the National Institute for Science and Technology and reviewed by physicists can get by with a heavier load of technical terms (but not designer-babble) than a central business parking study widely circulated not only to technical people but also to nontechnical readers such as developers, politicians, and the general public.

A report organized for convenience typically consists of these sections:

Cover
Title page
Client's authorization letter
Table of contents
Executive summary or abstract
Main text
The team
Appendices

Cover and title page. The object of the cover and title page is to convey information at a glance. A skilled graphic designer, given the key words, will find fresh and snappy ways to project the message (see figure C-0). The title page needs to include the name of the project and location, the names of the client and designer, and the report's delivery date.

Client's authorization letter. A facsimile of the letter from the client or agency authorizing the job is sometimes reproduced near the front, especially on publicly funded work.

Contents. A table of contents makes sense if the report is bulky and the reader needs a navigational aid. Smart graphic designers can exploit the contents page, as they do in magazines, to highlight the report's chief parts and help make the report an experience, not a chore. For generations of readers reared on MTV and *WIRED* magazine, such touches are critical to engagement.

Executive summary. The executive summary or abstract has the same role as in the proposal: to allow senior client officials and others to seize on the essence without having to read the whole report—the task of the middle-level technical staff. The executive summary isn't always the same as an abstract. The abstract typically exists so librarians and researchers have an easy time filing the report or finding it in the catalog; an abstract tends to be shorter than an executive summary. Some design firms equate the two terms, and the abstract reads like the executive summary.

The purpose of the executive summary, as I shall call it, is to describe the assigned problem, the methods used to investigate it, and the solutions. Since conciseness is its aim, no summary should run longer than two pages (750 words) without good reason. Clients have been known to restrict it to a single page. Your style should be concise without being terse, technical-term free without being patronizing, friendly but not chummy. Identify the main parts of your summary with bullets or numerals.

Main text. Divide the main text into logical sections. Consider three sections or chapters—the problem or objectives of the assignment; the process used to uncover the answers; the recommendations and their rationale. Another way to divide the text is by phases; according to the work done by the different parties to the job; or by key influences on the project.

For example, an environmental report tracking the impact of new construction on a large, sensitive site could divide the text into a chapter on the geography, geology, climate, and vegetation of the site; a chapter identifying the possible presence of cultural artifacts on or near the site, and the historical, aesthetic, and ethical issues involved; a chapter comprising a synopsis of the field and laboratory methods used; and a final chapter of recommendations on environmentally proper use of the site.

The style of the main text needn't be as tight as the executive summary, because it has to take up a greater volume of detail. Nonetheless, you need to make sure every word that doesn't carry its weight is relentlessly cut.

The team. A report is no stronger than the work of its project team, so the players should be listed and their roles defined. Writing this section is much like the resumes segment of a proposal—name, rank, and job title, followed by a few paragraphs detailing this person's role in and contribution to the result. Be sure to list not only your staff and that of associated firms, but also those on the client's side who contributed.

Appendices. Appendices are the place where you deposit material that is awkward to describe or that amplifies what you have already stated in the text. Appendices may include economic, demographic, or other statistics; maps and site plans; photographs and renderings; a list of references; and a schedule diagram showing the time implications of your recommendations.

(The following sample executive summary is a mildly fictionalized version of that for the Chelsea Piers Sports and Entertainment Complex, New York City, completed in 1995. Butler Rogers Baskett were the architects and planners; Cosentini Associates were the mechanical/electrical engineers; Thornton-Tomasetti the structural engineers; Edmund Hollnader LA Design PC the landscape architects; Douglas/Gallagher the graphic designer. Chelsea Piers Management was the developer.)

Scenario

Your firm of architects and planners and a developer have been asked by the State of New York to explore the feasibility of converting some decaying piers owned by the state on the lower Hudson River waterfront into a sports and entertainment center that will attract New Yorkers and visitors, generate commercial revenue, and relate to the community. There are four adjacent piers and a connecting headhouse; you are to assess the physical condition of the piers, investigate various scenarios for replacing them if necessary, and compare the relative merits of a number of options that have surfaced for adaptive reuse of the restored piers.

These options can include, but need not be limited to developing: 1) participatory, nonspectator facilities for basketball, ice hockey, swimming, bowling, and sailing; a small children's sports-oriented amusement area; and a range of food-service facilities; 2) spectator facilities for basketball and bowling for junior and high school sports, with these facilities also available for participatory activity without spectators; 3) a marine-oriented facility for sailboats and small powerboats, with appropriate food service and facilities for children; 4) a reduced sports focus, with greater focus on entertainment, to include small theaters for stage shows and film projection, and a larger theater for multimedia entertainment.

Your firm has now explored the technical feasibility of such a project, initial capital investment and possible sources of funding, operating revenues and expenses, the time frame, and likely attitudes from neighborhood and community groups. Your report comprises your recommendations, along with preliminary planning drawings and 3-D sketches to supplement your recommendations.

The typical framework for an executive summary of a feasibility report based on this assignment might appear as shown below. In many cases the shorthand format shown is satisfactory. On occasion, depending on instructions from the client, you should flesh it out.

Executive Summary

Problem
   Piers built in 1910 to accommodate new luxury liners. Headhouse designed by architects Warren & Wetmore. Piers deteriorated with demise of passenger liner trade. Piers later used to house the city's automobile towing pound. New uses are to meet demand for recreation facilities, commercial revenue, generous public space, and private financing.

Process
   Inventoried public participatory sports facilities in New York City, especially for ice hockey, golf driving range, basketball.
   Consulted state and city authorities as to financing incentives available to supplement private investment.
   Explored types of commercial nonsports uses.
   Investigated structural condition of piers.

Recommendations
   The Complex should have a sports focus, with secondary but significant entertainment functions. Focus should be on participatory over spectator sports, although spectator space should be provided for ice hockey and swimming.
   Develop piers 59 through 62 and the connecting headhouse as a single phase, with completion dates staggered over six months. Pier 59 is to house

a golf driving range. Pier 60 is to house a sports center consisting of facilities for swimming, running, rock climbing, beach volleyball, aerobics, weightlifting. Pier 61 is to house an ice-skating rink. Pier 62 is to house roller rinks integrated with a public park.

The headhouse is to contain commercial space owned and/or operated by the developer, including such activities as network television productions, a feature film studio, a photography studio, and offices, as well as parking and truck access.

Restaurants and snack bars are to be dispersed throughout the Complex, including a major theme restaurant.

The infrastructure, including the piers, is in poor condition and will require $27 million to rebuild, including structural, mechanical, electrical, and plumbing services, emergency access, lighting, and security.

Public space, indoors and out, will be planned to allow for skyline views.

Because the six-lane 11th Avenue cuts the Complex from the community, an overpass bridge is critical to connect the Complex to the adjacent neighborhoods.

The existing headhouse facade erected after demolition of the original Beaux-Arts structure will remain, but a graphic embellishment program to enliven the facade is essential.

A public esplanade will allow foot access to every part of the Complex.

A lease should be given to a cruise operator to operate cruises around Manhattan island, and docking should be possible for small boats.

Budget for design, construction, furnishings, equipment is estimated at $100 million, not including infrastructure retrofit. The city has agreed in principle to a combined tax abatement and deferral plan, to expire by the year 2045.

We the architects have developed a series of computer-generated sketches depicting assorted views of the proposed Complex, along with a series of animated sequences in a CD-ROM format.

Note how this summary offers its conclusions in short, bite-sized, single-topic chunks that inform but don't bore.

Short Reports

Not every report calls for the amount of depth and detail implied in the foregoing example. In many cases, such as a feasibility study for a fire station on an uncomplicated site, or development of a program for an inner-city primary-care facility, you can simplify the normal trappings of a full-fledged report.

For example, you could dispense with the table of contents; reduce the executive summary to a simple statement of the problem and your recommendations; and desist from chopping up the main text into chapters, in favor of a single text subdivided into bulleted entries. In case of a fire station or a community center, this breakdown could be:

Objectives
Options
Limitations
Opportunities
Investigative process
Recommendations

In formulating a program for an inner-city primary-care facility, you could split the principal text into the five divisions developed a generation ago by Houston architect William Peña in *Problem Seeking*, namely:

Establish goals
Collect and analyze facts
Uncover and test concepts
Determine needs
State the problem or program to be solved through design

Emerging firms with limited resources should console themselves (as noted in chapter 3's discussion of brochures for firms with limited years of practice and tight budgets) that clients are looking for content as much as lavish presentation. That doesn't mean the report cannot sparkle graphically—catchy graphics need not cost a fortune. Focus on a good, straightforward text. Even an office with modest resources should be able to afford having the text edited by an outside editor for clarity.

Investigative Reports

Many firms devote part of their annual budget to publishing research findings gained from experience in practice or as the result of a special interest by a partner or employee. It combines marketing value with responsibility to the design profession, and contributes to the general advancement of knowledge.

Potential topics for investigative reports are:

Energy-conserving designs
Assisted-living housing concepts
New directions in planning public schools
Trends in designing for sports, education, healthcare, retail—or any building
    type in which your firm has experience
Urban design observations from travel
Space-age materials applied to furniture design and construction
Advances using water in landscape design
Emerging concepts in intelligent building design
Techniques for designing sustainably on low budgets

Such reports have many benefits. They are an outlet for useful, practical information that otherwise no one would ever see. They are a valuable marketing tool, selectively left with important clients or attached as supplements to proposals. They are an appealing device for attracting and keeping high-quality staff. They are morale builders for enterprising staff wanting to sink their teeth into something different from normal routine. In some cases the content carries such authority and widespread application that it is sold, generating revenue to offset costs.

These reports need not be elaborate, although a touch of graphic pizzazz or whimsy accompanied by an engaging writing style helps their acceptance. Still memorable today is a series of travel observations by the late William Caudill from Russia in the early 1970s and Egypt in the mid-1970s. And in the days of the Great Energy Crisis of 1974 Caudill wrote a catchy report on practical ways to design buildings that won't guzzle energy (see page 29, left). All these he illustrated with small pen-and-ink sketches in a style reminiscent of Le Corbusier. Such reports, whenever they tax busy in-house staff, may be outsourced to a professional design writer.

Another form of firm-sponsored publication is the periodical. It is issued several times a year and distributed to staff and clients. It differs from the client newsletter (chapter 5) because its content is so substantial that it resembles a professional journal, and because it is devoid of internal staff and business news.

An outstanding example of this type of professional, content-loaded publication is the *Arup Journal,* begun in 1986 and distributed three or four times a year to staff and, in the words of former Ove Arup Partnership partner Charlene Silverman, "those we work with and those we want to work with." Unlike client newsletters, it is not used as an out-and-out marketing tool. See cover and sample pages from the *Arup Journal* on page 29.

This fine journal uses significant engineering projects for detailed presentations. Included are photographs, crisp color drawings and renderings, and lucidly drawn details. Above all, there's a direct, jargon-free text that doesn't compound the mystery of structural engineering by using cryptic language. One month, the journal gave over an entire issue to a Sydney speech by former chairman Jack Zunz. The speech was the preamble for an in-depth report on the structure of the Jørn Utzon opera house, for which Arup were the engineers. The journal is much sought after for its content and precise layout.

Internal Newsletters or House Organs

It is every firm's responsibility to keep employees apprised of what's happening. Topics cover such matters as work-week and overtime policies, insurance matters, use of personal cars on company business and vice versa, and other human resources activities. Where a small firm might use a bulletin board for this purpose, larger firms write and distribute an internal newsletter, sometimes known as a house organ.

The internal newsletter also can serve as connective tissue for multi-branch firms, and is useful for keeping all informed on such matters as anniversaries, upcoming company picnics, congratulations to staff having children, or company athletic achievements.

The fact is, however, that the printed internal newsletter is riding an ebbing tide. Firms, large or small, more and more use an on-line network to share information within the firm. The intranet, and even standard e-mail (see chapter 11), will in the next few years replace the printed vehicle, which is still somewhat cumbersome to produce and time-consuming to distribute.

Write the internal newsletter in a style that is simple, chatty, humorous without being cute, arranged into logical categories, and equipped with telephone extensions and e-mail addresses for follow-up information. The newsletter should be done properly, just like the client newsletter; this is not the sort of writing, design, and production to leave in unqualified hands. Follow the guidelines offered for the client/marketing newsletter (chapter 5). You need not follow a regular schedule; some announcements won't wait. On occasion, invite the staff to contribute opinion pieces. Aim for high-quality writing, regardless of the medium.

While the house organ is not part of the firm's overall marketing communications arsenal and may not win you new clients, it is a handy medium for partners to confer with staff, boost morale, and reinforce team spirit.

Internal newsletter topics and categories may be:

News about staff
Promotions, interoffice moves
Professional licenses achieved
Honors and appointments
Continuing education accomplishments
Marriages, offspring
Employment anniversaries
Out-of-the-ordinary work-oriented travel

Company announcements
Working hours and overtime
Use of automobiles (personal and company)
Health insurance
Sexual harassment guidelines
Maternity leave policies

Design projects
New work
Completed projects

Kudos
Published articles about the firm or its people
Design awards

Extracurricular activities
Accomplishments of firm in running, baseball, bowling, or other leagues

Obituaries

None of us is immortal, and it pays to be prepared to deal with the death of a member of the firm so that the obituary is handled capably and with taste.

Newspapers, magazines, and the broadcast media as a rule write the obituary themselves, based on information supplied by those who knew the deceased's background and accomplishments. Persons of unusual celebrity are commonly interviewed by their hometown newspapers while still alive—no doubt an unsettling experience all around. More often, either the family or a representative of the firm telephones or e-mails the information to the paper's or TV or radio station's assigned reporter. Most papers carry a contact phone number on their obituary pages.

In the case of a death, the firm should prepare and issue an announcement, on paper, which is in reality a form of press release. The announcement should follow largely the press release's ground rules (see chapter 5). A photograph may be added. You might post it on your firm's Web site, if you have one.

The announcement typically follows this sequence of elements.

Headline (include name, age, principal achievement)
Opener (same data as headline plus place and cause of death)
Review of main accomplishments
Birthplace, education
Career development
Personality (optional)
Surviving immediate family

Obituary

MARIO G. SALVADORI,
Engineer And Inner-City Teacher, 90
By Paul Goldberger

Mario G. Salvadori, an engineer whose passion for structures was equaled only by his devotion to teaching about them, died on Wednesday in Manhattan. He was 90, and lived in Manhattan.

At his death, Dr. Salvadori was honorary chairman of the engineering firm of Weidlinger Associates and the James Renwick Professor Emeritus of Engineering and a Professor Emeritus of Architecture at Columbia University. He was best known in his last years, however, for his determination to use the principles of architecture and engineering as a way of teaching science and math to inner city students.

Responding to a call for volunteers in the New York City public schools in 1975, Dr. Salvadori, then 68, taught a junior high school class in Harlem. His success at explaining complex structural concepts through such real-world examples as how bridges and skyscrapers are built led him to develop his ideas into a formal curriculum, which ultimately became the basis of the Salvadori Educational Center on the Built Environment, now based at City College. The non-profit center trains teachers and supervises the use of Dr. Salvadori's curriculum in more than 25 schools in the South Bronx, Harlem and elsewhere.

Dr. Salvadori, a lifelong pacifist, had a gentle, patient manner that belied his stature as one of the world's leading structural engineers. He took particular delight in encouraging inner-city students to build models of buildings and bridges out of ordinary materials like toothpicks and string, and would even encourage them in class to set up economies in play money to teach them about the economics of structure as well as the physics of it. He showed the students how to make arches out of folded paper, startling them by revealing that the paper could be strong enough to support several bricks.

"I teach them why buildings stand up—that is, the basic principles of architectural structures, which is also the subject of my first-year course in architecture at Columbia," Mr. Salvadori wrote in 1981. "To my surprise, the children seem to absorb the ideas better and quicker than do my university students. Their enthusiasm is unbounded and their questions come like bullets from a machine gun."

In a speech in 1990 at the International Design Conference in Aspen, Colo., he asked "Are children capable of influencing the environment? I believe the answer to this question to be a resounding yes, on one condition: that they be empowered to understand, appreciate and wish to modify that environment."

In 1993, when Dr. Salvadori received the Hoover Medal, given jointly by the nation's engineering societies, Jonathan F. Fanton, president of the New School, said of him: "He is shattering myths about how science and math must be taught, how inner-city children learn, and what they are capable of learning." Dr. Fanton concluded: "He has made the teaching of engineering a humanitarian art in itself."

Unlike many engineers who think in purely mathematical terms, Dr. Salvadori was a scientist who constantly sought ways to connect his craft to art and society. He designed the concrete structural system for Eero Saarinen's CBS Building in Manhattan, among many other celebrated buildings.

"His main concern was that great architecture be achieved," the architect Eugene Kohn said of Dr. Salvadori in 1995. "Some engineers say you can't do this or that, but Mario never did. In my view, he's on a par with Louis Kahn or Paul Rudolph."

Mr. Salvadori was born on March 19, 1907, in Rome and was reared in Genoa and in Spain. His father was an engineer, but Mario hoped to become a concert conductor, and in 1925, at 18, he established what he later said was Italy's first student jazz band.

Dissuaded by his parents from a musical career, he received two doctorates from the University of Rome, one in civil engineering and the other in mathematics. An outspoken critic of Mussolini's Fascist regime—he later said that his exposure to Fascism helped inspire him to seek more creative and open teaching methods with children—he left Italy in 1939 for the United States. Through a contact established by his parents, he first worked as a time-and-motion engineer at Lionel Trains in New Jersey.

His interest in teaching was already apparent, however, and by 1940 he joined Columbia as a temporary faculty member, the beginning of a 50-year association with the university. He was appointed a full professor in 1959.

For three years he worked as a consultant to the Manhattan Project, unaware, he said later, that his research was connected to the atomic bomb. In 1945, Dr. Salvadori joined with Paul Weidlinger, who had recently established an engineering firm in New York. While his name was never on the door, he was the firm's most prominent presence, serving as a consultant until 1960, then as a partner from 1960 to 1991, and then as honorary chairman.

At Weidlinger, he established a particular expertise in the analysis of structural failure. While he helped design numerous new buildings, Dr. Salvadori was often called in as a forensic engineer investigating building failures in situations ranging from design and construction errors to earthquakes.

Dr. Salvadori is survived by his wife, Carol, a son, Vieri; a stepson, Michael Kazan, and three grandchildren.

Writing in School

7

A critical mark of the enlightened, well-rounded, successful design professional is skilled communication through writing and speech. The groundwork for this must take place in the schools, where the prevailing—and essentially justified—focus on design must be amplified by a deeper concern for the written and spoken word.

It is only after a year or two in a school of architecture or other design discipline that students realize with a shock that academic life isn't made entirely of design; there is, in fact, a copious volume of writing to be done, as indicated in this partial list:

Themes and papers for the history, theory, or professional practice course
Text for presentation boards
Reports for courses in technology, engineering, and materials
Essays and exams for required humanities courses
Job applications at graduation
Grant and scholarship applications

Many vehicles exist for honing writing skills. Required and elective course writing assignments in history and theory, professional practice, research, urban design, construction technology, and environmental studies can all serve as training grounds that you, as a student, can exploit. You'll deepen your awareness of the written word and sharpen those skills to your advantage, obtaining better grades and more attractive job offers.

Before you settle down to carry out a course assignment or apply an explanatory text to your review boards, read through the following useful guidelines for clear writing. While they will not (necessarily) make you into an Ernest Hemingway or a Toni Morrison, they will give you a leg up in writing clear, understandable, and, above all, effective prose. To paraphrase Marshall McLuhan, if your message fails to clearly convey your purpose, you have no message.

Your first consideration in developing a clear style is to stop thinking of the act of writing prose as an awe-inspiring venture. A lot of your writing will be for your studio critics or course lecturers. These individuals are people first and faculty second; therefore, don't throw a lot of convoluted text at them. If you want to get your instructor into an amiable frame of mind, giving you the benefit of the doubt between an A and a B, make sure your writing doesn't suffer from an excess of formality and difficult construction. Writing style and talking style should not be that far apart.

Poor wording:
The new business school campus is characterized by a monumental scale incompatible with the context of the surrounding built volumes.

Better wording:
The new business school is out of scale with its neighbors.

Another aid to clear writing is to keep your sentences short. Writing long sentences that make sense takes a talent well beyond yours or mine. It's hard to balance several ideas in a single long sentence and still make sense. You'll do far better to limit your sentences to making a single point. This may give you a string of shorter sentences, but you'll have no problem with stating your message clearly. A good rule of thumb is to limit sentences to twenty words or less. This doesn't mean that sentences longer than this don't communicate; it's just that much harder to be effective. If you find a sentence getting out of hand, it's all right to use semicolons to divide it.

Poor wording:
For my thesis I elected to investigate the science of acoustics and to explore its role as a determinant of architectural form, knowing that spatial acoustics are influenced by the shape of the room, the volume of the space, and the absorption of the room's surfaces across a range of frequencies, and that the construction of the edge walls, floors, and ceilings have an impact on acoustical comfort.

Better wording:
For my thesis I decided to investigate the impact of acoustics on architectural form. The acoustics of a space are influenced by its shape, the volume of the space, and surface absorption across a range of frequencies. Key factors in acoustic comfort include the materials and construction of edge walls, floors, and ceilings.

Avoiding Designer-Babble

Consider the benefits and limitations of using specialized designer lingo. Designer-babble or jargon is the use of words in strange, exotic forms, or using common words to denote uncommon meaning. Designer-babble commonly stands between you and clarity, whether you're reading it or presenting it to your instructor. As a student, when searching for models of good writing, avoid passages of text that have a supposed cleverness of verbiage that is in fact muddy or obscure; it usually conceals an absence of content. Used by small groups of like-thinking designers, jargon can serve as a kind of handy shorthand. But beware of assuming that everyone outside the group will understand your meaning when you refer to "syncopated plastic adjacencies" and "referential disconnects."

Do not, however, confuse designer-babble or jargon with technical terms. Every profession and trade has its own terminology that is used to conduct business. For example, there is no way, as structural engineer, that you can get by without using such terms as shear, moment, deflection, point loads, Vierendeel truss, or space-web. If you are writing a class report about Gothic architecture, you may well have to use such terms as triforium, finial, lancet arch, ogee window, half-timber, and more.

But don't lose sight of your audience. Your instructor will have no problem with such terms. But as soon as you begin to combine technical terms into oblique sentences and paragraphs, you won't impress your instructor so much as cause annoyance. Your instructor may be devoting a weekend afternoon to grading your class's papers; the last thing he or she needs is to have to wallow in a sea of verbal obscurity.

How can you tell when you cross the line from clarity to designer-babble? Put yourself in the shoes of the reader. Rigorously screen every phrase in your text. Whenever you have the slightest doubt as to the meaning, simplify the word, the phrase, and the context.

Note that after you go into professional practice, your reports, proposals, and correspondence will be read by several levels of reviewers. First are the client's technical people, and they will probably grasp your design terminology. But most clients lack technical staffs; even when they do exist, most key decisions, such as the selection of design consultants, are typically made at a higher level. That level includes administrators, politicians, senior management executives, selection boards; these are made up of laypeople. You don't want to alienate those individuals with obscure terms and references. If some technical terms cannot be avoided, insert a small glossary. Better be safe than sorry.

The following "before" and "after" examples are based on examples of designer-babble in chapter 1.

> *Before:*
> [The building's] formal strategies are consistent. . . . The detailing ethic is the same—it's forever.

> *After:*
> Form is consistent . . . the detailing is forever.

> *Before:*
> Projects are either investigative or accommodative.

> *After:*
> Designs either stretch the envelope or follow norms.

> *Before:*
> Activated axiomatic topologies of nonnomadic tribal elements . . . have been interpreted within the archaeological context of the site.

> *After:*
> The architect selected design features typical of nonnomadic tribal cultures and fit them into the archaeological nature of the site.

Another tip for getting your message across clearly is to choose words that have specific meanings. English, like most other languages, has words that range from the specific to the vague and indefinite. The vaguer the term, the greater the chance of misunderstanding. It is true that a hammer is a pounding device; a chicken is a mobile egg-producing grain-consuming unit; a door is an interspacial transition element. But you'll make more sense as you write class assignments to use words on the lines of hammer, chicken, and door.

Note the following example from the design of facilities for education:

> *Poor wording:*
> Modem-accessible outlets were dispersed on a two-foot module throughout the instructional spaces.

> *Better wording:*
> Dataline jacks occur on a two-foot module throughout the classrooms.

Closely linked to the admonition to deploy specific rather than general terms is an appeal to use simple terms and phrases. To "rank" a list is surely better, and less pretentious, than to "prioritize" it. For other examples of dos and don'ts, see page 19 in chapter 1.

The enterprising tenor of our society, as reflected by corporate figures such as Bill Gates and Donald Trump, is mimicked by an equally adventurous tone in the new media. Not only such hip journals as *WIRED* and *Fast Company*, but also more and more of the traditionally stiffer professional and business media have caught the excitement. The buzz shows up not only in invigorating, untamed graphics, but also in the writing. Two ways to achieve writing with impact and excitement are to use the active sentence form and to include deliberate references to people in your text (discussed below). Be sure to apply both these guidelines and you'll note in a flash a higher level of appeal shining through your writing. See the effect of the following sentence, which uses the passive form. It is taken from a student's report on landscaping design for arid zones.

> It was decided that plant types requiring a high year-round level of rainfall would not be selected. Instead, planting would be kept to a minimum; various methods of finishing the landscape through special ground colors and textures were chosen by the designers.

Why not write:

> The designers decided to avoid rain-thirsty plant species. Instead, they put in very few plants, and embellished the landscape by means of special ground color and textures.

Be sure to work people into your writing. Nothing turns readers on more than an infusion of individuals. While the public media have operated on this principle for years, the trend has now infiltrated professional and business publications. Writing reflects this, and the well-attuned journals make a point of weaving people into their text. You should do this too, even in unglamorous situations, such as the following examples. Your professors and mentors are more likely to identify with your message if couched as though people were involved, rather than as a dry-as-dust event carried out by anonymous participants. So avoid the "before" examples here and turn to the solutions for a better way. (In these examples, the "after" versions are somewhat longer, but much more direct and appealing.)

> *Before:*
> Community elements took exception to the methods used by the city in securing their input into the planning and design process. *(from a half-page handout to the judges at the review of a problem for a new community center)*

> *After:*
> Several mothers of young children, headed by Mrs. Bess Wright, complained to John Olsen, a member of the city department of housing and community affairs, that his department was making decisions without checking with families in the community.

> *Before:*
> The community will benefit by converting the old warehouse into a library, day-care center, and neighborhood meeting place. *(from a student presentation)*

> *After:*
> The converted warehouse will benefit everyone in the community. Parents can drop children off in the day-care centers. Students and their parents, as well as visitors, can use the library, and young and old can meet and socialize in the warmly appointed ground-floor spaces planned for this purpose.

Making Your Point

Above all, your writing will flow more clearly when you are clear in your own mind as to the points or argument you want to make. Whether you are presenting a project at a faculty review or writing an essay or other written assignment in a history or structures class, begin by asking yourself, "What is my message?" The simplest words assembled in the most elegant composition won't help you communicate if your reasoning is muddy and your basic logic flawed. Before you even hit the keyboard, list on a pad the points you want to make, arrange them in a sensible progression, eliminate—if you can—all but the critical ones, then start to write. A useful tip is to try to express your message in a single sentence, then keep that sentence in front of you as you write. If you are able to write such a sentence without trouble, chances are that your writing will flow clearly and easily. If not, go back and rethink your argument or approach.

For two excellent student papers, see pages 118 and 120.

Gender Bias

Forty years ago a woman student looking around her in the design studio would see almost nothing but men. Today, over 30 percent of those enrolled in bachelor's degree programs are women, and over 40 percent in master's degree programs. For years, however, echoing writing patterns in the design professions as a whole, course assignments, writing, school bulletins, and curricula descriptions failed entirely to reflect this change in the makeup of the student body. Nor did it mirror the changes, albeit somewhat slower, in the makeup of design school faculties.

Guidelines for avoiding gender-explicit writing fall into four types:

• Find a word that is gender-independent (e.g., manufactured, not man-made; staff hours or hours worked, not man-hours; drafting staff or even drafter, not draftsman). Avoid inventing awkward-sounding terms: use "chairman" or "chairwoman" (if you don't know the gender, use "chairperson") or "council member."

• Ignore the situation, and state that whenever you use "he" or "she" you mean both. This is a copout.

• Each time you face the possessive form *he, write he/she, his/her, him/her,* etc. This is virtuous but clumsy.

• Use the plural whenever it makes sense. Note that the plural (they, their) is gender indefinite, whereas the singular is gender-specific (he, his; she, her). Take advantage of this.

Refer to chapter 1 for more detailed examples of gender-neutral writing.

In the sixties the use of what was then known as sexist language was very much a cause célèbre. Champions of equality preached against the inequities of biased language; company executives, especially publishers, held seminars to discuss the problem; human resource departments issued detailed guidelines on how to write without gender bias. Today the battle is not won. But the attitude of a new generation has changed. Positions are less sensitized, more laid back, more tolerant.

That doesn't mean that gender bias in writing or speech is not critical. It has re-emerged more as a general awareness than as a cry to battle. Just as Calvinist doctrine preaches that you cannot achieve grace through good works alone, but that hard work, moral virtue, and business success are evidence of grace, so awareness of gender-free prose tells your instructors, contacts, and prospective employers—many of them women—that your writing aims for a new, higher standard. In the end, as a student you should let yourself be guided by whether your text, or anyone's text, makes a serious effort to avoid references to male or female stereotypes.

You can also safely take an example from the daily and professional press. As you read articles, note how the media—reflectors of trends on language as in most other matters—use gender-independent language. Your instructors, too, are aware of the problem and can help you sort out awkward situations as they emerge.

Above all, be aware. Write a lot: avoiding gender-specific writing comes steadily with practice.

Rules in writing are designed above all to convert a potentially obscure text into one that its audience can understand and use. That doesn't mean you cannot bend or break a guideline if by so doing you enhance the meaning of your work. Shakespeare, who loved short words for their punch, wasn't afraid if the occasion was right to insert a long word. The long word stood out by contrast, and added emphasis to the text, as these examples show:

> Blow, blow, thou winter wind,
> Thou are not so unkind
> As man's ingratitude.
>   —*As You Like It,* II/7

and

> The sense of death is most in apprehension.
>   —*The Tempest,* III/1

Beware of trying to be clever with sudden artifice merely for the sake of surprising your instructor or judges, unless this adds insight, impact, or triggers a response. Thus we know that sentences should be short and unburdened with more than one or two ideas. But consider a situation where you are describing, in an assignment for your professional practice course, the lengthy process a project undergoes, from a gleam in the client's eye all the way to occupancy and beyond.

One way to convey this information is to use short sentences. ("The owner met with the architect and three weeks later a program emerged. The architect then developed a series of schematic drawings. These established the broad outlines of the museum. . . .") But to symbolize this long process, you could show it in your writing, perhaps: "Three weeks after the first meeting between owner and architect, a program emerged, followed in early summer by schematic drawings, which established in broad outlines the character of the museum, and which led to the design development stage, where the basic concept was fleshed out and yielded enough information so the contract documents could be prepared prior to sending the project out to bid."

I do not recommend sixty-four-word sentences. But if you can bend the rules and get away with it to accomplish a stronger, justifiable text, go for it. Ernest Hemingway once allegedly lambasted an editor for daring to correct a split infinitive in his manuscript. "When I split an infinitive," he supposedly said, "I [bleep] want it to stay split."

Among the most common assignments of students in schools of engineering, architecture, interior design, and landscape design is the written essay, often known as an article, theme, paper, or report. The assignment may originate in a history and theory course, a technical course, a course in professional practice, a related professional design discipline course, and courses in the humanities. Sometimes the writing is linked to a studio problem in which the instructor calls for a written summary or digest to accompany the drawings, model, or animation.

When tackling such an assignment, look first for the instructor's intent. Are you to write a succinct report on a lab test on concrete mixes? an assessment of a historic style? a review of a significant contemporary or historic interior? a discussion of professional ethics?

Set down your thoughts and ideas derived from your examination of the material, do background research, and develop your own thoughts. Record this data in the roughest possible way: use a handy notebook, pad, or computer screen. Don't worry about how it looks or the order of the entries. The main purpose is to brainstorm and trigger a stream-of-consciousness thinking process.

Next day, review the assemblage of notes and scribbles, and begin to impose a logical order. A close scrutiny of your notes will almost always suggest an arrangement of the material. Usually it will look like this:

Introduction—define the topic and why it's important (5%)
Subdivision of topic into principal subtopics—these should show how each
    subtopic or subtheme builds on the previous one (10%)
Discussion of each subtopic (six, each 10%, say)
Conclusions (20%)
Restatement of topic and its importance (5%)

An essay of this type is not unlike the sonata form in music. A sonata typically consists of a medium-speed first movement that sets the tone, a slow second movement that brings it out in more detail, a sprightly third movement that reinforces the ambiance, albeit more happily, and a final movement that captures the vein of earlier material and ends usually with a bang on trumpets and drums.

There are variations to this suggested approach. It is the fashion in the media today to kick off every article with a chatty little paragraph of human interest ("Jane Rodriguez was crossing Michigan Avenue after lunch when she stumbled into the pothole that had survived the spring road repair campaign . . ." before the article lumbers on to a discussion of road paving materials). This has merit if you are trying hard to capture the reader's attention; when an instructor must correct thirty papers, it can work well. But be sure this kind of opening serves to set the scene quickly for the article, and that you move on promptly to the core topic.

Once you begin writing the body of the article, bear in mind the guidelines taken up earlier in this chapter, and keep the piece simple. Avoid clever turns of phrase, hackneyed expressions or clichés (e.g., "they lived in a *sprawling mansion*"; "the two spaces were alike as *two peas in a pod*"), and pointless flaunting of obscure terminology. Include your opinions if asked; when you do, make sure they are supported by facts.

A few seasoned writers claim to be able to compose as they write. The act of writing, they say, stimulates their brain cells to come up with the proper ideas and ways to frame them. If this works for you, and your instructors like your work, great. If not, you'll do better to clarify your ideas *before* you write them down.

Consult a manual of style (see Resources) to make sure your format, punctuation, and arrangement of references (and footnotes, if you choose to use them) are consistent. Do not imperil your grade by neglecting these important parts of writing.

Above all, recall the need to have a clear point of view: lacking such a point of view, no amount of verbal acrobatics will help you compose an effective essay.

Note these two examples of papers by students who completed their assignments with success.

Scenario

You are to identify a building (or a related group of buildings) that you have visited or are able to visit by the deadline and develop an article suitable for submitting to a professional architectural magazine. Once you have identified the building, plan to visit it during hours when it is accessible. Spend whatever time you need to walk through and observe it as a whole as well as observing its parts. Bring a notebook and, if you wish, a sketch pad and a camera. Record what you see, then develop a 1000-word article describing the building as well as giving it your assessment.

The article is to consist of these five parts:

1. Title or headline
2. Deck (a twenty-word expansion on the headline)
3. Description [Cover as many of the following points as feasible, not
     necessarily in this order]:
       Context (relationship to its site and to adjacent buildings)
       Style
       General configuration and massing
       Principal materials (exterior and interior)
       Structural system
       Electric and day lighting
       Interiors and furnishings
       Special spatial features (e.g., atrium, grand stair)
       Access (parking, ADA—Americans with Disabilities Act—concerns)
       Landscaping
4. Your conclusions and evaluation
5. Credits (architect, consultants, owner, sources)

Devote about two-thirds of your text to description, one-third to conclusions and evaluation. You may include up to two pages of illustrations.

MANTYNIEMI
Raili and Reima Pietila Design
Official Residence for the Presidents of Finland
by Patrick Brown
[Patrick Brown wrote this piece as a student at the School of Architecture, Washington University, St. Louis.]

The President's new residence in Finland was a ten-year project for the husband-and-wife team of Raili and Reima Pietila. They won the national competition for the building in 1983. The house was completed shortly before Mr. Pietila's death in 1993. The building is the first to be designed specifically as the president's residence. The president has lived in various existing manor houses since Finland became independent in 1918. The house obviously has tremendous symbolic importance for the people of Finland. Nature was the source of inspiration; the house is very well integrated into the landscape. Finnish artists from a variety of disciplines collaborated on the project. The result is a complex, unique, and highly articulated building. Mantyniemi is an important expression of Finland's national character.

The name Mantyniemi means "pine tree cape." The building sits on a sprawling, wooded site that juts out into the Baltic Sea. Though the setting is rural, the house is actually in Helsinki, a 20-minute drive from the city center. The vegetation on the site is typical of a Finnish forest—mostly pine and birch trees, with ferns, astilbes, and moss covering the ground. The trees on the site were meticulously preserved during construction. The landscape designer supplemented these trees with other native vegetation to create a garden that does not rely on bloom for beauty.

Mantyniemi consists of three buildings—a gatehouse, a servants' building, and the main house. The main house is approximately 25,000 square feet, and contains the reception rooms, the private quarters, and the office wing. The building stretches out along the contours of the site. The entrance façade faces north and is clad in granite. The south façade faces the sea and is almost entirely of glass. The office and staterooms are to the east, at a higher elevation, whereas the private living area is to the west, at a lower elevation. The reception rooms—including the dining room, two drawing rooms, and an office—spread out in a fan-shaped pattern. A corridor to the north links these rooms to the flanking office and private wings.

The architects integrated the house into the Finnish landscape. They considered both the specific conditions of the site, and the geological and climatic conditions of the country. Finland has been emerging from the sea over the past 15,000 years. Helsinki is rising at the rate of sixteen inches per century. The house responds metaphorically to this fact. Mantyniemi seems to be rising from the glacial deposits of the site. At the same time, from the south, the building has a crystalline form, like an ice formation that is draped across the rocky site.

The architectural expression of the interior is complex and sculptural.

Folded white planes form the ceiling and walls. These surfaces capture and reflect the white sunlight of Finland. Because of its northern location, the sun angles in Finland vary greatly from winter to summer, creating a variety of effects. Concealed spaces between the ceiling and roof are filled with warm air in winter, to provide insulation in the frigid climate. The lower ceiling rises two feet just inside of the southern windows, giving the impression that the glass extends beyond the roof. The south-facing windows are very tall and narrow, because the architects thought that a short window was not appropriate for viewing the tall, slender pine trees that surround the house. These windows were originally designed with small, branch-like mullions. This idea was abandoned, however, because very heavy window frames were required for security reasons.

One of the most striking things about the house is its complexity. I had the opportunity to visit with Raili Pietila at her home in Helsinki [in the summer of 1997], after I visited the house. She showed me the huge volumes of technical specifications that were required to build Mantyniemi. There are, for instance, over 150 doors in the house, and only a few are the same. The form of the air ducts and the slats that cover the openings are not recognizable as HVAC elements. Elements such as lighting and fences—even the long stainless steel poker that hangs next to one of the main fireplaces—were specially designed.

Artistic collaboration played a key role in creating Mantyniemi. Finnish artists designed the landscape, furnishings, tapestries, artwork, and even the table settings in the house. A staircase links the public and private portions of the house. Along the wall of this stair is a huge ceramic relief work by the artist Rut Bryk. The quality of the welds in the staircase does not equal the craftsmanship of the adjacent artwork. Still, the design quality of the house and its furnishings seem to complement each other. There is a uniform softness of tone to all the fixtures within the house. What one notices most of all is the variety and intricacy of the reflections of sunlight in the house.

Mantyniemi stands as a testimony to the creativeness of the Finnish people. As a national symbol, this building sends an invaluable message as Finland steps up its industrial production. Perhaps the quest for gold will not inflict upon Finland the mediocrity so characteristic of development here in the United States. Instead, Finland has in its geography, climate, and people the means to achieve a unique national expression.

Curiously, not all Finns like Mantyniemi as strongly as I do. I talked to a number of people in Finland, and they are not as proud of their president's residence as I think they should be. Apparently, the current president has made some unkind statements about the house. He likens the experience of living in this house to "living in an Alvar Aalto vase." My friends tell me that he thinks the house is cold, impersonal, and museum-like. The current president is also apparently too overweight to move through some of the house's narrow passageways. This commentary seems to have harmed the Finnish people's opinion of their "first" house.

I'm not sure what this portends for the future of Finland. Emerging nations tend to want to avoid being different, and prefer to imitate their wealthier neighbors. Mantyniemi is a masterpiece. Will the people of Finland fulfill the promise of Mantyniemi? Will Finland maintain its cultural identity as it gains in economic strength? It remains to be seen.

Credits:
Maj-Lis Rosenbroijer, landscape architect
Antti Paateru, interior architect
Irma Kakkasjarvi, textiles
Reijo Paavilainen, Kinni Paharinin, Rut Bryk, Mais Kaarna, contributing artists

Sources:
"The President's Residence, Mantyniemi, Helsinki," by Olga Gambardella, *Domus*, May 1994.
"Raili and Reima Pietila, Mantyniemi, The Residence of the President," by Raili Pietila, *A+U*, June 1995.
"Finland's New Presidential Residence," *Progressive Architecture*, September 1994.
Reima Pietila: Architecture, Context and Modernism, by Malcolm Quantrill, Rizzoli, 1985.
Reima Pietila, Intermediate Zones in Modern Architecture. Museum of Finnish Architecture, Helsinki, 1985.
Author's interview with Raili Pietila, July 1997.

Comment

This is a well-argued article, with an accurate, discerning description clearly based on a site visit. The writer expressed his opinions and, aware of a surge of praise as well as criticism around this building, nevertheless forged a well-balanced article. Note the short, snappy sentences and the virtual absence of puzzling jargon.

Article B

A HOUSE FOR HEALING
A New AIDS Residence Gives Hope to New York's HIV+ Homeless
by Gonzalo Fernandez
[Gonzalo Fernandez wrote this article as a student in the
School of Architecture and Environmental Studies at
City College of The City University of New York.]

Almost twenty years since the first case of AIDS was diagnosed, a cure is still out of reach. Nowadays patients are living longer, however, thanks to new combinations of drugs and treatment. But there are many people who cannot afford treatment because they are homeless. In 1990 a group of people of different minority groups formed HOUSING WORKS INC., a nonprofit organization that provides permanent housing and medical and social assistance to New York's HIV+ homeless population. Since then they have helped more than 30,000 New Yorkers with housing and medical and psychological treatment throughout the city. In June 1997 HOUSING WORKS INC. opened a new building that provides housing and assistance on site for residents of the Lower East Side.

The AIDS Residence and Day Treatment Center is located at 741–749 East 9th Street in Manhattan and was designed by Allan Wanzenberg and Associates. This five-story, reinforced concrete structure was built on two adjacent lots forming an L-shape, with the longer side facing East 9th Street. The shape of the site and local zoning regulations forced a long, narrow, design.

To preserve a residential atmosphere, the entrance is announced by a glass marquee in front of a glass wall. The lobby is also kept at a residential scale with no grand spaces or information boards that might hint at a health institution; a reception desk and waiting area give a private atmosphere that helps residents feel that they are in a secure and private environment.

The common spaces are located on the ground floor. A foyer or corridor divides the game room and the dining room. The game room is in a comfortable setting with game tables, a TV set, and plenty of sunlight. This space is also used as a meeting area for local community groups that visit the center. The dining room seats 80 people three times a day. Next to it is the "sun porch" that leads to the garden. Yet this space receives no natural light because it is located in the north facade and faces a six-story building.

Nevertheless, the residents use the porch as a secluded and quiet space. At the moment the garden is under construction. The design was provided through the generosity of landscape architect Edwina von Gal who donated her time and resources to completion of the project. The design consists of small pockets of bamboo trees along a paved weaving walkway ending in a water fountain. The design was conceived as a self-maintaining garden because of the limited funds allocated for its maintenance. Also on the first floor is a retail space run by the Center. This space will house a small diner for the community and will be run by residents as part of their work training.

The day treatment center is located on the second floor surrounding the double-height lobby. The three departments that form the center (administration, clinic, and social services) face one another. This is done for two reasons: one is to provide a feeling of service and openness for the clients; the second is for efficiency, as only one receptionist and waiting area service the three departments.

On the next three floors are the suites. Each floor has its own laundry room and lounge. Each suite is on average 300 square feet and completely furnished. To nourish a sense of independence no two studios have been decorated in the same way. The furniture was donated by high-scale patrons and corporations such as Crate & Barrel (furniture and china) and SAMSUNG (appliances).

Some of the pieces were designed as modules that can be changed or combined in many ways as the residents' needs change. On the roof is the community room overlooking the World Trade Center where residents can meet as a community in a friendly and familiar atmosphere.

The simplicity of the design, the distribution of the spaces, and the finishing materials ably provide the residents with comfort and a sense of independence. But most importantly the Center provides an atmosphere in which they can feel like functional members of the community.

Reproduced by permission.

Comment

This is a well-documented report on a highly sensitive and timely topic. It aptly combines description and assessment. Sentences are short, the style simple and clear, and the vocabulary straightforward.

Assignments

Here is a method for organizing an assignment in a history and theory class.

As the Modernist movement nears its one-hundredth birthday, it is becoming the subject of history, both as an architectural style and as a sociological event. Steps are under way to anoint as landmarks some of its best-known examples. You are to write about this phenomenon. Refer to any precedents where a social, religious, or economic movement spawned a design style which, in its turn, came to acquire historical status and pressures to preserve its prime examples. Write 1000 words, and support the essay with illustrations.

1. Begin by reviewing sources. This will disclose a number of styles that emerged from religious, social, political, or economic roots. One is the Gothic style. Another is the Baroque. A third is the Arts and Crafts movement. Analyze these styles for causes and effects. Then examine Modernism. Finally, hazard a projection as to Modernism's future in the new millennium.

2. Create an outline. Establish an outline of sections for the text, with relative lengths for your own use. For example:

Introduction (5%). State theme, why it's significant.

Precedents (15%). Origins, evolution, spread, demise, opposition to, and revivals of one or two historic styles.

Modernism (10%). Origins, growth, emergence as a style, impact of 1932 International Style show at the Museum of Modern Art, New York.

Criticism (10%). Sterility attributed to Modernism; its temporary eclipse by Postmodernism.

Revival in the 1990s (20%).

Comparisons of Modernism to selected historic styles (20%).

Key players and their roles (10%) (e.g., Gropius, Le Corbusier, Mies van der Rohe, Rudolph, Venturi, Meier).

Conclusion (10%). Modernism, today and in the future.

References.

List of illustrations.

Master's theses and doctoral dissertations are, at least in many schools of architecture and design, extended forms of studio work that culminate in a public review. They differ from regular studio problems in the amount of research and investigation required and, especially in the case of the dissertation, in the depth and length of documentation.

Schools differ in their precise demands. Some place greater weight on research or theory; others focus on the design solution to a (preferably) realistic problem, and often demand of the student several solutions, with one then chosen for final development. Some schools consider the investigation and the design of equal weight, figuring that in the world of professional practice both aspects are essential.

Theses place a premium on original thought and findings. Dissertations raise the bar a notch either by demanding totally new ways of examining an existing theme (for example, water as a design element) or by inviting research into a currently pressing theme that demands the intense scrutiny of a dissertation (such as computer-aided design; intelligent buildings; desert landscaping; the new workplace).

The volume of writing demanded of the doctoral candidate is colossal. Key components of the dissertation include an abstract or summary; a statement of the problem, argument, or issue; development of the argument—typically the central and longest segment; and conclusions. The design complements the written work; displayed on boards or through other media, it features writing to identify the drawings and, often in a short sentence or paragraph, to give the theme of each board.

The text of the dissertation is commonly targeted for a faculty committee, at times augmented by guest professionals and lay persons. Because of these outsiders, and because it is good practice, the writing should be simple, straightforward, and clear. While privileged use of esoteric terminology whose meaning is clear to the faculty judges may seem to bring a short-term benefit, it is not provident over the long haul. Even if you are committed to an academic career, where such privileged writing is quite common, as a candidate you are on firmer ground by employing a more broadly accepted vocabulary and simpler language forms. Dissertations are sometimes published; your chances for publication improve when your work is well organized and clearly written.

A student presentation board or set of boards—the outcome of a design studio problem or thesis—has an immediate selling job. It increases or decreases your odds of winning a good grade. It could also get you possible contacts because of the professionals who may come to judge the panels. Whereas the trade show exhibit panel has to stand and "speak" alone, the student's board is supported by the student's own verbal presentation and possibly a 3-D model. Many of the precepts for trade show exhibit panels still apply, however. Refer to chapter 5 Exhibit Panels (page TK).

Simplicity is important—of drawing, text, layout. But because the review jury has more time to give, because the judges are in effect a captive audience, and because they will judge you on concept and detail, you must provide added information. Typically, that means concept, circulation, structure, form and finishes, siting and landscaping, choice and application of energy sources, lighting, and probably acoustics.

You then must choose between too much clutter or too many boards. Normally the studio critic determines the number of boards, and you work within this framework. The verbal presentation tends to rework what shows on the boards, but as a savvy student you can use the boards as a platform for orally embellishing your solution. How to choose and organize the spoken word is covered in chapter 13.

As you prepare design boards for a pinup or faculty review, remember that drawings alone are not enough. What you write or letter on your boards is just as critical in conveying your design intent.

The written message typically includes the title, an explanation (brief or long, depending on the type of problem) of the concept, and drawing labels or legends or both. The amount of writing may be substantial when you seek to explain a technical, financial, or management issue.

Consider both the content and the form of your text.

Content. First, make sure your theme or argument comes across. Whether it's the reorganization of a huge, 4000-student high school into small, 500-student units; a community college that respects its context; a midrise suburban commercial building that complies with green standards; the design of a two-mile bridge span; or a contemporary workplace environment that's totally flexible—say so in an easy-to-read headline. For text of some length, use a verbal shorthand to avoid unnecessary items such as articles (a, the) and useless adjectives and adverbs. Divide the text into small, logical parts, and assign a number or bullet to each part. Study tabloid newspapers; they are expert in compacting mounds of information into the least number of words. You probably cannot rival "STIX NIX HIX PIX" (Small-town moviegoers ignore hayseed films), but something along the lines of "ABANDONED WIRE FACTORY IS SITE FOR COMMUNITY COLLEGE" does the job.

Format. Whether your lettering is by hand or machine-generated, what counts in the end is whether it can be read. Even if your review jury is sitting close to the boards, don't irritate them with lettering so small that they have to rise every other minute to pick out the text. Test letter height in advance to see how far it can be easily read. You'll do better to edit down the number of words and make them larger than to cram too many words on to your boards. Remember that you can use the lettering on your board as a simple but useful set of cues as you give your oral presentation.

Common Faults

Certain faults appear and reappear in student writing in general. Watch out for these. Avoid them when you can; there will be times when you cannot, such as a long sentence to make a complex point or a multisyllabic word for which there is no substitute. The list that follows spells out some suggestions for avoiding common faults.

Tighten sentences—make fewer words work harder.

Shorten paragraphs—twenty lines should be ample.

When describing a project, don't ignore the user.

When evaluating a project, avoid unspecific, essentially meaningless words such as "interesting," "impressive," "intriguing," "amazing," "surprising." Be specific, or explain why and how something is "interesting."

If you wax poetic about a building, do not get so carried away that your meaning is lost.

Be sure to include basic credits—i.e., the client, the primary design professional and associated firms, the principal consultants, the contractor, and the photographer (essential if your text is to be published).

Some schools of architecture and design offer courses on verbal communication skills. These are not "English 101" courses, but are geared specifically to the writing demands of the design professions. The course typically takes up principles of good writing; gives uses and abuses of technical terminology and jargon; and shows how to write letters, proposals, reports, brochures, e-mail, and the other written work products of a typical practice. Also usually covered are tips on making a lucid oral presentation. Such courses give students a double payoff: early warning about the career benefits of clear writing and speech, and the opportunity to master the art by practicing it in class.

Think of the principles and suggestions in this chapter as guidelines, not as rules. The intent is to trigger in your mind an attitude, rather than to think of suggested practices as dogma. With practice, these guidelines will become second nature.

For examples and samples of writing correspondence, brochures, proposals, reports, texts for exhibit boards, and other written products, refer to chapters 2–5. For tips on writing successful grant submittals and job applications, turn to chapter 8. Turn to chapter 10 for writing for the media. Finally, refer to chapter 1 for detailed tips and examples on clear writing.

Job Prospects

Nowhere does the quality of your writing count more than when it's used to advance your own career prospects. If you are a graduating student looking for your first job or a restive employee in a design firm, government, or a corporate or institutional facilities agency who is looking for a change; if you are a junior faculty member in quest of a tenure position or promotion; or if you have your eye on a juicy grant that will take you to Harvard or Rome or accord you time to pursue a cherished project—your chances depend greatly on how you present yourself through the few pieces of paper that will serve (along with references and an interview) as your ambassadors.

This chapter tackles the most common categories of applications and submittals (for developing a winning dossier for academic promotion or tenure, see chapter 9). It also offers useful guidelines on writing a letter of reference that will enhance your protégé's chances.

Career options for design professionals include:

Private practice
   design
   project management
   technical expertise
   specification writing
   estimating
   office administration
   construction contract administration
   business and general management
   business development (marketing)
   public relations and communications
Government service
Corporate facility staff
Education
Writing/journalism
Product development
Research
Real estate development

You usually look for work in one of five ways:

Identify a firm you want to work for, and apply;
Look in the classified section of the newspaper or browse the Web sites of
    known firms;
Contact a recruiter who specializes in design professions;
Send the word out over your personal or electronic network;
Advertise in print.

There is another variation, known as informational interviewing. Here you visit target firms with the understanding that they have no openings but use the interview as a way for both parties to get to know each other, and thereby create contacts.

Play out as many of these scenarios as you need to. Whether you are a graduating student or have been in practice for years, in general try to follow this procedure:

Assemble your assets. Avoid listing mere activities; focus instead on successes and accomplishments: computer savvy, education, registrations, travel, languages, contacts.
Develop a resume, cover letter, and attachments. Some combine the cover letter with the resume, but it is better to separate the two.
Send the package. Use first-class mail, private express mail, or messenger. Send by fax if okayed by the firm, but some fax machines print on flimsy paper and thereby weaken your impact. Send by diskette or e-mail if acceptable to the firm.

You can organize your resume as either a narrative or a listing of your qualifications. A crisply written narrative is better able to convey character; a listing can transmit a greater volume of facts. Use the first or third person, whichever seems most comfortable to you.

The main attribute of a winning resume is that it mentions accomplishments and results, not merely activities. Use specific verbs such as "increased," "completed," "exceeded," "launched," "built." Terms such as "conducted," "coordinated," "managed," "administered" will do only so long as they are seen to culminate in a worthy result. Avoid phrases such as "participated in," "researched," or "was team member" as they give no clue as to the success or failure of your efforts.

Opinions vary as to the order in which to list your past activities—most recent ones first or oldest first. Most recent first works best. If you have a long record of positions, you might list them by type of work or position. Reviewers read from the top down; chances are what you did last week is more relevant than what you did eight years ago.

Include in your resume the following items, assuming there is something positive to say about each item (as a student or recent graduate, the amount of information will be more limited; how to deal with this challenge is covered later in this chapter):

Positions held and results achieved. Be quantitative if you can (percent under budget; millions of dollars in project-managed construction; successful initiatives).

Publications. What you have written—so long as each is germane to design—and media where your work has been published; focus on quality over quantity.

Education. Stick with colleges, unless you went to a secondary school whose status or location could help your case.

Computer savvy. List software you know, especially CAD, and its version or release; and programs you have written or adapted.

Registrations. Name states, and whether you have a certificate from the National Council of Architectural Registration Boards (NCARB), the Council of Landscape Architectural Registration Boards (CLARB), or the corresponding engineering or interior design council.

Travel, where relevant. "Photographed examples of mud architecture as used in modern low-rise office construction in India for an article in Texas Architect" beats "traveled to India, Pakistan, Russia, Thailand, Bali, and Malaysia."

Languages spoken or understood, especially design and construction terminology.

Military service, where relevant.

Cover Letter

Your cover letter should be short—two-thirds of a page—but needs to dwell on the following:

What you are interested in, and why (say this up front).

Show enthusiasm for working for the firm. Research the firm so you know its strong points and agenda. (Unfortunately, when responding to a classified ad or in dealing with a recruiter, often you may not know this.)

Special qualifications. Select them from the resume and briefly restate them here.

Indicate readiness to travel. Many firms with global practices look for globetrotter staff.

Show confidence. Use words like "will," not "would"; "must," not "should."

Ask for an interview.

Let the content determine the length of the cover letter. If you are a student, don't pad it with irrelevant efforts. If you are a mid-career practitioner, gear the length to your audience, including only those items that will help your cause. If you can, determine the name and title of the person to whom your letter should be addressed.

For an example of a cover letter, see page 132.

Strengthen your message with enclosures and attachments. Include page-size reproductions of projects relevant to the job, the final project schedule print-out of a completed-on-time project, or the executive summary page of a key feasibility report. Make sure each is clearly identified and captioned, with a brief statement as to why it is relevant. If the job sought is an academic one, enclose a listing of published work.

Double-check the graphic quality of the enclosures. Eliminate any but the most engaging and clearest items. You do not want poor artwork to torpedo an outstanding written message.

Indicate that more material is available on request.

Some employers, especially high-technology companies with a high volume of job applications, now process resumes electronically. They use optical scanners to identify desired skills by searching for industry key words, phrases, or acronyms—such as "chief designer," "project manager," "JAVA," "AutoCAD Release 14," "top 5 percent," "fluent Mandarin."

Computerized scanners are said to prefer nouns over verbs. Key nouns such as those listed above may get noticed more than action verbs such as "exceeded." Insert the important verbs anyway; not every firm scan-reads resumes—that is more the province of large corporations and recruiting agencies than of the design professions.

You may also find preformatted resume-writing software packages that reflect some employers' wishes for easily identifiable key words (these packages vary from the one-size-fits-all to more targeted ones, but at this writing I know of none that targets design). Software for the job hunter is often contained on the employer's Web site. You download the software from the Web site, complete it, and e-mail it back. This process not only ensures its arrival, but also enables you to check out the Web site for other openings.

No matter what the medium, your bottom-line motto must always be "think accomplishment, not effort."

In the booming design and construction climate of the mid- and late 1990s, graduates from design schools, especially those at the top of their class, created a job hunter's market. Some large design firms have even sent recruiters to these schools. But building construction is notoriously cyclical, and an economy that roared in your first year may be sliding when you graduate five years later. This places a premium on marshaling your assets in a convincing way as you apply for a job.

As a student your volume of experience is limited, so make the best of what you have. Consider:

• Your school work, especially studio work in building types that are a specialty of the firm you're courting, or projects that won you a high grade or that graphically sparkle. Also consider an in-depth, well-written report on a technical or design topic, or an assignment for a design writing course;

- Practical summer or part-time experience. Focus on accomplishments rather than on activities, whether in the office or in the field. Even menial work is significant because it gave you an inside look at the operations of an office;
- Computer savvy;
- Travel (see earlier comments; don't list cruises in Norwegian fjords unless you can demonstrate a design benefit);
- Published writing on design or construction topics;
- Languages, but only if your knowledge is technical and fluent;
- Social or other contacts to make your prospective employer take notice.

Keeping these provisos in mind, follow the steps and advice stated elsewhere in the chapter for job hunters already employed. Be sure to focus on germane professional items; only in exceptional cases should you include entries along the lines of this one, sent to me by a recent graduate who was obviously short on relevant material: "High school: junior and senior years, member, later secretary of the Jefferson High School Chowder and Marching Society."

Consider the following successful student resume.

Scenario

You are about to graduate with your first professional degree. You decide to prepare a one-page list-type (as opposed to narrative-type) resume that places you in the best light for a solid, entry-level job offer. You have worked summers for professional design firms as well as in a retail store.

Resume

GEORGIA DUPLESSIS
1-A Avenue of the Elysian Fields,
New Orleans, LA 70100
T: (504) 123-4567, F: (504) 123-4568
e-mail: gduplessis@cpr.com

EXPERIENCE
Summer 1997. Portofino Associates, architects, Baton Rouge, LA
Technical assistant
I reviewed the firm's archives under partner's supervision, then reorganized them for easy access. Researched and compiled sources to aid designer of new Botanical Garden, freeing her for added assignments.

Summer 1996. Haussmann and Moses, urban designers and planners, Fenton, TX
CAD operator
I drew base plans for master plans for inner-city districts in Dallas and Fort Worth, using AutoCAD R14 and DataCAD. I created original map symbols that proved effective and more flexible than off-the-shelf symbol libraries. Also took part in field surveys.

Summer 1995. Neiman-Marcus, Houston, TX
Assistant office manager
Duties included secretarial support of office manager and three buyers, using conventional and on-line media, and customer service. I diplomatically handled numerous complaints to the satisfaction of customers and my boss, even persuading one to drop a lawsuit over an accident that the customer conceded was her fault.

EDUCATION
1992–95 Colby College, Waterville, ME. B.A., 1995
1995–98 Tulane University, New Orleans, LA. B.Arch. (expected 1998)

PROFESSIONAL AFFILIATIONS
Chaired Tulane chapter of the American Institute of Architecture Students.
Member of Tulane Cercle Français. Cercle traveled to West Africa to study natural temperature control techniques.

PUBLICATIONS
"A Student Looks at the Design Professions," *Architectural Chronicle,* May 1996
"The Getty Museum as Urban Design," *CRIT*, May 1997

SPECIAL SKILLS
Fluent on common computer software including CAD, spreadsheet, database, and word processing on Mac and PC platforms
Fluent in technical Spanish and French

HOBBY: Mountain climbing

REFERENCES: Available upon request

Note that this resume wherever possible states an accomplishment and not merely an activity. A little narrative is added in the summer jobs held, for a more personal touch.

Be aware that employers cannot ask you questions about your race, sexual preference, or religion, nor can they let your age affect their decision. There is nothing to prevent you from inserting such information, but it could place the interviewer in an awkward position and thus is best left out.

Arrange your material on the page so each heading is in bold type and the dates stand out. Be sure to incorporate important key words, such as "exceeded," "launched," "created software," and others, as previously noted.

Once you are in the field, you are virtually certain to change jobs several times in your career.

Changing Jobs

Scenario

You have worked at Gazebo Associates, landscape architects, for six years, and you feel it's time for a change. Your heart is set on working for Green & Associates. They have advertised in key local newspapers for a designer and production person, and you decide to go for it. Here is one possibility for your cover letter and resume. Their advertisement:

LANDSCAPE ARCHITECTS
For a versatile Filmore County firm. Degree, plus 4-6 yrs exp in design, constr docs, production & field superv. Communications skills essential. 2 yrs of office AutoCAD 13.0 exp required. Mail resume and enclosures to Green & Associates, 4 Eucalyptus Street, Rosefield, MS 38000

Letter and Resume

Ms. Olivia Green, Partner
Green & Associates
4 Eucalyptus Street
Rosefield, MS 38000

Dear Ms. Green:

I'm confident that I'm the right staff person for the position described in last Sunday's *Boston Herald* and *Mississippi Times*.

You will see from my resume that

- my experience includes four years in the office of Michael van Nyhuis, where I worked on developing contract documents and later did field supervision on projects that included the Riverfront Walk in Minneapolis and four midsized parks in Columbus, IN. All came in on budget and were completed on schedule.
- I was recently promoted to associate project manager, only six years after graduating from the landscape architecture program at the Harvard Graduate School of Design.
- At Harvard I was deputy editor of Harvard Design Magazine.
- I received the Rich Travel Prize and used the money to document through sketches and notes the great English eighteenth-century natural parks at Blenheim and Althorp, relating their message to today's environmental practices.
- I have fluent mastery of AutoCAD 14.0 and LandCADD, and related software.

I have studied and worked out of state since I left for graduate school, but my Mississippi roots go back four generations. I'm anxious to return to this state and bring my experience and enthusiasm to work in your firm.

I look forward to an interview with you.

Sincerely,
Mary Ellen Brown
Encl:
Resume (one page)
Project sheets (Minneapolis; Columbus, IN)

MARY ELLEN BROWN
6C Brattle Street • Cambridge, MA 02138
T: 617/459-2001 • F: 617/459-2002
e-mail: brownme@mzu.com

EXPERIENCE

1993–97
Mary Ellen Brown began as a designer in the office of Michael van Nyhuis. There, after only eight months as a junior designer and production person, she was promoted to associate project manager and a year later to project manager. In that position she coordinated the design, production, and later field supervision of two significant landscape projects designed by Mr. van Nyhuis: the Minneapolis Riverfront Walk and four midsized parks in Columbus, IN. Both projects, which were unusual in their complexity and in one case faced persistent poor weather during construction, were completed on budget and on schedule. Both projects were published in *Landscape Architecture* and *Garden Design*.

1991–93
Brown's first full-time position was as a designer in the San Francisco headquarters of the architecture, interior design, and landscape architecture firm Vancic & Ericson. There she completed, in record time, under partner Janko Vancic's direction, schematics for the three-acre St. Absalom park, playground, and fountain on Russian Hill. She used the occasion, with the partners' support, to create a detailed study of the workings of a large, multidisciplinary firm, which she developed into a much-praised paper presented at the 1992 northwest regional convention of ASLA in Seattle.

COMPUTER SKILLS
Expert use of AutoCAD release 14.0, and LandCADD, augmented by custom creation of landscape symbols and textures. Also Adobe Illustrator, and Atlas and Foxpro linked to GIS.

EXTRA-OFFICE EXPERIENCE
On a Rich Travel fellowship, Brown spent six months at Blenheim Palace and Althorp House researching Georgian parks developed under the influence of Capability Brown. Identified and sketched every tree, flower, and shrub species in the two locations; her report has come to be used as a text in the landscape architecture curricula at the University of Pennsylvania and the University of California at Berkeley.

The other six months of the fellowship Brown spent in post–World War II new towns, including Cumbernauld and Milton Keynes, tracking intended versus actual uses of open land.

EDUCATION
In 1987 obtained a B.A. from the University of Mississippi at Oxford. Graduated summa cum laude in 1990 with a Bachelor of Landscape Architecture degree from the Graduate School of Design, Harvard University.

REGISTRATION
Brown holds the Council of Landscape Architectural Registration Boards (CLARB) certificate.

References are available on request.

Scenario
Now consider another approach, using facsimile. You are a structural engineer and found the following advertisement in the newspaper:

ENGINEER
Growth-oriented consulting engineering firm has outstanding opportunity for a self-motivated structural designer accomplished in innovative structural design, with significant management skills. Constructive team member. Good communications skills. 12+ years experience required. Submit resume by fax to: Levy Associates, attn. William Thornton, FAX: 404/201-0000.

Fax and resume

Cover page

TO: William Thornton, Levy Associates
FAX: 404/201-0000

Mr. Thornton:
I was glad to see your advertisement in Sunday's *Atlanta Constitution*. I have long admired the work of your firm, and would like to be part of the team. I have held positions of increasing responsibility at three of the nation's most eminent structural engineering firms.
After you have reviewed the attached resume, I look forward to the opportunity of an interview.
George A. Williams, PE

(Note that Williams decided to send a "listing" resume instead of a narrative, the brevity suggested by the required fax format. The firms listed in the resume are real, but the applicant's positions and functions are fictitious.)

Resume

George A. Williams PE
400 State Street,
Oak Park, IL 60300
Telephone: 708/210-0001 (home)
Facsimile: 708/210-0002 (home)
e-mail: gawpe@mzu.com

WORK EXPERIENCE
LeMessurier Associates, Cambridge, MA. 1993–present
Senior engineer. Leader of design teams on 20 high-rise and other large buildings. Project engineer on 15 renovation, facade investigation, and repair projects. Launched innovative design quality control procedure.

Weiskopf & Pickworth, New York, NY. 1988–1993
Senior engineer. Project manager for 30 large-scale preservation and conservation projects. Developed advanced technique for nonintrusive analysis of the building fabric.

Weidlinger Associates, New York, NY. 1984–1988
Designer on 12 buildings ranging from 4 to 32 stories. Realized improved coordination between owners and contractors using project Web sites.

EDUCATION
Georgia Institute of Technology. B.S. in Civil Engineering, 1982
Columbia University Graduate School of Architecture, Planning and Preservation. M.S. in Preservation, 1984

REGISTRATIONS
P.E.: New York, Georgia, Massachusetts, Colorado, Texas

MEMBERSHIP
National Society of Professional Engineers

TEACHING
Adjunct professor, City College of City University of New York

PUBLICATIONS
Composite Structure Materials. Titanium Press, 1997
Conserving Historic Structures. Vernon Press, 1990

LANGUAGES
Spanish (fluent)

References on request

The Portfolio

The portfolio is a packet of personal qualifications. Consider it when your materials are more graphic than written. It contains chiefly reproductions of completed design work, suitably annotated, and is typically accompanied by a transmittal letter and a resume. For details, see chapter 3 on portfolios and Harold Linton's work *Portfolio Design,* described in the Resources section.

Grant Submittals

Winning applications for grants and awards follow tactics similar to those used in successful job applications. You are pitching your skills to a person or a committee who very likely doesn't know you and who will match those skills against certain criteria. Your chances of winning are a direct function of how shrewdly you select your good points and how lucidly you write them up.

Grants sponsors typically offer money or prestige or both. They provide funds that permit a winner to do independent work. Grants may be applied to research and travel leading to exhibition or publication. Recipients are usually individuals, but in some cases institutions are eligible. The best-known grantors in the design fields include the John Simon Guggenheim Memorial Foundation, the Graham Foundation, the National Endowment for the Arts, and the J. M. Kaplan Fund. The New York Chapter of the American Institute of Architects offers grants from the Allwork, Stewardson, Keefe, and LeBrun Funds. Grants can range from $2500 to upwards of $30,000. The Boston Society of Architects administers the prestigious Rotch Traveling Scholarship. Some grants tend to favor recent graduates; some, practitioners in mid-career; and some, scholars. The Loeb Fellowship program, for example, is one year of mid-career for study at the Harvard Graduate School of Design.

Students are eligible for a variety of important research and travel scholarships. Principal sponsors are design schools. A special program that recognizes only written work is the Douglas Haskell Awards for student architectural journalism, named after the late *Architectural Forum* editor.

In the end it is up to you to identify and screen awards programs. Deadlines vary widely, as do entry requirements. The Russell Sage Foundation in New York City keeps a database of charitable foundations, accessible by discipline, among other criteria. Most sponsors send out notices about upcoming grants for posting on design-school bulletin boards and for publication in design journals and society newsletters. In some cases candidates are nominated by their design-school deans.

A large part of the work of submitting is faithful completion of the many boxes typical of most application forms. You'll gain the most points, however, by the way you write a component known as "the Statement." This asks you why you selected your topic and how you intend to apply the award money.

Your statement needs to deal with these queries, typically in this order:

What is to be the end product of your study?
Why is the end product important?
Who is its audience?
How will it benefit this audience?
How does it conform to the values of the sponsor agency?

How will it reach the audience? What are your publication plans? What are your special qualifications for tackling the project?

Your style should be simple and concise—the 100 to 200 words you are given do not allow for rhetoric; keep technical terms to a minimum and eschew jargon—applications often go through a two- or three-tier review process, and you don't know how many reviewers will be from outside the design professions. The following are abstracts of selected winning grants at the Graham Foundation for Advanced Studies in the Fine Arts.

Abstract A

Julie Campoli, Elizabeth Humstone, and Alex Maclean
VERMONT LAND PATTERNS
Research Leading to Publication

With aerial photography and computer enhanced images, the completed work will illustrate how rural landscapes have changed over time. It will demonstrate to a general audience how the shift from traditional to suburban settlement patterns has created areas of sprawl in rural areas, emphasizing the effect of small scale, incremental development. As they see the land both from the air and through history, readers will begin to recognize these patterns and develop the ability to predict how their own land use decisions will affect the landscape around them.

The book will demonstrate how small towns have traditionally handled growth and how they can be used as models for future development. With aerial views and historic photos and maps of dense downtowns and village streets it will reveal the strong urban tradition of rural areas, demonstrating how a traditional settlement pattern of compact settlements surrounded by open land can sustain development for generations.

The book will feature traditional and contemporary examples of urban centers, neighborhoods, highways, villages, and farm land, highlighting the contrast between patterns and demonstrating alternative approaches. It will illustrate several transformations in detail: a rural road to a commercial strip, a crossroads hamlet to a manufacturing village, productive farm land to large lot housing subdivisions, and the suburbanization of downtowns.

Courtesy Julie Campoli and The Graham Foundation, 1995.

Abstract B

Indiana University Press
DRAWN FROM AFRICAN DWELLINGS
Publication Support

Drawn from African Dwellings will be the first comprehensive study of West African architecture, with a focus on Senegal. The study assumes building practices, living, and ecology are inseparable. It sets into relief some of the structural patterns common to formal aspects of the house (setting, design, decoration, orientation, etc.), and oral traditions and religion. *Drawn from African Dwellings* is ground-breaking in its effort to redefine "tradition" as a mobile, living entity that may not be relegated to the past. Such an understanding will make a critical difference in how we view the growth and change of different cultures that populate the world. The study takes a fresh look at the idea of housing that challenges our preconceived notion of a house as a fixed dwelling or the notion of home related to an Eurocentric view of comfort, security, and individual property.

The book relies on a diverse body of oral accounts and written documentation collected during several years of library research in in Dakar, Paris, London, and the United States since 1977, and from extensive field work in Dakar and inland Senegal. Although the information presented is condensed and highly selective, the book comprises 320 pages, 151 duo-tone drawings, and 225 photographs.

Courtesy Indiana University Press and The Graham Foundation, 1995.

Abstract C

Christiane Hertel
RECONSTRUCTING DRESDEN
Research Leading to Publication

This study is an investigation of the aesthetic and political implications of the reconstruction of Dresden's Baroque center, which was almost entirely destroyed in February 1945. Emphasis is on the rebuilding of Matthaus D. Poppelmann's Dresden Zwinger (1711–28) immediately after World War II, and the current reconstruction of George Bahr's Frauenkirche (1726–43). Reduced to a heap of rubble, its ruin had been declared a war monument dedicated to the victims of Dresden. After the fall of the Berlin Wall in 1989, a citizen's initiative brought about the decision to rebuild the church. This decision has been very controversial.

The primary purpose of this study is a critical comparison of these two reconstructions, their guiding principles, their public perception, and both continuity and discontinuity in the values attached to these two landmarks of Dresden over time.

Courtesy Christiane Hertel and The Graham Foundation, 1995.

Letters of Reference

At some point in a career nearly every design practitioner is asked to write a letter of reference for a professional colleague, student, or friend. An employee (not one of yours) is switching jobs; a designer applies for a one-year midcareer study grant; a firm principal is being nominated for fellowship in a professional society; a practitioner is nominated for the Carlsberg Prize.

When you write a reference letter, consider these issues:

Use superlatives ("brilliant," "outstanding," "incomparable"). While they may be considered improper in other types of writing, superlatives are good in a reference letter to ensure that the candidate is not being damned through faint praise.

Send copies of your letter to the candidate unless instructed not to. That way a successful candidate will be grateful; a losing candidate can't fault you for not trying.

Be sure you have the necessary background data on the candidate to help you compose your assessment. Nothing is more embarrassing to the candidate than to have your letter include errors of fact.

If you don't want to write the letter, decline immediately—say you are already endorsing another candidate, or you are busy, or you are going out of town on a long trip.

Scenario

Liu Sung-Yee, a former associate, has been proposed for fellowship in the American Institute of Architects, and his sponsor has asked you to write a letter in support of his nomination.

Reference Letter

Mr. Reginald Hay, Chairman, Fellowship Jury
American Institute of Architects
1735 New York Avenue, NW
Washington, DC 20006

Dear Mr. Hay:

Liu Sung-Yee would be a superb addition to the College of Fellows.

I support his nomination for personal and professional reasons. I have known Sung-Yee for over twenty-one years, from the time he first went into practice as a junior designer in the office of Gómez and Abernathy to his present role as principal of a 140-person office. In that period he has managed to accomplish what is possible to few. He has the ability to excel as a designer—buildings and interiors projects from his office have been on the list of national honor awards four years in a row. And he has the special gift to inspire students as professor of architecture at the University of Washington.

His designs portray a special genius for creating innovative forms logically shaped by modern structural and mechanical technology. Yet he also insists on calm and tranquillity—qualities you know are eternal but that these days are too often brushed aside in the race to be original.

There can be no real genius without character. Sung-Yee meets the test in things both small and large. He is totally a man of his word. A promise to return a phone call or to deliver a book review to a magazine is never broken; the word "excuse" is not in his vocabulary. Last year he held out gallantly for a fellow practitioner wrongly accused of unethical behavior by unscrupulous competitors, and obtained his reinstatement. And aware that the quality of our built environment can only be as good as the demands of an enlightened client, he dedicates several hours a month to teaching appreciation of architecture in the public schools of his native Seattle.

I cannot think of a more worthy candidate for Fellowship, and commend him to the Jury's consideration with immense enthusiasm.

Sincerely,

Francis X. O'Connor, Partner

Jansson & O'Connor

This letter is enthusiastic and specific.

Writing in Academe

9

Design educators devote more time to writing than do any other design professionals except perhaps journalists. This chapter offers guidelines that will help writers in academe enhance the impact of their writing upon students, tenure committees, journal editors, and book publishers.

Faculty writing typically consists of:

Sponsored research reports
Recommendations on school programs and policies
Applications for promotion or tenure
Comments on or endorsements of applications for promotion or tenure
Scholarly papers (topics may include design theory and practice, aesthetics, teaching methods, pedagogy, criticism, technology, history, academic administration, drawing and visual presentation, computers)
Books
Studio problems

Much of this writing is no different from the reports, proposals, and correspondence discussed in earlier chapters. Where the paths diverge is in the unique subject matter—issues of student performance, curricula and syllabi, teaching philosophy and concepts, and design criticism—which has tended to center in the schools rather than in design practices. Faculty face the challenge of expressing intangible, often theoretical concepts in language that is scholarly without being elusive, and down-to-earth while reflecting the special wisdom expected of the educator.

Academic writing has, often unfairly, been saddled with a reputation for obfuscation. The assumption that critical or scholarly writing has to be obscure to be important—Eleanor Roosevelt is said to have once remarked that you always admire what you don't understand—is not unique to design. Princeton historian James McPherson cited the dilemma professional historians have (allegedly) in reaching broad general audiences, writing in the *Princeton Alumni Weekly:*

> Soon after [my best seller] *Battle Cry* [*Battle Cry of Freedom: The Civil War Era*] was published, a member of the program committee of a professional association formally invited me to participate in a session about the book at the association's annual meeting. I was flattered and . . . said yes. Six months later I received an apologetic letter from the same committee calling the whole thing off. No

coherent explanation was given, but in my re-reading of the correspondence, it seemed clear that a majority of the program committee felt that a book which had reached a large audience of non-professionals was not sufficiently weighty to merit a session at a professional meeting.

A colleague at a California university recently remarked to me that I would be forced to choose between becoming a "popular historian" or a "historian's historian." He strongly hinted that I was in mortal danger of becoming the former.

Excerpt from "What's the Matter with History" by James M. McPherson.
Princeton Alumni Weekly, 22 January 1997, reprinted by permission.

Several schools now encourage clear writing for faculty through courses and special interdepartmental liaison programs. As of fall 1996, the Multimedia-Authoring, Teaching and Research Facility (MATRF) at Clemson University has catered to faculty who wish to write and develop multimedia materials for their courses. The program allows them, according to the publication *mirare* (Latin for "to see"), "to prepare themselves to teach undergraduate and graduate courses in desktop and electronic publishing, multimedia development, interface design, and human computer interaction." Architecture, the arts, and the humanities at Clemson are combined in a single college, headed by architect and dean James Barker. A key part of the program is links to the English and the speech and communications departments.

Papers and Research Reports

Articles, papers, and research reports need specific structure. With a bow to slight variations due to content and audience, a topic may be broken down as in the following outline:

- State and define the topic.
- Why is it important? What are the issues?
- What are its main components?
- What is the role of each component?
- Who or what are the principal influences?
- What is the likely outcome?
- What is the desirable outcome?
- What are the arguments in favor of the outcome? against it?
- Is there need for further study?
- What are resources for added study?

Notice the structure of the outline. Begin with the topic, break it down successively into its logical parts and details, then begin to retrieve the various strands. At the end, bring the parts together into a conclusion that states an opinion justified by the preceding arguments. An admirable source for developing this attack in greater depth is Barbara Pinto's *Pyramid Principle: Logic in Writing and Thinking,* which forces logic into the writer's thinking. This logic inevitably translates itself into better writing.

Most publishers of academic papers will supply an author's guide that spells out the desired format and style; how to deal with footnotes, bibliographies, illustrations, and other apparatus such as the index and table of contents; and in what form to submit the whole. Publisher's guides also counsel on the quality of writing, and you are wise to read those sections before you start, as they define for you that publisher's expectations. A favorite general guide is the *Chicago Manual of Style: The Essential Guide for Writers, Editors, and Publishers*, now in its 14th edition.

Refereed journals, such as the *Journal of Architectural Education (JAE)* or the *Journal of Architectural Historians* publish papers refereed by the author's professional peers—usually three to six. Each issue prints the ground rules for accepting a paper. The process is complicated and can take months. *JAE's* guidelines for its authors take up three pages. The object is to yield papers that are critical and fair; concern for good writing is contained in a rather mild paragraph included by *JAE* as one of seven instructions given to each referee:

> If necessary, comment on the mechanics of the author's writing, grammar, style, usage, etc. Although specific editing of these is not necessary at this time, it is important to know the extent to which these might influence or impede one's understanding of the article's content.

Perhaps the greatest challenge in writing learned papers is the use or invention of jargon. It's represented in an exaggerated way in the Roger Lewis cartoon in the *Washington Post*. For examples of other jargon, see chapter 1.

Isolated examples of designer jargon are often held up for laughter, as in this cartoon. Yet a case could be made that they are taken out of context and that, if you read or listen further, the real meaning will emerge. The reality is that

Cartoon by Roger K. Lewis, FAIA, first published in his "Shaping the City" column in the *Washington Post*.

sometimes it does, sometimes it doesn't. Another case could be made that even in context, papers full of difficult language are permitted, because the language is quite clear, but only to a narrowly defined group who use with precision terms that only they understand. For example, in the late 1980s such a group of architects and designers flourished by seeking to transpose from the world of literary criticism into the world of design the tenets of deconstructivism of Jacques Derrida. The architectural champions of deconstructivism borrowed freely from Derrida's obscure vocabulary. Some claim that these closed groups are entitled to confer among themselves using what Dean John Meunier at Arizona State University calls "privileged academic discourse" (PAD) that will help them develop a theoretical base for their work. But is this necessary or desirable? It took an architect and writer of the caliber of Michael Benedikt to discuss deconstructivism in language understood by the design profession and serious laypeople. Study the two excerpts from his book *Deconstructing the Kimbell: An Essay on Meaning and Architecture*—(in chapter 10, on writing criticism.)

It is hard to imagine that papers composed of obscure references and jargon are likely to fulfill their presumed purpose—to secure awareness of a subject. Any author who makes a practice of communicating in language of limited currency risks serious hurdles in advancing a career through publication, as well as mystifying prospective clients or employers.

This chapter is therefore a plea for using only known vocabulary to express known concepts. Invent new terms for novel concepts gingerly and then only if no word or combination of existing words will do the job. The following excerpts are from a highly successful paper. The subject is the Phoenix [Arizona] Homesteads project, a Depression-era federal effort in rural rehabilitation, affordable housing, sustainable community, and vernacular design. Homesteads is now an historic neighborhood on the National Register. Mary Hardin, an assistant professor of architecture at Arizona State University in the early 1990s and now associate professor at the University of Arizona, consulted on remodeling one of the houses, and in the process came to know the origins and attainments of the project, warts and all. At the 1995 national conference of the Association of Collegiate Schools of Architecture (ACSA), Hardin shared her findings, then wrote up the results, excerpted below.

Paper

THE PHOENIX HOMESTEADS PROJECT
Overlooked but Not Forgotten

(The Project)
Ensconced in the heart of Phoenix, Arizona, four miles from the downtown core, is an 80 acre community that has flourished for nearly 60 years as a verdant oasis in the concentric rings of stucco and asphalt developing around it. The Phoenix Homesteads Project was an experiment in rural rehabilitation, affordable housing, community sustainability and vernacular

design that was surveyed, platted, constructed and landscaped by the federal government in the midst of the Great Depression. That it came to a free enterprise conclusion and survives as a desirable residential neighborhood is a fact that challenges many of the myths that lend form to the desert city today. Lessons drawn from the project's inception, realization, and ultimate success could inform modern endeavors regardless of the decades that have intervened.

(The Myth of the West vs. Government Intervention)
Accounts of self-sufficient pioneers, scrappy prospectors, and resourceful entrepreneurs who tamed the elements dominate the lore of how the West was won. Explorers on horseback were followed in close succession by pioneers in their covered wagons, prospectors towing mules, and homesteaders traveling the railways and wagon roads.

(Differs from Stereotypes)
The Phoenix Homesteads project, which remains intact as a historic district, merits study as an experiment in cooperative living and working that differed widely from the stereotypes about the development of the West that prevailed during its inception and linger to the present day. Many homesteaders of the late 19th and early 20th centuries failed in their efforts. Some did well enough to gain the deeds to their land; but others gave up within months, forced out by hardships and economic circumstances. In retrospect, they are seen as innocent victims of greedy capitalists, venal government officials, a hostile environment, and an irreversible national movement toward an industrial economic base and an urban-based population.

By contrast, the homesteaders of the Phoenix Homesteads project were successful and prosperous, supported by the government until their personal efforts allowed them to repay their debts in full. Regardless of its socialist origins, the Subsistence Homesteads program concluded in parallel with the American dream; hard-working citizens were able to "pull themselves up by their bootstraps" and enter the mainstream of suburban life.

This project is also interesting as a model for comparison to contemporary affordable housing communities because it incorporated means of vocational and social support as well as residences that used local materials to best advantage. Operating costs of the homes were kept low by the sensitivity to the micro climate, and some costs of living were defrayed by the cooperative facilities (shared equipment, social and recreational spaces) and the edible landscaping.

The author manages to advance at a good pace through the subject matter, using precise but simple language, alternating short and long sentences to maintain interest in the topic.

Studio Problems

In schools of architecture and design, studio problems challenge the studio instructor to distill the essence of a program that might normally run to many pages into a single page with enough information to enable the student to create a viable design. Here is an example of a well-conceived studio problem.

Assignment

A PLACE FOR UNIVERSITY STUDENTS TO LIVE

Morphology: The science of form

Morphon: An element of form

Metamorphose: To turn or change something else by enchantment or other supernatural means

The project consists of "three halves." In the first half you are to study the individual elements of the program as though each were an isolated problem. Your research will provide useful historic information; however, "creative research" entails making inventive decisions as to what is useful for your purpose rather than cataloging every fact. Your real exercise is to "idealize the morphons"—that is, to work out the best way to deal with each element. What is an ideal room? What size? What height? Should the window have one-way glass or shutters? How should it be furnished? Such questions do not apply only to spaces. You might decide security is better served by a moat than by bars. You are also required to analyze the site in terms of route, services, orientation, scale, context, etc., and do some quick sketches of these forms.

At the end of the "first half," you are to submit drawings that boldly demonstrate your research, your "morphon design," your philosophy and reasoning. This work will be assessed and returned to you at the start of the "second half."

Probably only a small proportion of your initial ideas will survive if your final design is to be coherent and strong. The process by which they are sifted and synthesized into a clear organic whole belongs in the mysterious "second half." For a week you will work on another project, freeing your mind but priming your subconscious to provide perspective and inspiration. It is said that people learn to swim in winter. The metamorphosis will culminate in the "third half" when, very rapidly, you will complete the overall design.

Assigned by Jo Noero, associate professor, School of Architecture, Washington University, in fall 1997. Reproduced by permission.

Comment

This studio problem differs from most in that it requires the student to develop not only a design but, first, the program—in this case, student housing on the Washington University campus. Note how Professor Noero gets into the student's psyche by explaining the reasons behind his instructions. Although the terms "morphology," "morphon" and "metamorphose" are recondite, he takes the trouble to explain them up front and within the text.

Academic promotion, at some point leading to tenure, is a test of the ability of the candidate and the candidate's shepherds to organize the candidate's dossier or portfolio and express the rationale for promotion in clear language. The candidate is asking the school and the university to make a long-term, if not lifetime, commitment.

Much hinges on the dossier. Supporting items, such as prior work, are commonly sent to a board of referees—some of whom are chosen by the candidate, some by the school. If supporting papers are obscure because the candidate has used privileged academic discourse—that language used by small subcultures as a kind of shorthand to communicate among themselves—the candidate risks opposition from referees who cannot comprehend the material. Members of one generation often tend to speak or write what seems like mystery-laden language to a different generation, thereby muddying the prospects of a dossier's contents being understood.

Published works that are heavy on PAD may work in your favor for a time but against you once the materials have reached people who may be mystified and perhaps annoyed by what seems to them obscure or turgid. Each candidate must call the shots on this sensitive issue.

Promotion procedures vary with the school or university. Some schools demand a "long form" dossier for in-house use and a "short form" dossier for external use, such as by the provost. The heaviest dossiers emanate from three categories of promotion: to associate professor with or without tenure, and to full professor.

Elements of a typical dossier where writing skill is especially important include:

- the candidate's self-evaluation
- supporting matter in the form of prior work, such as designs and published papers or reports
- letters to referees from the candidate's department head requesting an evaluation
- letters of evaluation
- letter of recommendation to the dean from the department head
- the dossier's summary page, including a crucial three- to four-paragraph statement about the candidate written by the department head or the head of the promotion committee (only this document typically goes to the final approval level, usually the university board of trustees).

The Candidate's Self-Evaluation

The self-evaluation must fuse an assessment by candidates of their own worth with the values of the department and the university. (Promotions of individuals in a professional school, with their focus on practical achievement, may clash with the traditional academic focus on scholarly performance through research and publication.)

The self-evaluation should accordingly seek to record high performance in line with some or all of the following criteria:

The overall focus or scheme of your work and accomplishment, and its importance to your discipline. This may be research, design, criticism, teaching.

An assessment of each element of your work—how does it assist the work of others? to what degree does it build on the work of others?

What is there about your teaching, research, and design work that is in tune with your department's needs, vision, and values? with national values?

Is your work suited to further development?

How do you view your educational role in the department, and how have you acted on it?

How have you communicated your concerns to others in your field and those outside your field, such as design clients and the general public?

What has been your role and influence in the intellectual life of the university?

How have you remained in touch with the professional life of your design discipline, as a designer, association committee member, journal editor, consultant?

If applicable, reasons for a meager publishing record.

What are your personal aspirations for the future?

An astute declaration of criteria for tenure was created at MIT by School of Architecture and Planning dean William Mitchell. The document forms part of the school's "Guidelines for the Preparation of Promotion, Tenure and Appointment Cases." The criteria are summarized here with permission. They are typical of major research universities. Direct quotes are from the document.

The standards were created to offer a level playing field for all tenure-track faculty members, whatever their specialty or domain. They are tough, and justified by the school on the grounds that "only extraordinary people should be given tenured appointments—particularly in an era of pressing resource constraints and one in which mandatory retirement no longer applies." The school distinguishes three kinds of concerns:

Intellectual leadership
Teaching
Equity and consistency

Intellectual leadership is defined as "a demonstrated track record of recognized intellectual achievement, and consequent stature as a leader in some domain of importance" to architecture and related disciplines. This record recognizes four models or combinations of models:

Humanities model. This calls for one substantial published book based on a dissertation and one book not so based. It also requires evidence, through letters, of a high reputation among leaders in the field—home and international. At least six scholarly papers in refereed journals may be used to replace the second book.

Science and engineering model. The candidate is expected to produce at least six research papers in refereed journals, plus evidence through letters that the research is important, that it has influenced others, and that its author is a "national leader" in his or her specialization. Also required is a high rank in a listing of workers in that field.

Design practice model. Here the track record can take the form of "a built, published and critically discussed work." The assumption is that this sort of record is "equal in significance for the field of architecture to the public intellectual track record of a leading scientist or humanities scholar, but is simply different in the form of production." It acknowledges that "publish or perish" for architects and designers can take a different form from the traditional books and papers. The record calls for "at least two major built projects, premiated competition entries, significant theoretical projects"—all published in so-called mainstream design journals. A major published project is seen as the equivalent of a book or "pathbreaking" technical paper. Evidence is needed through letters that the candidate has reached the "stature of a leading designer and design thinker."

Artwork and design thinker model. This model requires "a track record of artistic production, exhibition of work and critical recognition." That means two (minimum) shows with published catalogs, or several "major public installations," reviews by "important critics," and evidence through letters that the work has been "innovative and significant."

Teaching is important but, at least under the Mitchell principles, doesn't take the place of a publishing or practice record. In a telling sentence, the memorandum declares: "Inability or unwillingness to teach . . . is a ground for denial of tenure. . . . Teaching excellence can strengthen a tenure case. . . . But teaching excellence alone, in the absence of the necessary publication or practice record, does not establish a tenure case."

The document admits that under today's more rigorous standards many tenured faculty would never have made the grade. This should not "be allowed to create ambiguity." Current standards have to be rigorously and consistently applied.

This set of criteria points again to the critical significance of writing in advancing careers. Even the tenure route through publication of built designs requires written descriptions that need to be models of clarity.

Supporting Matter

Depending on the candidate's strengths, supporting matter is heavy on published work, which may fall into such categories as books, papers in refereed and nonrefereed journals, research reports, transcribed invited lectures, articles for the professional press, supervised theses or dissertations; or built or unbuilt designs, suitably documented through drawings, photography, and succinct text arranged in problem/solution sequence.

Referees are independent appraisers of a candidate's qualifications. The letter to referees, typically written by the department head, asks the referees for a just evaluation of the candidate. Because of the vital impact of these evaluations on the candidate's prospects, how the request letter is couched is very important.

Letter of Request to Referee

The following example includes the principal components of a typical letter of request to a referee.

Dear_____:

    We are considering the promotion of Professor _____ from the rank of Assistant Professor to that of Associate Professor (without tenure). Our evaluation of the case for this promotion will take account of Professor_____'s intellectual contributions to her field, her effectiveness as a teacher, and her record of university and community service. To help us perform this evaluation knowledgeably and fairly, we need to have the comments of people who can critically assess Professor_____'s qualifications and record.

    We would, then, be most grateful to receive your written comments. We realize that you may not be in a position to comment on all aspects of Professor_____'s work, but whatever insights you may be able to provide will be extremely useful to us. In particular, we would appreciate any comments you can give us on the following:

    Her major research, scholarly, or design practice contributions and their significance;

    Her standing in her field (an indication of her peers of comparable age, together with your assessment of her relative position in that group, would be especially helpful);

    Her potential for future professional growth and leadership in her field;

    Her effectiveness as a teacher (if you have personal knowledge of this).

    The more precise and specific you can be in your comments, the more helpful they will be. We will treat your response with the greatest possible confidentiality, as described in the enclosed statement. For your reference, we are enclosing some information on Professor _____'s work. Please contact us if additional material would be useful to you.

    In order to meet our deadlines, we will need your reply by _____. I very much appreciate your help, and look forward to hearing from you.

    Sincerely,

Letter reproduced courtesy of Massachusetts Institute of Technology
School of Architecture and Planning.

Letters of Evaluation

In the letter of evaluation, the referee is called upon to produce a detailed analysis of the candidate's work. The letter becomes part of the candidate's dossier. The ideal approach is defined in the letter of request above. Moreover, at least half the referees are commonly selected by the school and not by the candidate, thus permitting a frank assessment. Frankness is enhanced further by stiff confidentiality guidelines limiting access to the letter to those who need to know.

With that in mind, the letter of evaluation still must be cast in language that is clear to a diverse array of judges. Each judge must be able to grasp quickly the salient issues spelled out by the referee/writer.

The referee's letter needs to cover meticulously the points suggested in the request letter sent to referees by the department or tenure committee head. A letter of recommendation to the dean from the department head, required in most schools, is a critical component of the dossier. It builds on the report from the departmental promotion committee, and can range from lukewarm to a very strong endorsement.

The summary sheet travels with the dossier and beyond—some schools request that several dozen copies be attached to the dossier for wider distribution. In one section of the summary sheet, the head of the department or promotion committee writes a few "succinct and persuasive" paragraphs (in the words of one school). The aim is to distill the essence of the candidate's qualifications. This crucial text is best drafted in rough, left to simmer for a day, then reviewed, tightened, and compared a final time against the substance of the entire dossier. Blessed with the endorsement of the department, this passage calls for the utmost care. The following example shows one way to write such a passage.

Dossier Summary Sheet

Jana Kopecka exemplifies the best ideals of this department. Appointed instructor only four years ago, she grew rapidly in her specialty: ecologically driven building design. She has proved herself able both to teach the topic cogently to her classes and to document her work effectively for publication in learned technical journals and in professional magazines.

Her talent in generating enthusiasm among her students for a topic that most consider important but lacking in emotional appeal has triggered a strong movement among students and faculty colleagues to found a building ecology center at the school. The center would integrate ecological concerns with distinctive design.

Also to be weighed in her promotion is her creative contribution to the university's responsibility in the urban community. Kopecka has on her own initiative worked with the public schools to bring design awareness into the elementary schools. She has organized a cadre of faculty, local architects, and landscape architects to work with school teachers in leading students to an appreciation of design and its potential in the places where they live, play, and go to school.

Two years ago Kopecka was promoted to assistant professor. Her promotion now to associate professor with tenure will secure and enhance her continuing contributions to her department and the University.

10

Writing for the Media

The media consist of professional and general-interest publications, broadcast media (radio and television), and, increasingly, postings on the Internet. These are described below and listed in detail in the Appendix, A Selective Listing of Design Media, page 218.

Every design professional and student has sights set on someday writing a piece for the media or having a project published. Some get there by taking up writing as a career, either on a publication's staff or as a freelancer. Others limit themselves to an occasional article at the invitation of an editor; or they write indirectly, preparing text about a building, landscape, interior, or other design project for submission to the editor, who rewrites it more or less drastically for publication.

This chapter deals with each of these contributors. But first, it provides a synopsis of the media as they are constituted, including a glimpse through the curtain of mystery that enshrouds the media's workings. Chapter 12 offers reflections on writing as a career.

Types of Media

Media fall into eight types, depending on audience and dissemination medium: professional journals, client-read journals, special-interest magazines, business publications, general press, newsletters, television and radio, and Web sites.

Professional Journals

Professional journals publish designs by design professionals, articles about the technical or business management framework in which design occurs, opinions, and news. The audience is your peers and competitors. Writing should be geared to the designer's level of understanding of that profession's technical vocabulary. Professional journal writing should not, but at times does, contain linguistic flights of fancy that defy comprehension.

Editors as a rule come from one of four backgrounds: design, English, journalism, or the arts. Some journals are blessed with large editorial staffs who do most of the writing. Others have a small cadre of editors who farm out writing to freelance contributors, limiting themselves to editing and some writing.

National professional U.S. design journals number a few dozen. They are supplemented by regional and local publications. Designers favor publication in professional journals for marketing and personal career advancement reasons, because it implies a third-party endorsement of their work. Also, graphically these journals tend to be of a high caliber, so projects look good in print and as reprints. A significant subset of professional journals is learned journals. Many are published by design schools and are repositories for critical writing and for publishing experimental or unbuilt designs.

Client-read journals offer design professionals a direct entrée to decision-makers. These journals are read by school administrators and school board members, hospital administrators and board members, developers, home builders, public officials, hospitality facility owners and operators, and judiciary and correctional officials. These publications, as part of their editorial coverage, regularly feature stories on the design of facilities. While not all match the visual caliber of the professional design magazines, their written quality is on a par with them, especially those that reach a national audience. Whereas the professional design magazines' selection procedures tend to favor the aesthetics of a project, the client-read magazines focus more on a facility's functional merits.

Special-interest design magazines play an important part in shaping the design tastes of American as well as overseas publics. They variously embrace residential design, interiors, garden design, historic preservation, and industrial design. Some, such as *Architectural Digest,* reach audiences as much as ten times larger than do the professional journals. They are handsomely produced, and are written in a style more accessible than that of the professional press.

Without quibbling with purists who consider all media not read by the general public as "business press," my definition is narrower, and identifies as business press only those media that cover business. Examples are *Fortune* magazine, *Institutional Investor, Business Week, Inc.,* and *Forbes.* Since building construction contracts total over $250 billion a year, what happens in construction is frequent grist for the business journals' mills. The writing is geared to a business audience and focuses on a building's economic impact on a company, market, or region. Some business newspapers, such as *The Wall Street Journal,* regularly carry reviews of design.

Newspapers and weekly news magazines attract writing on design matters because design has emerged as a popular topic. All newspapers have home and real estate sections, and many urban papers carry critical reviews of buildings, interiors, and landscape architecture. The critics are of national stature (at least two have won Pulitzer Prizes for criticism in recent years). Some newspapers, such as the *New York Times,* in the late 1990s consolidated their design coverage into independent sections, using color for the first time. General news magazines such as *Time* and *Newsweek* have full-time editors in charge of design coverage; the writing style routinely translates jargon into technical prose intelligible to the serious layperson.

New-age magazines such as *WIRED* and *Fast Company,* catering as they do to an audience steeped in acquiring information through video and the Web, not only cast their journals in bright colors, with acrobatic graphics, but also include content that often touches upon matters of design in stimulating ways. The magazine *@issue:* takes up the argument that good design is good business. Its lively, upbeat graphics practice what it preaches.

Newsletters

Newsletters offer a venue for a more clipped style of writing, on the premise that the reader wants news and wants it fast. Some newsletters also welcome short features. Publishers of newsletters include the larger chapters of the professional design societies. Some of these publications are of a high caliber; a few, in an effort to pack features into a limited number of pages, resort to minuscule type that challenges any reader.

Television and Radio

The vast majority of TV, cable, and radio channels are designed to entertain the public. They tend to contain a low ratio of decision-makers who hire designers. A few programs (such as Charlie Rose on public television), especially on cable, regularly interview design celebrities, thereby taking some of the public mystery out of the design professions. Local stations or local outlets of national networks make for an added forum for designers as seen by local corporate and government executives. Interviewed designers are on their own, with the risk of flubbing an interview through inexperience or nervousness (see chapter 13 for tips on handling the spoken word). Many stations do a couple of dry runs and tape the interview in advance.

Web Sites

Web sites created and operated by magazines, professional societies, and a growing number of design firms are a new form of media that is beginning to reach the level of respect it deserves. Some Web sites, such as Kent State University (Ohio) architecture school's www.saed.kent.edu, exist only on-line; others are published in print but also offer a Web site that provides additional reading, access to past issues and databases, and interaction through chatrooms. So do the major search engines and content providers, which have installed chatrooms and bulletin boards according to discipline, including architecture and design. Writing for the Web is affected by the nature of the medium (see chapter 11 for pointers).

For a selective listing of important design media and media directories, see the Appendix. Addresses are omitted, as are top editors, as both tend to change. Cities are supplied.

Articles about design projects may be constructed in several ways:

Straight descriptive story, type A. It has no criticism—you assume the project has merit or at least significance, or it would not have been chosen for publication. The design projects are chosen on their own merit and not because they fit a particular type.

Straight descriptive story, type B. Selected because it is a significant example of a type or classification (a small art museum; the work of a designer under 25; the work of a firm whose principals are married to each other; the work of graduates of a particular school; work designed by left-handed vegetarians). Such articles commonly leave unanswered the question of whether the project is published on its merit or because it fits a category.

Chronology of a project—extension of type A or B, above. Done when design and delivery run into roadblocks (presumably eventually overcome).

Critical review of a project.

A combination of the foregoing.

The steps in writing an article may vary slightly with each publication, and whether the writer is on staff or freelance. But all follow these basic procedures:

1. Identify your objective. Define for yourself exactly why you are writing the article. Is it to introduce the latest work by a celebrity designer? to record a successful blending of historic and Modernist design? to portray a skillful introduction of infill housing into a deteriorated community? Ask if the article is to combine description and criticism and, if so, will you be writing both or is another author tapped for the critical portion? A useful device is to write an interim headline that expresses the essence of the story. The interim headline wording may change before it goes to press, but it's a good beam to steer by.

2. Define the audience. Decide whether the audience is professionals, serious laypeople, or the general public. If the latter, skip some of your terminology to reach a less conversant reader.

3. Develop a schedule. The manuscript deadline as a rule is given to you by the managing editor if you are on staff, and by your contact editor if you are a contributor. Work backwards from that date, and establish these internal deadlines:

Conclude travel and/or research;
Finish breakdown or outline (more on this below);
Complete 50 percent of the text;
Complete 100 percent of the text;
Insert legends and other "apparatus" (see below; as a freelancer you may or may not be obligated to furnish this material).

4. Develop a framework or outline of content. To write, you need a framework of subheadings that will guide your article from start to finish. (A much-revered high school teacher of mine bequeathed to our class a superb device for building a foolproof framework: "Scan your notes and other source materials; grab a ruled pad; then record any idea or thought that occurs to you, no matter how dumb, and without worrying about the order; when you are at the end of your source materials, stop; read your notes through several times, and, wonder of wonders! an outline will jump out at you from the page." (This teacher assigned to us countless essays based on literature readings, and his advice was good ten times out of ten.) You will come up with something along the following lines:

Introduction. Bring in the chief point of the article, in a short, pithy paragraph that pulls the reader into the story. It should be sparkling but not overly cute. People like to read about other people, so if you can bring in an activity by or quote from one of the players on the design project, do so.

Body. Pull out your outline, which might have the following subheads or guideposts:

"Project had five challenges (list challenges 1–5)"
"How design team managed challenge #1 (site)"
"How design team dealt with challenge #2 (noise)"
"How design team handled challenge #3 (scale)"
"How design team handled challenge #4 (schedule/cost)"
"How design team handled challenge #5 (technology)"
"Designer's rationale for design silhouette and materials"
"Smooth/rough spots on project team"

Intersperse the text with short quotes from a designer or client, but avoid an article that is a string of quotations.)

Conclusion. Restate the story's main point, perhaps quoting a major protagonist. Hint at any futures heralded by the project's current status or condition.

5. Write the article. Pace yourself. Most writers have periods in their circadian cycles when they think more creatively, have greater stamina, and generally produce more and better copy than at other times, when the most strenuous self-discipline yields nothing but tailings. When inputting on the computer, save your text—this advice is commonly thrust at writers by purveyors of every software under the sun, and is just as commonly ignored. Most software allow you to set automatic saving every x seconds. Also, copy text to a disk twice a day.

6. Submit the manuscript. The publication's custom dictates the format of submission. If you are a freelancer, your editor will specify the format. Commonly you will need to ship a diskette on a specified software and platform, accompanied by a paper copy and originals of any drawings and photographic transparencies. Your freelance agreement should spell this out, along with requirements for securing permissions and clearances on all material you submit. A typical freelance author agreement is shown opposite.

Dear [Author]:

This letter will serve as the agreement between yourself and Smith Publishing, Inc., publisher of *Engineering Herald* (henceforth called "Smith").

1. You agree to write a 1500-word article provisionally titled "The Impact of Titanium as a Structural Material," tentatively scheduled to be published in the April 1999 issue of the *Herald*. The article should include a description of the material, its use in construction and nonconstruction applications, its advantages and limitations, recommended connection details, and relevant comparative cost information.

2. Please supply drawn details as appropriate, in camera-ready form. Four-color photographs should be in 4 x 5 transparency format, cleared for publication.

3. The article is due at our offices by 20 November 1998.

4. Smith will pay you $1500 on acceptance of the article. Should Smith find the article not acceptable, or should Smith decide for whatever reason not to publish the article, you will be paid a "kill fee" of $400.

5. Please submit the article in double-spaced hard-copy format, with an accompanying electronic version in Word, WordPerfect, or other common word-processing software, on a PC platform.

6. You agree to make any changes requested by our editors for reasons of style, so long as your meaning is not changed.

7. The article is a work-for-hire contract. You agree to assign title and copyright, including all rights in all print and electronic formats, exclusively to Smith.

8. You warrant that the work contains no slanderous, libelous, or unlawful matter, that it is original and accurate and does not infringe on any copyright.

9. Smith will reimburse you for appropriate expenses, including express mail and long distance telephone calls. Travel expenses must be approved in advance by Smith.

10. You agree that you take on this assignment as an independent contractor, and that you are not an employee of Smith nor entitled to benefits furnished to Smith employees.

Enclosed are two copies of this agreement. Please sign both and return one copy to me.

Sincerely,
Louisa Kwan   [Author signature]
Senior Editor   [Date]
Engineering Herald   [Social Security number]

6. Process the article. If you are a freelancer your editor may ask you to review the text in edited or page-layout form, or both, after shipping it to you by e-mail, fax, or the traditional paper "galley" form. Unless the meaning of your article has been changed out of recognition, do not harass your editor with minor alterations. Respond promptly; odds are the editor at this stage is under a deadline, and what may seem to you as a half-day's postponement could to the editor mean serious overtime charges from the magazine's printer. If you're a staff writer, the edited article will be sent, normally as an entire page, to your screen via your electronic publishing system, with instructions to cut or add copy to fit the space.

Text Reading Aids

Articles do not live by straight text alone. Respect for the reader's opinion requires that the publication furnish a variety of verbal devices that simplify or speed up a grasp of the article's main focus. They are written by the editor in charge of the story. Here are the most common of these devices (see also the illustrations on page 30):

Headline. The headline is usually set in large type. It crystallizes the essence of your article. Some editors like a two- to three-word headline that plays on words with a smattering of humor ("Gateway to Haven" for an article about the guest house at the entrance to the residential compound of a top figure in the computer industry). Other editors prefer longer headlines that give more detailed insight into the article ("Larson House Sets New Tone for Fire-Struck Oakland Hillside Community").

Deck. Decks expand on the headline, seeking to lure the reader into the article. They can run to 30 words and are set in large type. Readers commonly scan the magazine first, and are attracted by a nifty deck ("1920 St. Louis warehouse becomes a thriving base for training inner-city youths in space-age manufacturing skills").

Kicker. This single word, usually placed above the headline, is used to place the article in the context of a regular feature or series ("Criticism"; "Books").

Author byline and identification. Staff writers are identified by name only, as are contracted contributors who regularly provide news stories. Freelance writers receive an author's ID on the first page of the article, the last, or with the other contributors on a separate page. The author's ID should be relevant and specific. ("Vincent Durango, a landscape architect in private practice in Phoenix, advocates designing landscapes using native plant species," not "Vincent Durango lives in Phoenix in a house with seven gables.")

Pull-quote (sometimes known as a scan). Pull-quotes are 15- to 20-word excerpts from the text, set in large type and placed in the middle of the text as graphic attention-getters. If this chapter were an article, a practical pull-quote might be "Unless the meaning has changed out of recognition, do not harass your editor with minor alterations."

Subheads. Some magazines punctuate articles with one- or two-line subheads placed in midcolumn and set at the standard column width. They need to capture the gist of the next few paragraphs of text. If you are a freelance writer, check out the magazine's preference before you go writing a lot of sub-heads only to see them discarded or replaced by the editor. A new device is to highlight a few key text phrases per page and print these with a gray, light yellow, or other tone.

Photo captions. Captions have a role beyond telling the reader what is in the picture. They are a way of reinforcing readers' skimming of the magazine. Many readers, especially if in a rush or with a backlog of reading matter, never go beyond those captions. Thus they must perform as a secondary route through the magazine. Caption space is precious; write them to make every word pull its weight. Avoid using valuable space telling the reader what is obvious from the photograph. If you are a freelance writer, your agreement will tell you if captions are your responsibility or the editor's.

Other add-ons. These added text items are linked to illustrations: *labels* that identify items in drawings; *legends* (keys to plan spaces identified by numerals), used when the drawing is too small to accommodate labels; and *credits,* those highly sensitive paragraphs that identify the owner, designer and consultants, key team members, and contractors. Some magazines list with the article as many building product and material suppliers as they are able to identify and find space for; other journals list them in the back.

The Technical Article

The volume of writing about the technology of architecture and other design disciplines is increasing for many reasons: the electronic design office is fast becoming a reality; techniques are emerging for adapting buildings better to the physical and emotional needs of the user; novel methods reduce buildings' energy consumption and toxic waste generation; innovations are emerging in landscape and infrastructure design, construction, and management; we are seeing the advent of new exterior and interior construction and finish materials such as composites and new synthetics; and sophisticated entertainment and communication systems are finally making Le Corbusier's definition of the house as "a machine for living in" a reality. Writers are in demand to describe and interpret these developments clearly.

Most writing guidelines for the design article also apply to the technical article. In addition, observe these points:

Owing to the wide range of eligible topics, and the slim odds that a single publication harbors such a diverse range of experts, technical articles tend to be contributed. Because there are diverse ways, many of them in direct conflict, to interpret a technical development or product, it's the editor's challenge to ensure an impartial article. Much depends on the choice of author. Few freelancers specialize in every aspect of design technology. Occasional contributors are the technical staff of design firms, builders, and product manufacturers.

Editors must screen authors employed by manufacturers with special care. They need to head off coverage of, say, a controversial product or material in ways that favor its manufacturer, when an author from a competing technology might take an opposite view. Best is for the editor to pinpoint in advance the conflicting concerns, and make sure all are raised. The plot thickens when an advertiser advertises in the issue. Reputable publishers shield editors from interference in such cases, on the basis that readers subscribe to get objective information. Realistic advertisers will acknowledge this argument, and won't make a row so long as the article tackles the issue fairly.

Given the complexity and latent tediousness of many technical topics, writers should complement their text by soliciting or developing sketches, details, and sparkling 3-D images, with distinguishing colors. Word captions precisely, and refer to figures in the text.

The article should state, in the headline, deck, and first paragraph, the significance of the technical topic to the readers. If your readers are design professionals, the importance could be in opportunities for greater spans, new facing material options, reduced space required for hvac, or more versatile communications. If your readers are school administrators, developers, or hospital board members, compose the piece to fit those readers' concerns—for example, there's the impact of fiberoptic systems on providing an affordable educational makeover to computer-aided instruction or reducing a developer's long-term operating costs.

Keep it simple. No building technology is such that it cannot be expressed in straightforward, simple sentences, using technical language freely when the readers are technically trained, and defining your terms when they are not.

The Practice Article

The practice article may deal with project management, marketing, ownership transition, human resources management, and other topics tied to running a practice. Such articles are typically hard to illustrate, except in some cases through charts and diagrams and by inserting photographs of people for interest. This difficulty thus places the weight of meaning on the quality of the writing.

As in technical writing, the expertise is likely to lie beyond the editors' offices, because practice comprises such a large and diverse range of topics and issues. Fees, contracts and agreements, legal concerns, marketing, public relations, ownership transfer, project management, estimating, office business administration, employee training, construction contract administration, computerized practice—all of these and more are in a constant state of growth and change.

Organize the material for a practice article into a series of subheads to form a logical connection between points. To make reading easier on the eye, consider arranging material as a list of points, each point preceded with a bullet or some other graphic device. (Don't overdo bullets. Go for a good balance; you don't want an article to read like a punch-list.)

Since practice issues often trigger differences of opinion, a panel debate, duly taped, is an efficient way to gather material. The advantage is that panelists talk a lot more simply than they write, thereby boiling down the editing process. The disadvantage is that panelists always talk too much, and any seasoned editor will concur that only about 25 percent of a panel discussion is gold; the rest is tailings. Another method is for a writer to take heavy notes, and write up the event as a standard article, inserting a few quotes here and there for effect.

Editors seldom accept an unsolicited completed article. They prefer to discuss an idea or topic with you, then give you the go-ahead. Here are the main steps when soliciting an editor's interest in your developing a freelance article.

Overture. Propose your topic to the editor. Submit an idea or proposal to only one magazine at a time. Determine the slant of the editor's interest: aesthetic, technical, management, or some other area.

Preliminaries. Submit the outline, with headings, subheadings, and corresponding word lengths; list proposed illustrations (if the editor knows your work, you may be spared this step, but do it anyway for your own benefit). Discuss length, midpoint and final delivery dates, honorarium, and conditions for acceptance (if your manuscript is acceptable but not published, you can receive a partial fee, known ominously as a "kill" fee).

Development. Conduct the research. Prepare/assemble necessary or desired drawings and photography. Obtain permission for the use of any photography. Write the first draft (and submit it to the editor if requested).

Delivery. Complete and deliver the final draft. Comply with the editor's requested format, probably a typed, double-spaced copy accompanied by a diskette in a commonly used software and platform. Deliver the artwork. Drawings will likely be redrawn electronically by the magazine to fit its style. Assemble and deliver credits and permissions. Send a short two- to four-line bio. The magazine will rewrite this to its final form.

Final Touches. Review the edited draft from the editor. Chances are this will arrive by e-mail. Try to concede editorial changes so long as they don't alter your meaning. Respond promptly to requests from the publication—at this stage all are urgent. Arrange with the journal for reprints. Send an invoice (not all magazines require this).

Design criticism is a specialized form of expression that some design professionals do all of the time, and all do some of the time. Good critical writing demands solid academic and practical grounding in one or more design disciplines, a point of view, and the verbal skill to express this to a wide or influential audience. Often the critic's message travels in a limited circle that endorses its point of view, grasps the often esoteric language, and provides the underpinnings of a short- or long-term popularity. Yet the critic exists in every designer. The temptation to comment on buildings, interiors, engineering feats, landscape design, urban design and planning—especially the other person's project—is never far from the designer's mind.

The full-time critical writer bears a serious responsibility, especially if blessed with a large or important audience. Critics often exist on the staffs of newspapers and wide-circulation magazines. Writers such as Lewis Mumford at *The New Yorker,* and before him Montgomery Schuyler at *Architectural Record* when it was still a general-interest architectural journal, were widely read. In more recent years critics such as Robert Campbell and Paul Goldberger have brought an awareness of design to vast audiences; both have been awarded Pulitzer Prizes. Good critics provoke a growing public consciousness about design matters.

Some professional design magazines have been blessed with editors who take strong stands on current issues; by identifying, supporting, or condemning trends in design, they often impact the way a design profession evolves. Some practicing designers have also been critics, and a few, such as Robert Venturi, have notably shaped design trends, especially when—as in Venturi's 1966 book, *Complexity and Contradiction in Architecture*—intervention comes at a period ripe for change.

Academe above all has played host to the critic. It provides a fertile cerebral environment, the opportunity for debate in classrooms and common rooms, access to resources, and links to scholarly publishing outlets at university presses and scholarly journals. Critics such as Kenneth Frampton at Columbia University typify the best of these professional critics, though Frampton often demands a second or third reading before the uniqueness of his message sinks in. Like the best critics, he teaches one to see and to think.

Learning to Write Criticism

There is no easy way to teach the writing of criticism. But, as noted, it cannot happen without a broad base of knowledge and a point of view.

Words are symbols of meaning; if the symbol eludes the reader because it is too arcane and removed from common experience, there is no message. Some concepts may take many words to explain; you cannot try to cope with this merely by glibly inventing a host of new words. The challenge is to employ an existing, broadly understood vocabulary to explain complex ideas, not to succumb to the temptation of inventing a new term when the going gets rough.

A fine model is Michael Benedikt's book, *Deconstructing the Kimbell*. In this 1990 work Benedikt, who teaches at the University of Texas at Austin, deftly explains a movement once thought to be short-lived but that in various ways still permeates contemporary design attitudes. Benedikt sidesteps the pitfalls of explaining Deconstructivism by using words that mean what they always mean, and assembling them in conventional, nonthreatening sentences. Through his writing, Benedikt has probably done more to explain Deconstructivism than its designer champions. Below are two samples of Benedikt's writing, defining and describing a design theory derived from another, nondesign, humanist discipline.

IN INTRODUCTION

After many years in the air, with the publication in 1988 of Philip Johnson and Mark Wigley's MOMA catalogue *Deconstructivist Architecture,* and the appearance of *Architectural Design Profile 72: Deconstruction in Architecture,* a new "ism" was officially upon the American architectural scene: Deconstructivism.

Grumblings from working architects, historians, and teachers of architecture that it would soon pass, that it "doesn't work," that it's crazy, that it's just a style, that it really doesn't deserve a name of its own . . . all of these are typical of the kinds of things said at the inception of a new movement. Conversely, the notion that Deconstructivism in architecture is actually all over, come and gone, is also mistaken: Deconstructionist concerns, techniques, and terminology are to be found with ever greater frequency in academic journals of architecture, where they are presented with an ever greater air of normalcy. One must, I think, conclude that Deconstruction is very likely to continue to gain influence in the discipline and the profession, if only as a mode of discourse that supports the real and unstated enterprise of all designerly architects (save for feeding their children): the discovery/invention and execution of new formal systems, i.e., styles.

But Derrida's Deconstruction can mean more to architects (and artists) than a transitory aesthetic or a style, and it should not be allowed to devolve into the esoteric, promotional patter and stylish nihilism that it threatens to do. Deconstruction is primarily a philosophy of writing and reading philosophy. But it is also a probing enquiry into the workings of language, ideas, and the whole human cultural enterprise. As a theory, a philosophy, a method, in the hands of Jacques Derrida and others, Deconstruction had a considerable impact on philosophy and critical and literary theory in the late 1970s and early 80s. As a significant component of post-structuralist thought in the late 1980s, it was still making its way through all the arts and all but the "hardest" of the sciences, representing a pattern of thinking whose generality across the disciplines has been unequaled since systems theory in the mid-60s. Deconstruction's destiny, I believe, like system theory's, is to continue to be absorbed into routine intellectual, critical, and even scientific discourse. Already, key elements of its vocabulary have passed into the realm of common wisdom about method, expression, description, and meaning in all these fields, but its name—Deconstruction—and the name of its "inventor"—Jacques Derrida—may well soon be effaced. Who now speaks of W. Ross Ashby, James Miller, or Ludwig von Bertalanffy?

DERRIDA'S DECONSTRUCTION, THROUGH ARCHITECTURE

To read Derrida is to be swept into an uncanny stream of argument, exposition, and altered terminology that knows no rest or single direction. Language is questioned with language; whole passages swallow themselves up and disappear as meaningful. Homonyms vie with synonyms for possession of the argument. . . and yet "perfectly good sense" is always there, passing below and over, and just out of reach. One learns to swim in this foreign stream, or not.

One claims to have swum, or not.

It is my contention that very, very few people understand Derrida in any detail, certainly far fewer than claim to. In some way this is the fulfillment of Derrida's ambition, the cause and result of his method. Because it simultaneously uproots and affirms conventional rationality in certain imitable ways, and because it partakes quite freely of neologisms, wordplay, and evasions of resolution, the philosophy of Deconstruction is generative: of arguments, colloquia, papers, books of critical theory and criticism, and, perhaps, of buildings. But understanding Derrida in the first place—the belief that he is indeed saying something clear and deep and definable—is generative too.

It has created in the last fifteen years a minor industry in academia of lectures, published interviews, explicatory and ancillary books, conferences, debates, and innumerable bouts of academic one-upmanship.

Through all of this one must move carefully, skeptically, and with companions. Jonathan Culler, in his *On Deconstruction: Theory and Criticism after Structuralism,* educes a number of processes, or principles, from (chiefly) Derrida's writings on Deconstruction that we will find useful. Derrida applies them, of course, to particular texts and (usually by implication) to language as a whole, but he applies them especially to the kinds of texts and the kinds of language that make truth claims and generalizations based on ideas—in other words, to texts of metaphysical ambition. Here we attempt the translation to architecture with a selection of four such essential processes or principles . . .

Note Benedikt's skill in conveying abstruse concepts by keeping a tight handle on designer-babble and extra-long sentences.

A sharp look into what actually goes on in the mind of an architecture critic emerges in this graceful excerpt from an article by Robert Campbell in *GSD News,* published in 1994 by the Graduate School of Design at Harvard University:

> I believe very strongly that a true critic does not go to a building, or to any other work of art, with a checklist of virtues in mind. Every good building is good in its own way. You simply immerse yourself in the experience as fully as you can, and only when you're drowning in sensation do you begin to strike out for the shore of some kind of formulation. Of course you do develop convictions over time, but if you're a critic you hold them tentatively, and you try not to test the building against your reductive preconceptions.

Book Reviews

Reviewing books is surely one of the most widespread writing assignments, at school and in practice. Books are published at the rate of 50,000 a year, we are told, and would seem to outnumber available reviewers. Most professional publications review books. They typically assign this to a staff editor, along with other duties. It makes up a modest but stimulating segment in the publication. Often, especially for "significant" books that call for a longer review, the editor assigns reviews to outside writers. Reviewers may be sought out more for their expertise on the book's topic than for their writing skills. As a result, the writing level of book reviews is mixed.

Given meager page allotments and budgets, the book review editor personally writes a series of short (one paragraph maximum) mini-reviews to supplement the few long reviews. These short reviews reveal basic content rather than making an in-depth assessment, and are known in the trade as "flap reviews" because they draw heavily on what is printed on the dust-jacket flap.

If asked to review a book professionally for the first time, heed these tips:

Read the book. Inane as this may sound, it is the only way to make an accurate appraisal. Flap copy and press releases give a good clue as to the intent of the book, and provide synopses of the contents. They are, however, written by the publisher and aim to show the book in its best light. You need not pore over a book's every word, but read enough (and skim the whole) to form an impression. Then ask: Does this book meets the needs of its intended audience or not?

Arrange your material along the following lines:

> Open with a sentence giving an overall opinion. Avoid long lead-ups.
> Give the intent of the book.
> Summarize the content.
> Evaluate key elements of the content.
> Assess the author's qualifications.
> Compare the book to its competition for value and price.
> End with buy/don't buy advice.

You may be tempted to use the review as a vehicle for your own point of view or philosophy on the topic. In some cases, that's all right; but unless you are Shakespeare reviewing a book on playwriting, bear in mind that the reader wants first and foremost to know whether to buy the book or not, and only secondarily wants your philosophy. I continue to be dismayed by reviews that broadcast the reviewer's theories but neglect to say a word about the book.

For a well-cast and well-written book review, see the following. The reviewing magazine's own headline is in caps, the book's title in upper- and lowercase.

A TALE OF TWO CITIES: LESSONS FROM TWO COASTS
Parallel Utopias: The Quest for Community, The Sea Ranch, California;
Seaside, Florida, by Richard Sexton
San Francisco: Chronicle, 1995, 168 pages, $50.
Reviewed by Peter Katz

At first glance, *Parallel Utopias* looks as if it might be yet another style book, like the many glossy volumes that try to encapsulate the look of places from Ireland to India. But after reading it, one realizes this book is a much more ambitious effort. It compares two communities—Sea Ranch, California, and Seaside, Florida—that have become touchstones for new-town planning in two different eras. In so doing, author and photographer Richard Sexton wants us to understand each place as more than just a collection of houses.

The lavish photographs make a compelling visual argument for both places as ideal communities. But after reading Sexton's three essays and those of sociologist Ray Oldenburg and architect William Turnbull, I'm left wondering whether both, or just one of the places in *Parallel Utopias* has succeeded in its "quest for community," the challenge grandly posed in the book's subtitle.

As a resident of San Francisco, I've grown accustomed to hearing criticism that Sea Ranch "isn't what it used to be." Invariably the gripe is about overbuilding. During a recent visit, I was relieved to see that Sea Ranch, which was masterplanned by landscape architect Lawrence Halprin in the 1960s, looked better than these comments would have suggested. But I was struck by a criticism noted in *Parallel Utopias*—that Sea Ranch is dependent on the automobile. Says Sexton of Sea Ranch, "distances are great and all practical errands require a car." As a result, the development did not convey much of an outward sense of community.

Another problem with Sea Ranch relates to the expectations of those who have purchased homes in the development. Sea Ranch was marketed as a place where one can live surrounded by nature. Yet with the passage of time, residents are increasingly surrounded by other nearby homes. The sense of privacy that was promised to the first buyers is diminished with each new home that is built. This seems an inevitable consequence of a design ideology that can only work at unit densities far lower than those of Sea Ranch.

Seaside, started some 20 years later, follows different design ethos. Patterned after traditional small towns, Seaside's buildings assert themselves by shaping the public space of the streets and squares they face. Seaside is a place that seems to improve as it reaches full build-out. The few unbuilt lots that remain between homes read like missing teeth—gaps in the urban fabric. That is one reason why the town requires construction of a home to start within two years of the sale of a lot. Beyond its "look," Seaside seems to function like a real small town (albeit an upscale one), with everything reachable on foot.

Much has been written over the years about both Sea Ranch and Seaside: the philosophies that shaped them, the affluence of their residents, and the difficulty of applying the lessons of such second-home communities to year-round-round ones. *Parallel Utopias* captures much of that discussion. As such, the book is a welcome addition to the larger debate about community design now taking place.

But it's hard to reach a conclusion regarding the value of these projects as models for emulation based solely on what Sexton provides us. The Sea Ranch, for all of its beauty, fails in my estimation as a true community because of the ideas about planning and architecture that prevailed when it was started. Seaside, on the other hand, is the product of an era that is just now coming to appreciate the connection between physical design and the making of true community.

Architectural Record, April 1996, p. 23. © 1996 by The McGraw-Hill Companies.
All rights reserved. Reproduced with the permission of the publisher.

While this book is not about getting your designs published—a gleam in the eye of every designer—the process of writing is not complete without publication. The following remarks are not in-depth guidelines for publication so much as brief but realistic tips for the emerging designer.

Never approach editors with the attitude that they are a vehicle for your work. Treat them as professionals. Their job is to size up their audiences and to publish material that informs these audiences, perhaps uplifts them, maybe even entertains them. Their agenda may differ radically from yours, but respect it. It is their business, and they are calling the shots.

Recognize too that a media decision to publish your work is not a simple one, and hinges on such factors as the publication's backlog in your subject; its editorial calendar, which is commonly made up in the early fall for the following year and, although flexible, tends not to accommodate major changes without good reason; and your celebrity as a designer (lack of celebrity can sometimes actually help, as every editor loves to discover new talent).

Scenario

You have developed skills over the years in designing workplaces that respect the idiosyncracies of the design worker. You wish to share this knowledge with your colleagues through the pages of a respected professional journal. Following is a sample submittal letter.

Andrea Esterhazy
Senior Editor
Architectural Chronicle
1C Clinton Street
Chicago, IL 60600

Dear Andrea *[if you know her; otherwise "Dear Ms. Esterhazy"]*:
   I see from your 1998 calendar that *Architectural Chronicle* has scheduled a special section next October on the design of the new workplace. I want to propose an article on the human resources factors that should, but often fail to, influence workplace design.

   As associate partner at Harnischfeger and Haas one of my tasks is to research and apply good practices for accommodating office workers. Subtopics include ideal mixes of open and semi-enclosed offices; issues of privacy and productivity; access to on-line networks; and issues of individual controls over comfort, noise, and lighting. In the last five years I have researched and designed six projects totaling 400,000 square feet of state-of-the-art work space—all of it in successful operation.

   I can submit a detailed outline within two weeks, and can furnish drawings, details, and professional photography to illustrate a range of problems and solutions. I attach three examples, with brief text and picture captions.

I hope the suggestion appeals to you, and I look forward to your response.

Sincerely,

George Lodge

Associate Partner

Comment

This letter is brief and to the point, and doesn't presume to send an entire article before getting some encouragement in advance. Give Ms. Esterhazy two or three weeks to reply, then follow up with a phone call or e-mail.

The following list offers additional dos and don'ts on approaching the media.

Do

Identify the right editor (check the masthead).

Write or e-mail. Phone or fax only if the editor knows you.

State if drawings, details, and professional photography are or will be available.

Show that you are familiar with the journal's editorial calendar (ask for it).

Eschew hype, by voice or mail.

Exploit direct contact opportunities, such as seminars or conventions.

Don't

Follow up too soon, or more than once in three weeks. If it's obviously a "no-go," give up with grace.

Contact simultaneously more than one publication with the same idea.

Insist on reviewing the edited text.

Submit prewritten articles. Send an idea letter instead.

Going On-line

Words are words, you say. What, then, is so different about writing on-line versus writing on a piece of paper? On-line you create sentences on a preformatted computer screen for transmission by modem through telephone lines; on paper, you type words on a word processor and print them out on a piece of paper to be shipped through the mail.

But there are more important differences. The style and structure of the writing appropriate to each medium vary greatly, and there are advantages and disadvantages to writing on-line versus on paper. The listing below spells out some of the major differences.

Correspondence and in-house memos
Name and address block
    Print: Broken into three to five lines
    On-line: Typed into preset boxes or imported from address database
Salutation
    Print: Formal to semiformal
    On-line: Semiformal to none
Content
    Print: Text broken into paragraphs each containing one idea
    On-line: Text reduced to vital words; adjectives, articles, adverbs, even punctuation often omitted; content may be consolidated into one paragraph or a list
Closing
    Print: "Sincerely" or equivalent, with your name typed (unless your name is printed on letterhead, in which case typing your name is redundant); signature
    On-line: None
In-house memo and intranet
    Print: Text broken into single-idea paragraphs
    On-line: Text reduced to vital words; if responding to sender's request or query, single word ("Yes") often suffices

Brochures

Print: Printed "hard copy": no instant links among components or to outside sources. No simple feedback or interactive dialogue. High level of graphic design and quality control. Easy to read as no equipment required

On-line: On Web site: client or prospect gains basic information plus instant links to wider array of information; opportunity for interactive contacts between owner, designer, team members. Viewer can download contents, export files to own database. Graphic quality control and download time so-so, but improving

Proposals

Print: "Hard copy": easy to read as no equipment required. Superior quality control over visual materials

On-line: Electronic proposal forms available from government agencies (e.g., SF 254, SF 255) simplify production of proposals. Because available space is limited, paper and diskette formats both demand tight writing

Newsletters

Print: Interaction limited. Good graphic quality control

On-line: Interactive responses simple. Graphic quality and download time improving

Job applications and promotion

Print: Dominates designer hiring. Active verbs such as "completed," "launched," "achieved" work in your favor

On-line: Content and format arranged to ease electronic search for key words; this allows employer to match applicant's skills with own requirements (specimen "right" words or phrases: "project manager," "AutoCAD 14," "Spanish," "TQM [total quality management]," "schools," "environment," "energy conservation," "ADA").

Writing E-mail

No law says you cannot send a colleague, client, or project team member an e-mail composed in the same language, syntax, and grammar as you would using a standard paper letter mailed or faxed. Yet the no-nonsense, hard-eyed culture of our time has spawned a succinct writing style that is remaking how we communicate with others. It is chic to communicate by e-mail, not only because of its intrinsic benefits, but because of what it says about us—"this designer is clued in, innovative, enterprising!" Good manuscripts are still emerging from manual typewriters—but in the design profession it is no longer cool.

E-mail writing—whether sent through an ISP (internet service provider), such as Microsoft Network, America On Line (now incorporating CompuServe), or AT&T, or via a private company network—has the following features:

E-mailspeak. The writing style is more clipped, colloquial, less observant of customary courtesies. It is common to use hip, current forms and phrases that signal to the sender that you're in the know. See the list below for examples of e-mailspeak. Phrases such as "this will get the idea in Joe's face" are eminently more at ease in e-mail than in conventional correspondence. When old-time courtesies are used, the result can be antic (see the sample letters on page 173). The hectic, dynamic flavor of writing in the age of e-mail is also epitomized by a new kind of wordplay characterized by *New York Times* "On Language" columnist William Safire as "JammedTogether" names (examples: AutoCAD, BankAmerica, HarperCollins, FrontPage). There are also signs that the compression of e-mail is creeping into conventional writing.

Specimens of e-mailspeak	*Plainspeak equivalents*
Getting an idea in Joe's face	Making sure Joe gets the idea
Webster	One who often browses the Web
Ping	notify
Digerati	Folks who have risen to the elite ranks of those dealing with the on-line world
Pomo	Postmodern
IMHO	In my humble opinion
Charlie in engineering is a cypherpunk [Note: a cypherpunk is a crypto with an attitude. A crypto is one obsessed with codes and cyphers.]	Charlie is too concerned about playing his cards close to the chest, thereby keeping team members out of the picture

For additional examples, see *WIRED Style*, listed in Resources.

Responses. If the original e-mail message leans to the concise and unadorned, the responses can be positively anorexic. Since the mechanics of responding to e-mail are so simple—you click on the "reply to sender" option on the "compose" menu—answers may be short to the point of curtness.

Punctuation. Capital letters, hyphens, and other stylistic staples are sometimes omitted from e-mail messages ("steve, spoke with chuck thursday please send back up info on monday's job meeting asap williejo"). This underscores the utilitarian nature of the medium as well as the nonconformist mindset of many of its champions.

Forwarding. It is simple to forward a received message to a third party—or, for that matter, to disseminate it to a whole host—with or without comment. Forwarding e-mail without comment has emerged as the ultimate in zero-effort, zero-writing communication. Simply select the "forward to" option on the "compose" menu, enter the names, and "send."

Speed. E-mail travels as fast as the speed of your modem—if yours is a 28,800 or even 57,600 bps (bits per second), it moves like lightning, if not delayed in electronic post offices by rush-hour traffic. With a message's round-trip time measured in seconds, why compose a formal epistle when a stripped-down message is so much more efficient (if at times lacking in grace)?

Point of no return. E-mail is not a forgiving medium. A leisurely review of a letter typed on paper before you sign it may reveal typos plus thoughts inaccurately stated or inelegantly phrased; you can fix it and then mail it. No such luxury is given to e-mail: the hectic ethos of the medium demands instant dispatch. Warts? Fugeddabahtit! Once the "send" command is pressed, it's too late to fix, unless you undergo the indignity of a corrective follow-up. It is a sign of our age that there is less time to find and correct errors, whether in cybercommunication or cyberspace or cyberwarfare. A Wall Street trader reportedly composed an e-mail love note to a friend, and in a fit of haste with one wrong click sent it instead to 1000 coworkers. Some e-mailed back telling the unhappy man they didn't know he cared. Therefore, check e-mail just as carefully as paper mail.

Cost. E-mail saves money. Office managers have assessed the total cost of

typing a one-page letter
filing a copy of the letter
typing envelopes for recipient and cc: list
sealing the envelopes and applying postage
conveying envelopes to a mailbox, where
the U.S. Postal Service or express service collects them
flies them to destination cities
delivers each envelope to the addressee who, at least one day and
    often two days after it was mailed
opens the envelope
reads the message
responds (repeats above procedure)

   in comparison to
typing the message on screen
filing (two clicks)
pressing "send" and "copies to," at which point it
travels across phone wires or a radio frequency,
is opened (2 clicks) and read
a response is created, filed, and sent, all in the time it takes the sender to
    order and drink a cup of coffee.

It is clear which is the more efficient procedure.

Attachments. You can attach files from elsewhere on your system with a few clicks. Be sure, though, to check out your recipient's system. Some attached files must be decoded and recoded if crossing certain network and platform lines, using specialized software available free or at a small cost. To be on the safe side, paste the entire text of the attachment into your main message, then send as one message.

Enrichment. Some browser software allows you to embellish your e-mail text with borders and textured backgrounds, colored text, and funky text margins. Just because this is possible is no reason to do it, as it surely runs counter to the no-frills ethic of professionals conversing on-line. But always keep in mind the character of the recipient.

Literacy. Employers expect you to be e-mail-literate.

The tension between e-mailspeak and old courtesies was never more pointed than in a 1997 exchange of letters in *The Times* of London. A July 3 letter (not shown) first raised this issue, and a week later the following two responses appeared in the newspaper under the heading "Sign-off of the Times."

Sir, Mr. Adrian Dodd-Noble suggests (letter, July 3) the "your obedient servant" is perhaps an unsatisfactory closing for an e-mail.

Could I be the first to conclude an e-pistle to the editor with a "smiley."

Yours, [smiley face art]

David T. Staples

[street address and e-mail address given]

Reproduced by permission.

Sir, The march of technology must not be allowed to erode courtesy and civilization. In a civilized society, any written communication should be signed off with a suitably courteous salutation, whatever "netiquette"—or perhaps nerdiquette—may or may not require.

I remain, Sir, yours truly and electronically,

Henry Robinson

[street address and e-mail address given]

Reproduced by permission.

Some software also allows you to fax your message electronically, using special software, without having to insert a paper copy into the fax machine. Writing the computer-generated facsimile message for direct transmission takes on the features of writing for e-mail.

The following are examples of e-mail messages and responses. Note the concise, sharp style used in e-mail. The first shows a prime design professional e-mailing to his consultant, and her response.

E-mail Correspondence Sample A

From: Alvaro Nuñez
To: Gblandings@azu.com
Sent: March 31, 1998 2:20 P.M.
cc: Robert O'Connor
Subject: Furniture for Robison

Georgia: Carpenters and painters are out of the Robison House. Still no word on delivery of first furniture consignment from Milan. If Robisons are to move in June 1 as in contract, we'll need some action. Best—Al

From: Georgia Blandings
Sent: March 31, 1998 2:32 P.M.
To: Anuñez@azu.com
cc: Robert O'Connor [intranet converts to on-line address]
Subject: Furniture for Robison
   Al: Milan's New York supplier tells me furniture on ship docked in New York harbor. Expect delivery to site in three business days. Thanks for the nudge.—Georgia

The second example is from Mr. Nuñez to the senior landscape designer.

E-mail Correspondence Sample B

From: Alvaro Nuñez
Sent: April 2, 1998 10:13 A.M.
To: Dcheng@azu.com
cc: Robert O'Connor
Subject: Weekend fiasco
   David, this rain-sodden weekend [Cheng was out of town at a project meeting] was chaos on the site of Adams municipal park. Only two members of Citizens Group, which was supposed to unload two truckloads of dirt for the shrub and tree planting later this week, showed. Cats-and-dogs both days. Three trucks arrived, unloaded the dirt, which now sits in one corner, in no shape to be dispersed for the planting. Can you meet 12:30 in conference room B for a working lunch to sort this out?—Al

From: David Cheng
Sent: April 2, 1998 10:18 A.M.
To: Alvaro Nuñez [intranet converts to online address]
cc: Robert O'Connor
Subject: Weekend fiasco
   Yep

From: Robert O'Connor [partner in charge]
Sent: April 2, 1998 10:22 A.M.
To: Alvaro Nuñez
Subject: Weekend fiasco
   al—i'll join you—bob

Be sure to fill in the subject line at the top of your message. It draws readers into the text.

The Web Site

The original Internet, now broken up into the internet (or extranet) and the intranet allows you to connect via modem to the Web site. The Web site, after you clear away all the definitional underbrush, is a sequence of electronic screens internally connected and linked to other Web sites as determined by the site's owner/operator. It is composed of a combination of text, photographic and other images, and an array of devices, icons, buttons, and blue- or other nonblack-colored words linking you to other parts of it and other sites.

A design firm's Web site typically may include some, many, or all of the following contents, depending on the firm's goals, ambition, and budget (the entries, except for the first, are in no particular order):

A welcome screen or home page, which also serves as a directory or index to the site's other parts

Lists of completed projects, divided, if the list is long, into appropriate categories, such as by building type or type of client. As many projects as feasible should be hyperlinked to, and shown large on, individual screens (see next item)

Screens showing one or more images of completed projects, augmented by design, technical, and sometimes operating data

Staff biographies, with or without faces

A list of articles published about the firm's projects, hyperlinked to full texts

A list of published articles and books written by principals and staff (articles hyperlinked to full texts)

A directory of qualification forms on file with government agencies (e.g., SF 254, SF 255), and hyperlinked to full texts

The design firm's vision/mission/goals statement. Compose this with care and ingenuity so it comes across as a factual, realistic, believable document, not an array of overblown generalities that could apply to any firm in any profession

News about the firm (new projects, promotions, awards). Can also serve as an internal newsletter

Office announcements (these are accessed only by office staff supplied with a password and ID)

Project management status reports (these are accessed by team members and designated others)

The name of the webcaptain (a better term than the gender-specific "webmaster") and other key contacts, with mailing addresses, key telephone and fax numbers, and e-mail addresses

An emerging sign of status is for individual designers and students to strut their own Web sites, not necessarily a part of the official school or firm site. It supplements e-mail and affords more personal interaction with "visitors."

Web Site Benefits and Challenges

What's in it for your firm? In creating a Web site, the design firm can realize benefits but must also look out for challenges.

Marketing. The firm's qualifications show up as more dynamic than is possible in even a very sophisticated paper brochure (the CD-ROM as a vehicle for your firm's qualifications is described later in this chapter). The Web site brochure assumes client prospects are hooked into the Internet and in the habit of browsing for design firms' home pages. The first option is likely; the second is not, unless you have alerted the client through some other medium, such as mail or voice mail. Try to get your Web site onto the major search engines, such as Yahoo!, Lycos, or AltaVista, for added exposure. So you can monitor and classify your Web site traffic, leave space near the opening screen for a "visitor" to register (by e-mail, voice mail, or fax).

In-house resource. Saves time and bother by linking the user to relevant outside sites and search engines without being forced to sign off and then sign on again on another site.

Basis for preparing proposals. Saves time and lessens the chance of error by containing all the firm's databases needed to fabricate a proposal. Helps if the prime professional is linked to the Web sites of consultants.

Project management. Links members of a project team—in-house and external. Some firms establish independent Web sites for individual projects.

Morale builder. By incorporating chatrooms (and events) and bulletin boards, the Web site helps to interconnect the design firm's community, especially if the firm has branch offices. Much of this internal activity falls to the intranet, a communications network that firms over a certain size create to provide their staff with news, information, interactive features, workgroup potential, and a common e-mail platform. It is a private, internal resource, with controlled access. It also gives firms the option to offer controlled access to selected parts of the intranet to designated clients, vendors, and consultants.

Quality. Creating even a simple Web site entails selecting from a huge array of potential content, format design, and visual design options. Choose the best mix and the one most in character with your firm. Nothing hurts more than a dull, uninformative, stale, or out-of-date home page; you lose the browser on the first visit, and the browser may never return. To create traffic, seek to offer something compelling over and above facts about your firm—such as building codes, ADA regulations, building conservation guidelines, access to government Web sites, lists of consultants and contractors. These extras are known as "fish food."

Update. Appoint a webcaptain to update the site at predetermined intervals. Some parts, such as newly completed projects, can be on a looser schedule (bimonthly, for instance) than staff changes or new address, telephone, fax, and e-mail information.

Security. Designation and control of access is critical.

Modem speed. Worry about the client prospect still struggling with a 9600 bps modem. If your site is designed for a modem three or six times faster, you'll face some very impatient browsers as they try to download your stuff.

Writing on the Web

The needs of the Web site shape writing—its style, tone, grammar, punctuation, vocabulary, and physical arrangement—in the same way that any medium shapes, and is shaped by, writing. Writing for the Web site has much in common with writing for e-mail. Both are required to transmit information to and receive responses from people who are short on time and often short on patience, not as grounded in the graceful verbal forms of past generations, and living and working in an age that places a premium on unadorned facts delivered in a hard-hitting style with little room for embellishments.

But writing for the Web site has demands that go beyond even those of e-mail. Once you are browsing the Web, you face the additional challenge of linking words to other words, other screens, other sites. The psychology of directing the browser so the browser understands the message, links up to other significant sites, and doesn't become bored in the process makes the Web site seem not so much a writing challenge as a musical composition.

Questions arise: Which words on each page should serve as links? How should they be dispersed on a page? How many links are too many? too few? How big a text block is sufficient or too long? How much information should be conveyed by text? how much left to art? Behavioral scientists who analyze subjects' eye movements may have definitive answers. Meanwhile, we are left with a modest track record based on short-term experience that has yielded the following pointers:

• Humanize your Web site. Sites are identified by four fields of up to three numbers each, separated by periods (thus: 256.125.72.88). Selecting and registering a domain name (e.g., http://www.richardmeier.com) injects a more human, informal note. To register or be assigned an address, type InterNIC into your search engine and follow instructions.

• Write short text. Keep sentences short—12 words average. Users don't read so much as scan. A trained eye can pick up blocks of type around 40 words long (or 5–8 lines) without strain. Keep the measure (or width of a column of text) narrow, under 40 characters. If you go wider, you will need to increase the type size, the space between lines, or both. One expert suggests limiting text and graphics per screen to 100KB (a one-page single-spaced letter takes up about 8KB as text).

• Use simple words. Shun designer-babble and vocabulary that's too high-tech. You never know how versed in design terminology a potential client browsing the Web will be. Even designer-browsers have no time or desire to figure out jargon.

• Graphics only? Give photographs and other graphic items the benefit of some text. Viewers need words to orient themselves; they are uncomfortable without them. Equally, don't overpepper the screen with hyperlink words (except perhaps on the home or index page); it distracts from the page's basic message and makes the screen look like Swiss cheese.

• Revise your Web site regularly. Never feel that what you have composed is cast in stone. Your site is, or should be, in a state of continual development, shedding its skin to make room for new messages and improvements to the site.

• Consider reading as an experience. Unlike reading a letter on paper or as e-mail, surfing the Web site for information is an act of exploration, and text must support the experience, not hamper it through complex vocabulary or clumsy wording.

• Create headlines for the first or "splash" screen and other key screens. Make headlines simple, informative, and prominent in size or color.

- Help guide the reader. To assuage the feeling of anxiety felt by inexperienced navigators, make the wording and design user-friendly. Every screen should carry a common navigation bar indicating where you are and what to do to get to the next or previous screen and to the home or index page. Think about visitors negotiating a metropolitan subway system or hiking on a poorly marked trail—they'll probably choose the most likely path but can always fall back on signs or a trail map. Make important buttons large to avoid inaccurate clicking by a tired navigator.

- Avoid long categories. Stratify long lists into subgroups, each with a heading (for example, divide project lists into building types, long lists of a single building type into building subtypes—see the listing below). Experts feel six to ten entries is maximum for a list for easy screen reading. For example:

PROJECTS

Healthcare facilities

    Acute care hospitals

    Medical centers

    Special focus facilities (cancer; cardiac; mental; emergency; children; women)

    Long-term facilities (nursing; assisted living)

    Specialty centers (Alzheimer's disease; AIDS)

    Laboratories

    Medical offices

    Fitness facilities

- Eliminate time wasters. Screen what you post on to the site. Cut text and images ruthlessly. Visual images should convey useful information; cute, strictly feel-good images are distracting and possibly patronizing; avoid datasmog.

Check out the following selection of Web sites (current at the time of writing):

DESIGN FIRMS

www.arup.com (consulting engineers)

www.davisbrody.com (architects)

www.eastlk.com (Eastlake Studio, architects)

www.fitch.com (interior and environmental designers)

www.fk.com (Flack+Kurtz, consulting engineers)

www.hhpa.com (Hardy Holzman Pfeiffer Associates, architects)

www.jb2000.com (Jung/Brannen Associates, Inc., architects)

www.lera.com (Leslie E. Robertson Associates, structural engineers)

www.mjmarch.com (Maxwell Johanson Maher Architects)

www.richardmeier.com (architects)

www.smharch.com (Smith-Miller Hawkinson, architects)

www.som.com (Skidmore Owings and Merrill, architects)

www.tateandsnyder.com (architects)

www.wgcni.com (WalkerGroup/CNI, interior and environmental designers)

A directory of architectural Web sites may be found at:
www.architecturemag.com/resources/firms/firm.asp

Note that URLs sometimes change.

For examples drawn from the Web sites of the humble and the famous, see the following.

Web Site Sample A

Design Philosophy
Tate & Snyder Architects approaches each project with a focus on four critical aspects of architectural design:

- Regional context
- Environmentally intelligent design
- The relationship between the building and site
- Thoughtful and appropriate use of materials

www.tateandsnyder.com

Web Site Sample B

Hospitality/Entertainment at The Hillier Group

Places that are exciting and full of energy, spaces that delight senses. The environment should surround, envelop, immerse. This is total entertainment, a chance to escape, to experience, to BE somewhere, something else. Created by architects who know their craft, artists who know no limits. Because we want people to enjoy your facility and keep coming back. Combining an understanding of the design process with the practical knowledge of top-flight project management. Because we want our clients to keep coming back. From casinos to convention centers, riverboats to restaurants, hockey facilities to hotels around the world and back again, we've been there. Always with the same goal in mind—to make places where people gather together to have pleasurable and memorable leisure experiences.

And when unlimited creativity and imagination are married with experience, the results are truly astonishing.

For further information, contact Bob Blakeman.

www.hillier.com

1. Eastlake Studio
Help Wanted

Well, The facility management job has been filled. I guess we just took our time getting it off the web because we really like reading peoples' resumes. No, really.

So, just because we do not have a specific job position that needs filling does not mean we mind looking at resumes and portfolios. We like to keep track of people we feel might just fit into our extended Eastlake family. We have gotten some of the coolest resumes and portfolios around. Don't be afraid to be different with us (just remember to include pertinent information in a concise way.)

Eastlake Studio offers its employees plenty of opportunity, flexibility, excellent benefits, great co-workers, and a fun working environment. Appropriately, we expect plenty in return. Some (but not all) of those qualities just might be:

• Okay, first you are going to have to like computers. You don't have to love them and we promise not to quiz you on network cable color patterns but don't buy a new T-square for the interview, if-ya-know-what-I'm sayin'.

• Qualification one-and-a-half; You can't hate Macs. We know that Mac lovers can act a little . . . um, winsome is one way to put it, and it can kind of rub the PC people the wrong way. We really don't mind if you have a PC at home, we don't even care if you (e-gads!) like DOS! Can't we all just get along?.

• Secondly you should be able to really want to work here. Not just really want the money that you would earn while employed. Yes, every company wants this from their employees but since we are a relatively small business this becomes that much more important. People who can bring their care for the built environment and their ethics into the design are what we are looking for.

• Next, you are going to have to be able to manage information. We have a baby company that is in facility management called Facility Wizards and people tend to cross over on a project or two. Also, since we are only about twelve people you will definitely be on more than one project at any one time, even when its slow. If you are right out of school this takes a lot more energy than you might think. In general, be pliably organized.

• Be able to tell a joke. If nothing else it's good as a last second distraction as you bolt for the door.

• Be able to take a joke. Unless, of course, you are a lawyer, we want those jokes to hurt.

• Be flexible. Like we said we are somewhat small, and when something big comes our way everyone should be able to help out as best they can. Also, since even some of the junior members of the firm do construction administration and there has never in the history of western civilization been a building project to go on without a hitch, this is going to demand that you be able to adjust your routine.

We are pretty open minded. See that you are as well.

We are searching for someone who wants to work either in Chicago or maybe, although less of a possibility now, San Francisco.

If your idea of a good time is curling up with a C++ manual in front of the fireplace on a Friday night, we might not be quite what you're looking for.

By the way, the successful candidate must demonstrate fluency in the digital world and respect for our environment.

Now, these qualities might sound exactingly vague, but remember, we're not actively looking for anyone at the moment.

Resumes, work samples, and correspondence must be transmitted to us via e-mail at:

getajob@eastlk.com

If you want to attach any files, we'll also be looking in our America Online mailbox under the plain old EASTLAKE screen name.

Again, please don't try calling or sending us any atoms unless we ask for it directly. Also, due to the hundreds of thousands if not millions of replies we expect to receive, don't be disappointed if we can't get back to you personally.

Thanks, and may the Force be with you.

2. Eastlake Studio Portfolio: Lakeside Residence

Lakeside Residence

In 1993, a Chicago couple retained Eastlake Studio to design a home in Lakeside, Michigan, on a site they owned on the eastern shore of Lake Michigan. They wanted a home that would initially serve as a weekend retreat, and ultimately as a permanent residence. The three acre site is composed of two contrasting natural settings—an open prairie and a heavily wooded ravine, that empties into Lake Michigan about 200 yards north of the site.

The couple views their new home as a secluded retreat from their urban residence, but also as a place for entertaining weekend guests. While privacy from neighbors and the road was important, bringing the natural environment into their home directed the final solution. They envisioned a home in harmony with its surroundings, made of a scale in proportion to the prairie landscape.

Site Plan

Our solution sites the house on the edge of the ravine with an approach along the south edge of the site in order to keep the open prairie to the north clear.

The organizing principle for the structure joins a four foot planning module with a stepped circulation path. Four nodes distributed along the circulation path bring light into the center of the residence through large windows and skylights. The path also separates spaces oriented to the two basic site elements—prairie and ravine.

Morning spaces such as the master bath and breakfast area are located on the prairie (east) side, while large windows orient evening spaces such as bedrooms and the main living area to the site's most dramatic views on the ravine (west) side. In elevation, gently sloping curved roofs tie the complex plan together, link the ravine to the prairie, and reduce the scale of the large residence.

Living Room
The ceiling of the living room rises above as windows open to the ravine outside. A flagstone chimney provides a focus for activities within the room. For the building's enclosure, we chose materials that reflected the natural landscape of the site and the context of the area. Horizontal cedar siding, limestone fireplaces and aluminum roofing were combined to provide a subtle, understated image. The four foot planning module is expressed in elevation by vertical trim elements that separate segments of horizontal siding. Wood decks located on the private ravine side contrast with the stone patio and walks leading to the primary entrance on the prairie side.

Front Entrance
A cedar pergola marks the main entrance. The four foot planning module is expressed by the vertical trim elements separating the segments of horizontal siding.

Bird's-eye View
The irregularity of the plan is tied together by the curved aluminum roof.

The Lakeside Residence was also developed into an interactive walkthrough for the Chicago Villa competition sponsored by the Chicago Athenaeum.

Web Site Sample D

PLANNING ISSUES IN THE DIGITAL AGE
Library Design for the Future

Some pundits are predicting the demise of libraries in the electronic age.
Nonsense. We believe libraries will not only survive, but prosper.
Here's why.
Librarians have always been dedicated to assisting people in the search for information, and with constantly changing software, users will need even more assistance in the retrieval, manipulation and management of information.

Learning is increasingly understood as a social enterprise. Libraries are even more important as a place where users can interact and share knowledge.

Group learning facilities will increasingly benefit by being clustered together, both by allowing flexibility between media centers, on-line classrooms and group study rooms, as well as by allowing for shared staff support

Book collections aren't about to disappear. Given the economics of publishing and the high cost of scanning, centuries' worth of books will still need to be stored, made accessible and, ideally, made easy to browse.

Users want to study in inviting environments. Even though dorm rooms may be wired into the networks, they may not be ideal places for quiet study.

But libraries won't survive as is, and as with all important change, half the trick is figuring out how to get there from here.

Think "Service Oriented Information Center." The evolution of libraries into an expanded instructional role is blurring traditional distinctions between reference and instructional functions. The programming and design process can explore creative ways to help integrate staff as well as technology, and to optimize the delivery of services.

Think in terms of future functions, not today's space models. New types of spaces will be needed. With growing interaction between staff, users and equipment, planning for noise control will be important. Increasing demands for access to resources on a 24 hour basis will require redefinition of the library security envelope.

Be rigorous about wiring distribution and management. In today's tight budget world, your ability to respond is limited not only by equipment, but also by the physical limitations of your existing facility. Developing accessible but concealed paths for data wiring is essential.

Build in flexibility and adaptability. Thoughtful planning can make the difference in creating a building which can change in response to new unanticipated functions.

At Davis Brody Bond we understand the complex challenges facing you and can assist you in planning to meet them, from the earliest feasibility and programming stages to furnishing and fit-out.

We have a history of innovation in over 40 years of practice, involving many different types of buildings. We are comfortable dealing with the ambiguity of change and the challenges of the future.

We are among the nation's leading architectural designers focusing on library projects. Our awards reflect the care we take in the detail of design which not only makes our libraries function well, but also creates spaces people enjoy using.

And most important, we understand that you need a problem solver, not a preconceived solution. We analyze your particular library's needs to come up with a unique approach to your requirements.

Setting Up Your Web Site

This book is about writing, and isn't intended to serve as a primer for setting up your Web site. But these few suggestions will help you.

Option 1. Create a Web site by retaining a Web design consultant. Some are generalists, some specialize in creating Web sites for architects, engineers, and other design professionals. They charge an initial fee, plus a monthly fee for maintenance—a critical function for you or your consultant. As you work with consultants, always keep your audience in mind. You don't want your message to sink in a sea of well-intended but misdirected graphic virtuosity.

Option 2. Do it yourself. The main browser software companies offer do-it-yourself software. Microsoft has FrontPage, Adobe has PageMill, Netscape has Communicator, Claris has HomePage. These aids are for the general user and are not necessarily geared to the unique demands of the design professional. Special touches must come from yourself, and the setup software may be able to accommodate your choices. The software is similar to some word-processing software that offers a variety of suggested graphic output formats to make life easier for the graphically timid, but can't spawn works of great uniqueness and originality.

If you choose option 2, the best person to shepherd and maintain the site is, in the experience of many firms, a design professional with a bent for the Web, not a "dedicated" computer person. Either way, go through this four-step process:

1. Create a storyboard on paper, one sheet per screen, with extra sheets added for desirable hyperlinks. Draft the text or dummy text, and sketch or paste in the art.

2. Scan the sheets into your computer, using Photoshop or similar software, and evaluate them.

3. Encode to HTML, the lingua franca of the Web site. HTML (HyperText Markup Language) is a formatting language that marks up text files so they can be read on computers by browsing software.

4. Edit and revise.

Skeptics ask, "a Web site—who needs it?" Clearly there exists a bandwagon mentality: if my competitors have a site, I must have one. Beyond that, though, there are meaningful, practical arguments in favor of setting up a Web site: better coordination of project teams, closer rapport with site "visitors," in-house morale building, fast on-line access to remote resources, a more focused marketing process, and cost savings up and down the line.

Certainly design firms can run their businesses and win comfortable backlogs of work without a Web site. But as the new century succeeds the old, the Web will be the medium of choice for most office activities, and holdouts may be left crying in the wilderness.

CD-ROMs

A Web site is not the only electronic path to your markets. There's the CD-ROM. Firms that opt for a CD-ROM-based brochure can exploit dramatic features that go beyond what is presently available using Web site technology.

As a marketing medium for your firm, the CD-ROM has these benefits and limitations:

Used as a firm's brochure, the CD-ROM can be targeted more than a Web site, without the Web's temptations to digress.

The CD-ROM is amenable to dramatic multimedia effects, including 3-D modeling of sites for clients, virtual reality demonstrations of yet-to-be-finished projects, 3-D walkthroughs of completed projects, "talking heads" of principals narrating the firm's vision and accomplishments, live staff biographies, and sound throughout. A free copy of Fosterand Partners' CD-ROM was sent to subscribers of *Architectural Review* (see Fig. C-19).

There are no bandwidth limitations, as there is no transmission through telephone lines. Special effects consume great bandwidth; when accessed on the Web, they greatly retard downloading.

Updating is more burdensome on a CD-ROM than it is on the Web site. There are no great economies of scale in producing 500 copies of a CD-ROM at a time rather than 100, but any "published" CD-ROM is essentially out of date the day it leaves the press. (Web sites are updated regularly, some sites every day.) Software such aa Macromedia Director allows the CD-ROM's master disk to be updated in-house when the supply of copies is about to run out.

QuickTimeVR software is required for the viewer to capture the action on the CD-ROM. It is typically built into common browsing software such as Netscape's and Microsoft's, and is usually incorporated into the CD-ROM itself. Some magazines occasionally include a CD-ROM as a bonus to readers (see example, page 31).

To sum up, writing for e-mail, Web sites, and CD-ROMs differs from writing on paper largely in a loosening of the rules of traditional grammar and forms of salutation. There is a focus on brevity or, rather, on keeping length strictly commensurate with the needs of the message. In the moving-picture atmosphere of the CD-ROM, the writing of scripted, spoken content vies with written prose (most written prose today could benefit from the livelier language of speech). As the electronic medium begins to dominate the work and lives of the new generation of professional design firms, these changing standards of writing will end up dominating the language.

12 Writing as a Career

Career writers who write about design usually are trained design professionals, or they have degrees in English or journalism, or they come from the world of art history. No one field of training is best, so long as the resulting work is professional in content and form.

It is critical for career writers to know the practicalities of the design discipline they write about. Even if a topic does not call for the down-and-dirty aspects of construction or plant irrigation or cost control, the knowledge rests in the back of their minds. It imbues their writing with greater depth and authenticity than one finds in the subjective, aesthetic "facadism" that still pervades much writing about design.

Considering a Writing Career

Of the career options open to the design graduate or licensed design professional (see list in chapter 8, Job Prospects), writing has the fewest practitioners. This is because of the limited number of full-time positions and the equally limited opportunities for freelance contributors. Such a career does, however, yield great satisfactions. It provides regular contact with broad reaches of the profession; bracing travel; fellowship, often long-term and cordial, with leading players; and the delight of disseminating useful information and opinions with sometimes lasting impact on trends. There are also regular invitations to judge design and other award contests, to interact with students and faculty at design schools, and, if you reach top positions in the field, a comfortable level of income.

Full-time editorial careers begin typically at entry levels labeled editorial assistant or assistant editor. These junior positions commonly entail writing up short news and product items—although these two tasks have been known to develop, owing to the zeal of the players, into staff specialties with authority and compensation above the norm for those positions. As openings occur, junior editors are given more important writing assignments, contacts with eminent sources, and chances to edit the work of others, including contributors.

Top positions, such as managing editor, executive editor, or editor in chief, open up infrequently given the limited number of professional and special-interest design journals, but the same can be said about top positions in any industry. Criteria for these top appointments typically include a combination of talent, track record, the right balance of assertiveness and diplomacy, timing, and luck.

Some publications retain full-time correspondents in key U.S. and international cities. Others employ "stringers": part-time reporters and writers who keep a nose out for news, interview local design celebrities, and review design projects. They are paid by the word or by the published length as measured in column inches. Stringers are the eyes and ears of a publication outside of its immediate area, and their writing needs to match the style of the publication they service.

Candidates should send resumes, samples, and a hint at the range of their good contacts to the publication's managing editor or, in the case of newspapers, the section editor. These editors, despite rumors to the contrary, are always glad to have a reserve of names even when there are no openings.

Part-time design reporters are typically freelancers, and do this as a sideline to a regular job. Staff writers moonlighting for other design magazines whose top editor frowns on the practice sometimes resort to pseudonyms.

Some freelance design writers make a good living by combining writing with lecturing, teaching, editorial consulting, and writing an occasional book. (Refer also to chapter 10, Writing for the Media.)

Writing a Book

Writing a book about design demands an extra effort compared to writing articles and criticism, chiefly because of the mental and physical marathon such a project represents. A book has the value of casting a more permanent product upon the waters of design, generating a deeper level of discussion, and influencing trends. Notable examples include Venturi's *Complexity and Contradiction in Architecture*, Siegfried Giedion's *Space, Time, and Architecture*, Reyner Banham's *Theory and Design in the First Machine Age*, and Le Corbusier's *When the Cathedrals Were White*, in our era; the classic works of Vitruvius, Alberti, and Viollet-le-Duc; and, not least, the great pattern books—the generators of most of this country's domestic design and construction.

Before deciding to write a book, consider:

Books take time. It is not a three-days-a-week evening task. You will need to set aside hours every day, or days every week.

Books usually do not generate income through royalties until long after they are published. The book advance will not pay for your bed and board, unless you are a celebrity.

Check out your marketplace. Who besides you cares about the topic? Are those interested necessarily the ones with the cash to buy books?

Is your research done, or will it entail a major search for material? If you already have great expertise in the subject, you save research time.

Is a book the best medium for your topic? Would an article series be better, or an illustrated lecture series followed by a CD-ROM?

Does writing come easily to you? If not, don't underestimate the time you will need to complete the manuscript. But if the book is logically organized and clearly written and follows the writing guidelines mentioned throughout this book, it will need little editing and your editor will be happy. If it does not, expect to revise under the guidance of your editor, or have the manuscript heavily edited. Consider these issues up front, and make realistic decisions about your time and the likely financial return.

A book about your firm's design work is a good marketing item, and you may write such a book yourself. More commonly an outside writer takes on such a task, bringing to it a detached point of view more likely to appeal to a publisher and to the marketplace.

To find a book publisher, review the books of houses the publish books in your field. Decide whose publications—in quality of design, writing, and layout—best fit your purpose. Send a one-page outline of your idea to an editor there. This should yield immediate encouragement or a turn-down before you invest more time and effort.

If encouraged, develop a prospectus, an outline, and (if asked) a typical chapter. The prospectus is a two- to four-page description of your topic, why it is important, and who will make up the buying audience. How much of this buying audience is reachable by direct mail—an efficient selling medium for most professional design books? How many words will the book contain, and how many illustrations? The outline lists chapter headings and main subheadings, and proposed artwork. The typical chapter should come from the center of the book—not the introduction or the conclusion. Editors commonly demand it in order to assess your writing style, level of knowledge, and suitability for the intended audience.

Approach one publisher at a time, not several at once, and insist on prompt responses. If your proposal is accepted, your editor will give you a contract specifying your rights and obligations and those of the publishing house. The contract covers deadlines; the size, computation, and payment of royalties and advances on royalties; rights and obligations; and more.

Frequent or full-time design writers often engage an agent, who makes the initial overtures and retains a percentage of your earnings.

Writing Career Prospects

Career writers will face a new world at the turn of the century. Internet access to currently elusive data will greatly simplify the research process that still underlies most writing on complex topics such as design. And while I know of no software that will prepare a viable text based merely on inputting key words and linkages, such programs are technically possible. For example, for years design firms have routinely used master specifications on projects: the spec writer's task is to select texts from a range of alternative master texts, and edit these to achieve the intended meaning—no need to invent the text from ground zero.

None of this means an end to writing on paper, which is likely to remain the document of record for a long time to come. Nor will it mean the passing of the book and magazine; these have a physical convenience that has existed since antiquity. Electronic media, however, offer a vehicle for dramatically extending access to added information beyond the printed page.

On Your Feet

The quality of writing is rises immeasurably when it respects the style of people talking. This applies especially to electronic formats such as the CD-ROM, where speech increasingly rivals text as a communication medium. This chapter focuses on the challenges of speaking, its composition and delivery. The design professional faces these challenges in various kinds of speech.

Queen Victoria used to complain that whenever Prime Minister Gladstone came to brief her on affairs of state, he would address her "as though we were a public meeting." Speaking is an art and a science, with its own rules, opportunities, and pitfalls. What you say must be immediately intelligible; a listener who misses a word or phrase cannot relisten the way a reader can reread. Nor can you as the speaker retrace your steps and "unsay" a wrong word or thought. If you bore your audience, you will have a short career as a speaker. When preparing a speech, pay attention to these points:

Be sure content and delivery are direct. Listeners have no time for convoluted phrasing.

Shun statistics or lists unless you have visual backup.

Keep sentences short; it takes a practiced performer to deliver long sentences.

Restate your main points. There's wisdom in the old motto: "tell 'em what you're going to say; say it; then tell 'em what you just said." Restate, but don't repeat. A good example comes from Scripture. Note how the Psalms, written to be recited, not read, repeat each thought within a single verse:

1. The earth is the Lord's, and the fullness thereof; the world, and they that dwell therein.
2. For he hath founded it upon the seas, and established it upon the floods.
3. Who shall ascend into the hill of the Lord? or who shall stand in his holy place? —Psalm 24, King James Version

Gestures count. Just as the graphic format can make or muddy your message, so can your appearance, your gestures, and the physical setting.

People find it harder to absorb spoken information than written text. So the listener who wants to retain the content of a speech has to either take notes (distracting for the listener) or run a tape recorder (an obvious duplication of effort since the tape must be played back later, often even transcribed).

Client Interviews and Presentations

Speaking is a two-way street. Gauge your audience, pick up signals—of excitement, mild interest, or boredom—and adjust your delivery accordingly.

Like most speaking activity, the client interview is also a two-way street. It should not be a forum for the prospective client merely to pick up information about your firm; that should already be in your brochure, which the client has presumably at least scanned prior to the interview. The point of the interview is to give the client the chance to evaluate you and your associates—for example, how you deal with questions about the project's potential and limitations. The interview has these special considerations:

It is a dialogue, not a speech. The interview is a flexible occasion. Your presentation, ranging from simple slides to multimedia showbiz, may be interrupted at any time by a query. Some selection committee members deliberately interrupt presenters to see how they respond under pressure.

Beware the dangers of designer-babble. Designer-babble or jargon is even riskier in a verbal presentation than in writing. Odds are that your audience is composed of laypeople, and dishing out clever verbal ammo is a sure way to calamity. Avoid clunkers such as "the plastic qualities of a facade," or "the controlled clash of volumes."

Consider using audiovisual support. An endless array of aids is available to your firm's presenter. The 35mm slide or overhead projector is being supplanted by PowerPoint-generated 2-D offerings, computer-generated 3-D animations, and Virtual Reality productions convertible to screen projection using specialized equipment. Techniques for preparing such presentations are described in other works, such as Curtis Charles and Karen Brown's Multimedia Marketing for Design Firms (see Resources). Such whiz shows are two-edged swords, however; if overused, they will steal attention away from the presenter. Do not rest your case on too much high-tech razzmatazz. The client is looking you over as a problem solver, not a technical wizard. Control the show yourself (managed best from a laptop) or get a well-rehearsed assistant. Learn how to take questions. Respond briefly and to the point; no speeches. Avoid being drawn into a detailed discussion of a proposed project whose outlines you don't yet know.

Avoid techno overkill. Steer clear of showing complex engineering diagrams or elaborate computer printouts of project schedules or complex budget breakdowns. Most of the committee cannot follow them and may get a bad impression of your presentation. Use brief, simple descriptions—contrary to current wisdom, a word can be worth a thousand pictures.

Lectures and Speeches

A keynote speech at a national conference, an evening lecture to students, a speech to government officials—these contrast with a client presentation mainly in that you are granted a block of uninterrupted time instead of the give-and-take of an interview.

Preparation

According to Orvin Larson in *When It's Your Turn to Speak,* when asked how long it took him to prepare his famous "Reply to [Senator Robert] Hayne" speech of 1830, Daniel Webster said, "twenty years." Always assume that some day you will be asked to speak, whether it's about computer applications in the office, planning the new workplace, innovative landmark legislation, or building on wetlands. Start a speech file, making occasional notes and inserting pieces of information or a chance phrase in the areas of your expertise.

When you are to give a speech, schedule a silent hour and jot down ideas, however remote, on the assigned topic. Review your speech file for nuggets. Record all these on a notepad or, better still, on index cards—one idea per card. Arrange the cards in a sequence that allows a build-up. For example, if your theme is "design-build and the design professional's accountability," consider this possible outline:

1. The owner wants construction value for the money.
2. Traditional design-bid-build techniques sometimes suffer because design and construction don't meet until the bid stage.
3. Design-build provides single responsibility, and eases packaging subcontractor bids and phasing construction.
4. The design professional has the chance to take the initiative, by starting and managing design-build teams.
5. The owner receives more effective control over quality, schedule, and costs, but sometimes forgoes direct access from the designer.

Expand your outline to full length, adding examples. Except for quotes, avoid writing out full sentences that tempt you to read your speech to the audience; you cannot simultaneously read and look at the audience—a key virtue of a good speech. Limit your notes to short phrases. With a large audience (250 or more), you can get by with frequent glances at your cards; not so with a smaller group. Write notes large so they are easy to scan; set your word processor to 14-point type (minimum).

Rehearse the speech once or twice, including a dry run if you have visual aids; anything more will kill spontaneity.

Politicians and top executives write out speeches so they can hand them out to the press in advance and avoid embarrassing boners. That's why most such speeches are dull. As a design professional, you should feel comfortable enough in your command of the material to speak from notes. A read speech often sounds as though it was written for publication, not for oral delivery. And while writing as you would speak is a good general rule, a delivered speech sometimes triggers additional quirks of phrasing that would probably have to be edited out in a written piece.

Here are some examples of desired quirks that come out of speeches as opposed to writing:

Written:
We must consider cost, schedule, and quality control . . .
Spoken:
We have to watch over cost control and schedule control and quality control . . .

Written:

Architects, engineers, and landscape architects had big backlogs of work . . .

Spoken:

Architects were busy, engineers were busy, so were the landscape architects . . .

When you are preparing a speech, there are several other things to keep in mind:

Speed of delivery. Count on delivering about 85 words a minute, or 1275 in a quarter-hour. Radio announcers are trained to deliver 200 words a minute, except when they are reading the "fine print" of a commercial, when the speed seems to double. (I have heard hog callers approach this maximum.) If in doubt, slow down—better to speak too slowly than too quickly. Pause between sections; silence is a great attention-getter.

Sign posting. Consultant and author Antony Jay recommends resetting the scene for the forgetful listener at points during the speech—for example, "So here we are—the new site survey showed a high water table but the foundation had been designed to fit an earlier survey."

Audience size. The larger the audience, the more it reacts as one person, and the easier it is to influence. Large audiences react less to the subject matter, more to your personality. That doesn't mean you should dilute intellectual content, but you need to simplify concepts and work on your delivery.

Attention span. The classic attention span of the 50-minute lecture is shown in the chart below. Insert your lighter material in the 30–40 minute slot; the heavier stuff at the beginning and the end.

Humor. Jokes are a good way to loosen up a medium-to-large audience. With groups under 10 you may get embarrassed snickers. If you cannot tell jokes well or deliver a resounding punchline, pass them up. A flat joke is worse than none. Try for a connecting thread between your joke and your topic.

Audiences are sharper at the start and finish of a typical 50-minute lecture. Keep the heavy stuff out of the 30- to 40-minute time slot.

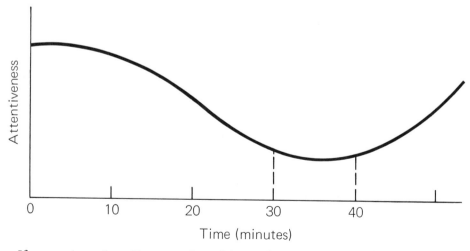

Press Interviews

If you are interviewed by a member of the professional press researching a story, develop a few notes on the subject and speak frankly. If you suspect you didn't get all the points right, the editor will welcome a correction by voice- or e-mail.

When speaking with a daily press reporter—who often interviews design professionals for reactions to daily events and, especially, catastrophes like an earthquake, a windstorm, or a bombing—be prudent. Because of deadlines, chances are you'll not have a chance to correct what you said. To avoid being misquoted, answer all questions with a complete sentence or rephrase the question in your own way before you respond. Never respond merely with a yes or no. For example: Reporter: "Do you agree that changes in the city zoning law will end up driving out low-income families?"

Poor answer:
"No, because of built-in safeguards."
(Next morning: "Designer denies that new zoning will displace the poor. He cited safeguards, but failed to describe them.")

A better answer:
"The changes in the zoning law are subject to an overall plan. The plan is aimed at encouraging families to live in the city—families of all incomes. Safeguards have been built into the changes. For instance . . ."

The aim is to get a complete answer into the reporter's notebook. Observe how seasoned politicians field questions from the press.

Broadcast Interviews

A speech to a live audience is one thing. A radio or television interview has some special ground rules. First, you cannot retract a mistake, unless the studio tapes your interview before airing it and allows you to tape over the mistake. Second, instead of addressing an audience in the dozens or hundreds, you are talking to an audience of perhaps two or three, clustered around a family room TV set or sitting in a car with the radio on. You do not have a captive audience; if they lose interest, they flip the channel, and you're history.

For broadcast, therefore, an informal, fireside-chat format is in order. No great oratorical statements or overwrought facial or other gestures. The TV camera exaggerates all. Avoid long sentences; people have been known to start out on one, then not know how to finish it. Your time on camera will likely be strictly limited: a couple of minutes to a dozen minutes or so if you hit Charlie Rose. So make your key points first; you won't know how much time you'll have. Look at the interviewer, not the camera.

Radio has its own special quirks. (See *The Associated Press Broadcast News Handbook* in the Resources section.) Silences are useful in a live speech and at times on television (you look wise, as though thinking deeply about your next remark). On radio, a silence of more than five seconds signals to your listeners that the transmitter has failed or, worse, that you just had a stroke. A kindly interviewer will help you bridge such gaps. A short opening statement written out in advance in colloquial language will get you off on the right foot. Typed-out material works better on radio, as no one can see you. (Just don't rustle the paper.) Gesture all you like when on radio—it may add animation to your voice.

14 Graphics: Medium for the Message

The success of your message is not just in the way it reads; it's also in the way it looks. If the design of a page, sheet, proposal, brochure, portfolio, Web site, or e-mail confuses the reader or is just plain unreadable (dark-brown 6-point sans serif type on a medium-brown background), you are wasting your time writing anything at all.

The following observations and guidelines for "good" graphics are divided into four factors: readability, appropriateness, image, and fashion.

Readability

The most innovative graphics will do you no good if the reader cannot make out the message. Therefore, whether you are a firm principal deciding on a new letterhead or a design for a marketing brochure or portfolio; a partner in charge of creating a cover and inside format for an important feasibility or planning report; or a doctoral candidate readying your dissertation, remember this adage. While Marshall McLuhan claims with some truth that the medium is the message, whenever the message is thwarted by the medium, there is no message. These pointers will help to prevent your message from being obscured by the graphic medium:

- Contrast type color and its background.
- Make type large enough to be read in comfort; don't attempt to pack too much information into a limited space. Even 7-point type is hard to read unless you are equipped with a magnifying glass. Line spacing that is too tight (say a point or less), like paragraphs that are too long (over 15 lines) in relation to column width, is hard to read. Long passages in sans serif type are usually harder to read than serif type.
- Avoid drop-out type (type printed in white or a color against a dark background). Too much is tiring on the eyes.
- Handle gingerly a type column of an unfamiliar shape. For example, in an article about seismic distortion, type may take the wiggly shape of a tall building deflected by lateral pressures. The concept is ingenious and can be made to work, but the reader must always be able to absorb the information.
- Provide adequate borders and margins. The eye needs rest. An inch all around a letter or memo is a minimum for comfort.

• Beware distracting backgrounds for drawings or type. A skilled graphic designer can balance out the discord and make it work. But it's a risky undertaking if the medium is in fact to be the message. In other words, clashing planes of color are okay if they are intended to carry a particular message to the reader, but eschew them if legibility is your object.

• Avoid using paper so thin that the type on the back shows through or so thick it is hard to turn the page.

Once you have dealt graphically with the basic goal of writing, which is to communicate, you face the question of graphic appropriateness.

There is in fact no absolute right or wrong in graphics. What counts is whether the design is right or wrong for its purpose. It's clearly inappropriate to print out a planning report on flimsy paper with a short-lived binding if it is to be widely seen and used by senior corporate or public officials. Even so, designers have been known to take the tack that public officials dislike ostentatious use of public funds, so a cheaply produced report should spell "economy." A news release printed in a large typeface on heavy-coated paper denies the purpose of the release, which is to be read briefly, the content edited for a news story, then the whole discarded.

Similarly, it makes little tactical sense to clothe a proposal to a cost-conscious inner-city school district in elaborate binding, glossy overlays, and a large range of color, when a straightforward assembly of pages, possibly with simply colored dividers, in a decent off-the-shelf binder, is far more appropriate. On the other hand, when a proposal is for design services to an oil-rich potentate, it is quite in order for the packaging to reflect a certain richness, as it appears to place proposer and client on the same level.

As Thomas F. McCormick, who was Public Printer of the United States in the late 1970s, told a seminar for graphic designers: "even some top-grade newsprint looks 'cheap and dirty'—but it's still the most effective paper there is for publishing daily news. But to put the *National Geographic* on the same paper would ruin it."

Appropriateness is also a matter of detail. Take typefaces. Your basic typewriter face, which most word processors carry (such as Courier New) is good for a news release. An elegant, old-line, serif typeface, such as Cheltenham or Clarendon, works well for a formal report on proposed restoration of a major historical landmark. A more playful typeface—or font, as it is known in the printing trade—is proper for an exhibit panel of your prize-winning design for an amusement park.

Page size is another graphic decision that shapes the impact of the written message. There is no reason to abandon the standard 8½- by 11-inch format (or the A4 size used by many overseas nations) for standard project correspondence. Chances are it will be filed, and odd page sizes aggravate.

On the other hand, if you want something read but not filed, it often helps to go to a different page size: it struts the document's difference and demands to be looked at. Any paper supplier will tell you that there are attractive, non-standard paper sizes cut from the basic 25- by 38-inch sheet that incur no wastage and thus no premium cost.

Image

Unlike appropriateness, which applies to the project, image applies to and expresses your firm. Graphic image is a key ingredient of any firm's communications. Each firm at some stage must determine what the firm is and how to express that through its public contacts and internal behavior. Do you want to convey an informal, convivial image, or one of sobriety and restraint? Is the impression you want to transmit one of tradition and concern for historic values, or do you seek up-to-the-minute cool? Would you rather project a concern for the client's pocketbook, or is your skill in creating innovative, envelope-bursting forms to bequeath to history? Do you want to stress youth? vigor? wisdom? experience? Do you go gently into that good market, or do you practice the hard sell?

Translate your decision into graphic terms. A conservative image may be expressed through dignified type, symmetry, subdued colors, bulk. A brash image shows through bright colors, unorthodox text arrangement, deliberately mixed typefaces. Budget-consciousness comes across by selecting resolutely bargain-basement materials, bindings, and common, popular fonts.

Note that paradoxically the impression of economy is not always cheaply come by. A famous graphic designer created a one-inch-thick report from pieces of paper of a dozen different sizes, and bound together by three off-the-shelf bronze marine fittings. The effect, while not cheap, was sensational, as though it had been knocked together in a spare moment, and you can be sure it wasn't ignored.

What about when appropriateness conflicts with image? If you are pursuing clients whose general culture matches yours, it's a nonissue. But suppose you are a firm known for clothing the building program in jagged forms and innovatively applied space-program materials, and you decide to compete for a regional bank headquarters with two notable, conservative firms also in the running. Your choices include:

Planning the proposal package and other marketing correspondence in a conservative graphic cloak;

Figuring that the client knows your firm, and the previous option isn't going to fool anyone. Stick with your image, along with a high-tech presentation if required;

Developing an inoffensive, bland (neither conservative nor innovative) marketing package that simply doesn't draw attention to itself.

My choice is the second. What's yours?

Fashion

Over and above any other concerns in expressing the written word graphically is the imprint of fashion. Graphic fashion tends to go in cycles—like hems, cuisines, and art—and is influenced not unreasonably by the technology available to produce the designs. The 1970s and 1980s saw rather formal arrangements of type in clean vertical columns, separated chastely from the artwork, with right angles dominant.

Today, great opportunities are inherent in computer-aided graphics through programs such as Photoshop and Illustrator and publishing systems such as QuarkXpress and Pagemaker, even in free software included in most laptops. An open, loose quality has captured much graphic design. There is a plethora of new typefaces; they are often mixed together; type is set in any desired shape, from rectangle to half moon to star; type, headlines, and artwork are freely mingled.

Thus fashion plays an inevitable part in the way your written message reaches your selection committee, client, project team member, or design honor award judges. That is as it should be, up to a point. After all, design has always expressed its society. Pitted against fashion, however, especially in firms of long lineage, is the tradition and culture of the firm. How such conflicts, where there are conflicts, are resolved is what makes good communication one of the more engaging of life's challenges.

15 Writing by the Product Manufacturer

"How will this product or material or equipment support my design concept?" That's the first question asked by architects, interior and urban designers, and landscape architects, as well as by consultants in the various engineering disciplines, lighting, and acoustics, whenever they read a manufacturer's promotional piece.

Because few manufacturers know ahead of time the designer's concept, the copywriters whom manufacturers retain to inform the nation's design professions about new and existing products, materials, and equipment face peculiar challenges. As they write their copy, they need to satisfy the following needs simultaneously:

The designer's need to have information that is accurate, complete, and in a usable form;

The company's need to sell a product;

The company's need not to give away proprietary information to competitors;

Product images that look professional without being boring, and images that evoke emotion without being crass, vulgar, or unconnected with the advertised product;

Dissemination in several formats (print; CD-ROM; on-line) linkable into the designer/specifier's information-seeking and decision-making network.

There are writing yardsticks that cut across all marketing communication channels. Here are some dos and don'ts for writing copy:

Do

• Write to press the designer/specifier's hot buttons. These buttons include the product's applications; evidence of superior performance when compared to existing products; appearance; alternate choices; ease of connecting to adjacent installed products; operating life; environmental attributes; price; delivery; manufacturer's support. From these data the designer will judge to what extent the product supports the design concept.

• Keep sentences short and snappy. You may even break some basic rules of grammar ("every sentence must contain a subject, verb, and predicate") in favor of a looser sentence structure ("There's more to see. More to choose. More to like . . ."—from an advertisement by Weather Shield). Where chapter 1 advocates short sentences—not above twenty words—product copy should aspire to even shorter sentences (" Fine artists aren't limited to just one color. So why should architects be limited to just pine?"—from the same advertisement).

• Shun the abstract and the trivial. Be concrete. Your reader isn't looking for flights of fancy, just the facts. ("New Hi-LR™ Optima RH95™ ceilings are specifically designed for open plan offices. With an NRC of .85–1.00 and Articulation Class (AC) of 190–210, they prevent reflected noise between cubicles. Sounds too good to be true? Listen for yourself."—from an advertisement by Armstrong)

• Use headlines of strength and meaning. ("817 hits. No errors."—headline for an ad by Pella Windows & Doors accompanying a photograph of a renovated warehouse within hitting distance of Camden Yards, Baltimore's ballpark. The name of the window series also happens to be "817".)

Don't
• Write so much copy that your message loses its selling focus. You seek a single, punchy message. There are exceptions: Rolls Royce and Mercedes Benz disregarded this notion some years ago; the advertising was noted for its excruciatingly long texts describing the cars' mechanical specifications in awesome detail. The idea was to convey to buyers the idea that they were getting their money's worth in quality and performance.

• Sacrifice the designer/specifier's information needs on the altar of superficial verbal brilliance. You are an information provider, not a poet.

In addition, individual marketing media have their own specific writing demands.

Direct Mail Copy

It's a safe bet that direct mail is only as good as your mailing list. The best-fashioned direct mail package won't yield a decent return if sent to the wrong destinations. What makes for a good list is part statistical mathematics, part trial and error, part common sense.

Direct mail from the product manufacturer typically comes in one of two formats. One format is the glossy, four-to-eight-page product piece (often a reprint of an advertisement, or a product catalog destined for or taken from Sweet's catalog); see example on page 32, top. The piece is best accompanied by a cover letter from a senior marketing executive. A second format consists of the postcard deck, made up of postcard-sized or double postcard–sized information cards and mailed to prospects three or four times a year.

The regular (8½ by 11 inch) format mailing pieces—whether original, reprints from an advertisement, or a catalog originally created for Sweet's—need to observe the basic tenets of promotional copy: attract the designer prospect's attention through some device; then, in the short attention span available, press one or more hot buttons. This will either close the sale then and there (unlikely) or else motivate the prospect to ask for more information by demanding an extended brochure, clicking on the company's Web site, or requesting a sales call. For the cover page of an effective direct mail piece, see the examples below.

Cover Letter

The cover letter is a powerful lead-in to the mailed piece. To spur the designer to read the full piece, the letter must get to the point fast and summarize succinctly the benefits to the reader of reading on. The letter should be short—a half page, perhaps. It is not the vehicle for formal courtesies and elaborate product prose.

Cover letter for manufacturer's direct mail piece

Dear Interior Designer:

You can see from the enclosed eight-page illustrated brochure that PDQ Company's furniture system for the new workplace covers a wide range of stylistic choices. What you cannot so easily see from the photographs and drawings are the benefits the system brings to you and your clients. These include:

- Flexibility to adapt to frequent staff moves, all effected simply by your in-house custodial staff
- Built-in modem, lighting, and comfort-control connections
- Multiple-file storage at each station that offers security in case more than one shift of workers is assigned to the work station
- Top quality by seasoned Maine cabinetmakers and other craftspeople working in our technically advanced manufacturing plant
- Our own technical staff available to you 24 hours a day

Read our brochure. If you need more information, consult our Web site (www.pdq.com), call us at 207/555-0000 and ask for David Jones, or e-mail me at djones@pdq.com.

Sincerely,
David Jones
Executive Vice President

(Note that this letter, sent from the mythical company PDQ, focuses on what cannot be readily seen from the photographs, namely, benefits derived by specifying the company's workplace system. The text is brief, and zeroes in on the types of features an interior designer needs to know.)

Postcard Decks

Postcard decks are among the simplest and most targeted of direct mail vehicles (see page 32, bottom). Postcards—actually, the space on them—are "sold," typically by business magazines, to product manufacturers, publishing houses, service providers, or other vendors. The cards are mailed in translucent plastic wrappers, in batches of 20 to 100 cards, to circulation lists. The manufacturer writes copy to fit on one side of the prepaid postcard or double postcard. The recipient is encouraged to return the cards with an order or with a request for more information. Given the tight 3½- by 5½-inch space, designing the card and writing the copy is a challenge. One way is to show an image of the product on half the card along with a short caption; the other half is taken up by blank lines for the user to fill out when requesting more information. Another way is for the manufacturer to write about 100 words of copy describing the product, service, or a brochure offer. Good copy should put the most important information up front, and follow it with the details, which can use bullets for easier scanning. Overcome the temptation to set everything in 4-point type so you can squeeze in more words. Stick with a 7-point minimum, and select your words with greater care.

Postcard

Brick Information on CD-ROM

The Brick Institute of America's *Technical Notes on Brick Construction* are on CD-ROM. The digitized version contains all the text, drawings, photographs, tables, and charts on design, detailing, and construction, with brick included in the printed version. Excellent search program and the details are downloadable. One hundred full-color photos show brick in applications. Available for $119.95 (20% professional discount to architects and other construction industry professionals) VISA/MC welcome. Brick Institute of America, 11490 Commerce Park Drive, Reston, Virginia 20191. [phone contact number and system requirements given]

Reproduced courtesy of the Brick Institute of America.

This text is unadorned and to the point. In one corner of the card there is an image of the disk along with six bulleted items of information that restate the above text; this appears to represent the CD's jacket. The reverse of the card gives an equally succinct description of the printed version of the *Technical Notes*.

Advertising Copy

Advertising copywriters are known to be attracted more to the glamorous world of consumer advertising than to the serious material demanded by the business-to-business advertiser. Advertising copy often ends up either listless or saddled with a phony consumer tone guaranteed to alienate the designer who is just looking for facts and application information, not unrelated visuals and glitzy prose.

Designers are human, and respond to the same selling stimuli as other consumers. That, however, cannot justify copy that fails to provide factual information, or hides it under a blanket of showbiz glitz more appropriate to selling deodorant or chewing gum. Advertisers routinely test the impact of their advertisements, copy included, on focus groups made up of prospective customers to see what sells product and what doesn't. Informal conversations with architects and other specifiers consistently stress the designer's preference for ads that depict a product clearly, simply, with the copy tight, brisk, and focused on applications.

This classic advertisement, with the figure updated every few years, is a superb example of brawny copywriting, choice of image, smart psychology, and design.

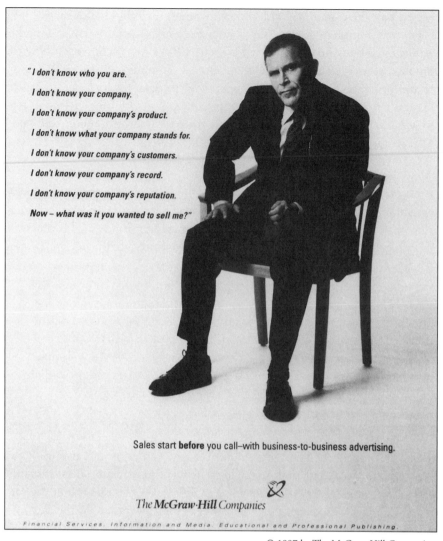

" I don't know who you are.

I don't know your company.

I don't know your company's product.

I don't know what your company stands for.

I don't know your company's customers.

I don't know your company's record.

I don't know your company's reputation.

Now – what was it you wanted to sell me?"

Sales start **before** you call—with business-to-business advertising.

The McGraw·Hill Companies

Financial Services. Information and Media. Educational and Professional Publishing.

For a classic example of brilliant advertising copywriting, see the ad above. A major publishing company's magazine publishers intended this ad to appeal to advertisers (it was in fact produced to advance the value of business-to-business advertising). It is a superior example of a smart concept, suitable image, and sparkling copy.

Writing Copy for Electronic Marketing

Product information systems are now at the point of enabling the designer to import product information, including details, into project drawings and specifications simply.

One way is for the manufacturer to place product information on a CD-ROM. The designer, aided by CAD drafting-engine software such as AutoCAD, drags and clicks the exact product drawing and specification right into the contract documents. Productivity gains of over 20 percent have been claimed for this procedure.

A second way involves the Web site. Many design firms obtain product information directly from manufacturers' own Web sites. (The manufacturer's copywriter should realize, however, that this form of access has not routinely replaced the printed page.) A design firm, if it is to rely on the Internet to keep abreast of new product developments, is compelled to designate a "watcher" on staff to monitor relevant suppliers' sites so nothing significant slips through the, ahem, net.

Writing effective copy for manufacturers' Web sites and CD-ROMs follows the same hot-button tactics that work so well for printed matter. The difference is mainly in the way the designer uses this new medium. The designer's attention span is already taxed by a lengthy downloading process. This process is especially burdensome when it involves a narrow bandwidth combined with a Web site heavy on graphics. The combination isn't geared to put the designer or specifier in a frame of mind to deal with a lot of superfluous matter, textual or visual.

Consequently your copywriting must be spartan, focusing on usable facts and removing all surplus words and syllables. Recognize that, with a click of the mouse, the specifier can move easily to the next screen or even to a competitor's Web site.

A brief glance at the Web sites of two national window and door manufacturers at the time of writing reveals a shrewd understanding of the designer's requirements. The Pella Corporation's site (www.pella.com) opens with a handsome four-color view through a large arched window overlooking the city of Santa Barbara, with the Pacific Ocean beyond; the image takes a few seconds to load. Below it are two lines of text ("Viewed to be the best"™ and "Welcome to the world of windows!"), followed by three paragraphs of short sentences totaling 100 words. Later screens use the line "how you make great window decisions" to introduce a series of clickable boxes with such labels as "energy efficiency," "beauty and aesthetics," and "product options." The site ends with the text, "Options and features to consider should include a true variety of glass systems and coatings; between-the-panes shading options; exterior cladding protection in a choice of colors; interior hardware styles and finishes; security features; interior washing; screens and windowpane dividers."

The tone of this passage, as well as the writing elsewhere on the site, is simple, friendly, informative, and suitable for both professional and consumer browsers.

Copy on the site of the Weather Shield company, another window and door manufacturer (www.WeatherShield.com), likewise is brief. The site consciously seeks to inform both a professional and a consumer audience—not an easy task. A simply worded welcome screen is followed by a selection box offering four choices: product information; design ideas; international services; and fun stuff (an array of small project images shown in vivid color).

A key feature is case studies, including a "Case Study of the Month," which include photographs (taking unusually long to download), brief descriptions, and a fact-filled interview with an architect. Ensuing screens give the designer the opportunity to obtain information about products from the manufacturer's line. There is also a dealer locator (type in your zip code to get a list of local dealers) and an e-mail literature request.

The following sample description of one of this manufacturer's product lines gives a sense of the straightforward, no-nonsense tone of the copywriting:

> Visions windows and doors mark a new generation in window technology. They're constructed using PVC vinyl with high-impact modified stabilizers to increase strength and prevent rust, corrosion, blistering, flaking, or peeling.
>
> The thick, multi-chambered frame design eliminates uncontrolled expansion and contraction, and provides superior insulation. Visions windows are designed to withstand heavy rains and winds with an interior drainage system that relieves pressure.

> Copy courtesy of Weather Shield Windows & Doors.
> © Weather Shield Mfg., Inc. 1998.

Buyer's Guides

The term "buyer's guide" embraces a number of publication types, some printed, some electronic, in which the caliber of writing has an impact on the designer's understanding. These works include:

Directories (cross-referenced listings of products and manufacturers, typically arranged to conform to the 16-category Construction Specifications Institute MASTERFORMAT®);

Annual "buyer's guide" issues of magazines;

CD-ROMs, such as ARCAT and SweetSource®, a quarterly CD-ROM shipped free to subscribers of any of Sweet's major catalog files. The CD-ROMs include drawings and details exportable to the designer's drawing.

The quality of copy in these guides and directories varies. Product descriptions in magazines are either written by the magazine's editors and qualify as editorial matter or supplied by the manufacturer and printed in space paid for by that manufacturer as advertising. Magazines' product editors lack the resources to research and assess each product they write up. Consequently, they evaluate manufacturers' claims from a viewpoint of logic and personal knowledge, and avail themselves freely of such qualifying terms as "allegedly," "reportedly," "according to the manufacturer," and "is said to have."

The best descriptive copy is made up of short sentences, a simple structure, and a level of technical terminology compatible with the presumed level of skill of the reader. If you have the space and enough data, divide the copy into logical groupings, such as basic product description, features, benefits, and key performance data.

The following examples show two types of write-up for the same fictional product: first as paid matter, then as editorial matter. Note the difference.

Sample A

SOUND ABSORPTION
DiCarlo-Smith DECIBEL bronze sound-absorbing panels are suitable for attaching to ceilings and walls. DECIBEL panels offer an exceptionally attractive high-tech look combined with sound-absorption of 2 sabins per square foot at frequencies between 1000 and 2000 cycles per second. DECIBEL panels may also be textured to include corrugations, as well as custom designs. A DECIBEL panel is air-permeable, non-fibrous, and totally resistant to harsh environments. Contact us.

    DiCarlo-Smith
    213/010-1001

Sample B

SOUND-ABSORPTIVE PANELS
Manufacturer's DECIBEL bronze sound-absorbing panels are suitable for attaching to ceilings and walls. Panels are said to offer a high-tech look, and are rated for sound-absorption at 2 sabins per square foot at frequencies between 1000 and 2000 cycles per second. Panels may be textured to include corrugations, and manufacturer offers custom designs. The panels are air-permeable, non-fibrous, and resistant to harsh environments, according to the manufacturer.

    DiCarlo-Smith
    213/010-1001

The manufacturer's task in composing market-oriented product copy is complicated. The writer needs to create interest-provoking language without turning off the designer/specifier with histrionics, lack of taste in the visuals, or preoccupation with the trivial.

The best advice to product writers who lack practical design experience (and many who write product copy fall into that category) is to meet and get to know designers and specifiers. Find out what the designer reads professionally, and steep yourself in the same reading matter so you can identify with the designer's vision and concerns.

16 International Style

Many design firms have projects overseas. Some firms have even established international offices. Keeping pace with this trend is the rising volume of written communication linking American design professionals and those from other English-speaking nations with the flourishing economies, short-term or long-term, of Asia, Europe, the Middle East, and South America, and the emerging economies of nations from the former Communist bloc. Forging solid links with these regions is a crucial test of the writing skills of principals who spearhead marketing or manage projects for design firms eager to establish an overseas presence.

It is vital, first of all, to become familiar with the mores and values of nations where you want to do business. In order to be successful, conversions both from English into the local language and from the local language into English must pass under the eyes of a person who knows each language's nuances and colloquialisms. Especially prone to gaffes are texts composed in English by associates for whom English is a second language (see these examples of predicaments caused by lax quality control). What counts in the end are not the words, but the meaning.

Swiss wine menu:
"Our wines leave you nothing to hope for."

Ad for a Hong Kong dentist:
"Teeth extracted by the latest methodists."

In a Paris lobby:
"Please leave your values at the front desk."

Taiwan Pepsi ad:
Original: "Come alive with the Pepsi generation."
Translation: "Pepsi will bring your ancestors back from the dead."

Sales pitch from a Copenhagen airline:
"We take your bags and send them in all directions."

Excerpt reproduced with permission from article "Speaking in Tongues" published in *@issue:*, v. 3, no. 1. *@issue: The Journal of Business & Design* is published by Corporate Design Foundation and sponsored by Potlatch Corporation's Northwest Paper Division.

When communicating on overseas projects, consider carefully the writing of such items as marketing materials, agreements, contract documents, correspondence, and speeches.

Marketing Materials

Special editions of your brochure need to be prepared for overseas markets. They show that you are familiar with local conditions and/or are ready to associate with a local counterpart.

The text must define unfamiliar English technical terms, shun jargon, cite dimensions and other quantities in metric units, and eschew cultural references that could cause offense. You clearly cannot afford to create a package to fit every possible target nation, but basic firm qualification statements stored in your marketing database may be adapted as needed. Most word-processing programs contain symbols that let you write, if needed, in languages using the Latin or Cyrillic alphabets. Some word-processing software extensions include kanji (a system of Japanese writing using Chinese-derived characters). The best rule is to keep text to a minimum; let the photographs and drawings do the talking. Overleaf are examples of brochure sections geared to the overseas market.

Agreements and Contract Documents

Because business practices vary by region and often by country, written words are open to misinterpretation. Local associates and consultants can advise on particular meanings.

Follow local conventions. Because words are more easily misinterpreted than drawings, the tendency is for firms to insert more of the design intent into the drawings and less into the specifications. In the United States it is also common practice for firms to carry the project through design development, then hand document production and contract administration over to the associated local firm. The local firm completes the documents to comply with local standards and regulations. Some firms use a short-form performance specification to accompany the drawings.

Project Correspondence

Project correspondence is especially sensitive to local cultural values and the nuances of words. Many nations have not yet adapted to the more informal American way of writing. Hence greater formality is in order (see the examples of correspondence to Japan and China on pages 208–209). On the other hand, many who also practice overseas assert that the world is beginning to adopt American forms of writing.

That does not mean you should ignore local etiquette, such as in forms of salutation and endings. Salutations and farewells of course vary from country to country and region to region, and it's not hard to find out the right form in advance. For example, a common error in addressing an individual from a Spanish-speaking nation is to address, say, Agostín Vázquez González, as "Dear Señor González" when that is in fact his mother's maiden name. The correct form is "Dear Señor Vázquez" or, in Spanish, "Estimado Señor Vázquez."

"When corresponding with clients whose native language is other than

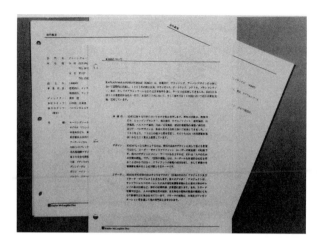
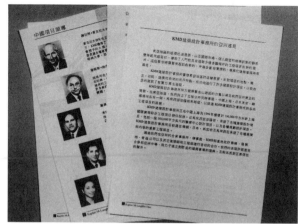

Japanese (left) and Chinese (right) versions of brochure sections listing qualifications of Kaplan McLaughlin Diaz, a San Francisco-based architectural firm with a large volume of Asian commissions. The three-hole-punched fact sheets are assembled in beige binders as needed for developing new business. Reproduced with permission.

English, style is not the issue," says Leslie E. Robertson, prominent New York–based structural engineer with a large global practice. Writing style is international, whether you are writing the United Kingdom, Malaysia, or Japan. "What you do have to worry about is the context of the words you use. Words have multiple meanings, and it's the context that provides the right meaning. Words have to be chosen carefully so they can be construed only one way." Misunderstandings occur when a letter in English is translated, as it often is, into the local language in order to inform non–English speakers about the project. When the recipient is influential, a poorly translated letter can create a lot of static.

Avoid lumping all nations in a region under a single umbrella of assumptions. Southeast Asia, for example, is not a single culture, but several. As she compares Chinese communication with Japanese, Lena Ning Zheng, director of China projects in the San Francisco–based architectural firm Kaplan McLaughlin Diaz, points out that China tends to adopt a subtle, classical, formal outlook in its dealings with foreign consultants, with scholarship honored in written and spoken communications. This at times clashes with the "let's get down to brass tacks" approach of Western or Westernized design firms. Japan, on the other hand, is by and large more welcoming to Western efficiency in verbal and written contacts.

Following are a request for information and a playful reminder.

Letter A

Mr. Tetsuo Nagae
Shimizu Corporation Civil Engineering
Midosuji Honmachi Building, 8F
No. 5-7, Honmachi, 3-chome
Chuo-ku, Osaka 541
JAPAN
Via fax/modem: 81 (6) 271-1595
Re: Miho Museum Bridge

Dear Nagae-san:

For another project we are seeking a free-draining material to be used for an area of paving not all that different from that of the Miho Museum Bridge. The paving being on grade, there is no thought of using the material in conjunction with grating. If possible, we would be very appreciative if you could provide to us the following:

• the name, address, facsimile and the like of the supplier of the material for the Miho Museum Bridge;
• a copy of the technical specification for the material; and
• the name and address of any United States supplier of a similar material.

It is our intention to enter the design of the bridge in one or more competitions. We will send to you copies of the entries as they are prepared.

We were told that Shimizu had entered the bridge in one or more competitions. If so, could you provide to us a copy of the submitted material?

Much to our surprise, ENR has honored LERA for the design of the bridge. With the written copy of this letter we will enclose copies of that material.

Best regards,
Leslie E. Robertson Associates

Letter B

Mr. William Palmer
The BCJ Joint Venture
P.O. Box 416, Tuen Mun Central Post Office
New Territories
HONG KONG SAR, CHINA
Via fax/modem: 852/2769-3814

Dear Bill:

Monday was a National Holiday; on returning to the office on Tuesday I was greeted by our two heaviest, tallest and strongest engineers. They held me by my heels, upside-down . . . but, even with a severe shaking, that greenstuff failed to tumble from my pockets. Now there is talk of the breaking of my fingers, one-by-one, in remembrance of each passing day. A bucket and a bag of pre-mixed concrete sits in my little office and the East River is just two blocks away.

Please exhibit compassion for this errant engineer by providing grist for our mills, oil for our bearings, wind for our sails—money for our bankers.

Best regards,
Leslie E. Robertson Associates

Speeches

Once established in an overseas nation, with a project well in hand, visiting principals are sometimes asked to speak at business, governmental, or professional functions. Contrary to the more informal delivery based on a few notes, as recommended in chapter 13, here it is prudent to write out your remarks beforehand and have them checked by a local colleague.

Other Qualifying Factors

The design and construction team on large overseas projects is typically composed of individuals and firms from all over the globe. Coordinating the process, with its array of different time zones, languages, and work methods, demands meticulous management. Thus communications, whether through the written word or by voice, are a critical component of success. Follow these pointers:

Recruit the ideal employee—a local design professional trained in the United States or other English-speaking nation;

Vet all written material for potential misinterpretation of words, phrases, and usage;

Become familiar with the host nation's culture and values;

Keep written material simple: eliminate pages, sections, paragraphs, sentences, or words that don't contribute to the message and that could raise the odds on a gaffe finding its way into the text.

For style guidelines in expressing currencies, measurements, time zones, and phone numbers in overseas correspondence, including e-mail, refer to *WIRED Style* (see Resources).

How to Measure Impact

Ernest Hemingway would turn over in his grave at the idea of using formulas to measure the quality of writing. Quality, he would say, is determined by the writer, by critics to a degree, and by the public.

He would be right. But that doesn't lessen the benefits of monitoring and measuring writing quality. It serves everyone—design firms, public and corporate facility staffs, the professional and general design media, the building product manufacturing and advertising community, design students and faculty, and, above all, the reader.

Managers in each of these groups should commit regularly—once a year at least—to monitoring their communication program. Do this by gathering representative samples of your entire printed and on-line output. Then subject each item to rigorous evaluation of content and format. Include in the review a marketing principal, a cooperative client, and, if possible, an impartial expert. This process alone will help principals and staff realize that quality standards apply as much to communication as to design.

Some years ago New York–based designer Ivan Chermayeff and I devised a set of editorial and graphic judging criteria. The criteria are flexible; you should modify them to fit the printed, CD-ROM, or on-line product you are judging. Here is an updated, abridged excerpt of these criteria:

- Planning, organizational logic
  Are the contents logically organized?
  Is the organization clearly expressed through graphics?
- Reader's wayfinding
  Are charts, tables, and matrices easily understood by the layperson?
  Are titles and headlines clearly worded?
  Are visual devices (pull-quotes, decks, subheads) used as aids to readers?
  Are illustrations clearly captioned?
  Are paragraphs limited to comfortable reading length (15 to 20 lines)?
  On the Web site, is there a logical progression of content from the home or "splash" page to hyperlinks and on to the final screen? Are navigation bars provided?
- Style
  Are words and sentences short and devoid of jargon (see the eight principles of good writing in chapter 1)
  Are spelling, punctuation, and abbreviation consistent?

Is the writing geared to the level of understanding of the audience's least informed reader?

Is the message clear?

• Illustrations

Are photographs of the appropriate quality for the medium (print, on-line, video)?

Are floor plans and other line drawings sharp, uncluttered, properly labeled, and equipped with scales and orientation indicators?

• Production quality

Is the paper stock appropriate to the purpose of the item? (Brochures can lose points for a design firm because they may be seen as too lavishly produced for a modestly financed client. Others suffer, by contrast, because they might seem stingily produced for a patron with luxury tastes.)

Is the printing good, not smudged?

Are the four process colors printed in good register, with no individual colors showing at the edges?

On a promotional CD-ROM or Web site, are images clear? Was the content chosen to minimize downloading delay by accommodating the audience's probable bandwidth?

• Sparkle

Is the overall impact one of freshness, imagination, originality?

We also devised a scoring method for judging editorial and graphic quality. Each item is rated on a scale from -3 to +3. Best is +3. Each of the columns—one for editorial, one for graphic quality—is then added up, and overall averages computed. (In the example below, numbers are imaginary, not based on an actual item.)

Subject	Editorial	Graphic Score
Planning, organizational logic	+ 2	+1
Reader's wayfinding	+ 2	0
Style	0	0
Illustrations	NA	-1
Production quality	NA	+3
Sparkle	+ 2	+2
Averages (rounded off)	1.5	1.0

Measuring Written Text

There are several ways to measure a written text. Assess clarity by selecting one or more representative samples from an article, letter, or other item; then compute an index of quality by applying an arithmetical formula.

The best known among these is the cannily labeled Fog Index, devised by the late Robert Gunning. It rewards clarity by penalizing you for using words that run to too many syllables. You are also penalized for overly long sentences. The index is tied to the presumed level of comprehension of the audience; this is measured by years of schooling. The Fog Index works as below.

1. Select a 100-word passage.
2. Count the number of words of three syllables or more.
3. Count the average number of words per sentence.
4. Add items 2 and 3, then multiply the result by 0.4.
5. The result is your Fog Index.

The Fog Index corresponds to the years of schooling required of the reader. Thus a Fog Index of 17 presumes 17 years of schooling.

Typical Fog Indexes of magazines scanned since 1996 are *People* magazine: 12; *Metropolis*: 13–18; *Architecture*: 15–20; *Architectural Record*: 15–20. For more information on the subject, see *How to Take the Fog out of Business Writing* in the Resources section.

Consider the following scenario. You manage marketing communications in your firm. You have recently come across examples of correspondence that, in your view, lack the kind of quality and impact on which your firm should pride itself. To bolster your point, you decide to compute a Fog Index on a sample passage. Having done that, edit the sample to improve its rating.

Applying the Fog Index

Sample passage (before editing):

"The undersigned and her collaborating team members undertake to implement the necessary contract documents for your secondary level educational facility in the requested time frame of 35 workweeks, with the understanding that in the eventuality of your adding programmatic elements to the scope of work, the completion date will be subject to postponement commensurate with the extent of the aforementioned scope increase. Nevertheless our firm has achieved an excellent level of accomplishment in its confrontations with difficult schedule requirements, and we feel to the highest degree confident that should this eventuality occur we will satisfy the demands of your committee to its satisfaction." [103 words]

Same passage, with words of three syllables or more shown underlined:

"The <u>undersigned</u> and her <u>collaborating</u> team members <u>undertake</u> to <u>implement</u> the <u>necessary</u> contract <u>documents</u> for your <u>secondary</u> level <u>educational</u> <u>facility</u> in the <u>requested</u> time frame of 35 workweeks, with the <u>understanding</u> that in the <u>eventuality</u> of your adding <u>programmatic</u> <u>elements</u> to the scope of work, the <u>completion</u> date will be subject to <u>postponement</u> <u>commensurate</u> with the extent of the <u>aforementioned</u> scope increase. <u>Neverthe</u><u>less</u> our firm has achieved an <u>excellent</u> level of <u>accomplishment</u> in its <u>confrontations</u> with <u>difficult</u> schedule <u>requirements</u>, and we feel to the highest degree <u>confident</u> that should this <u>eventuality</u> occur we will <u>satisfy</u> the demands of your <u>committee</u> to its <u>satis</u><u>faction</u>."

Note that the long-word count is 29. The sentence count is 2, making the average sentence length $103 \div 2 = 51.5$. Using Robert Gunning's formula, we find

1. Length of sample: 103 words
2. Number of long words: 29
3. Average sentence length: 51.5 words
4. $(29 + 51.5) \times 0.4\colon = 32.2$

The passage yields a daunting Fog Index of 32.2.

Sample passage after editing:

"Our project team commits to completing required contract documents for your high school within the stipulated 35 workweeks. Please realize that should you choose to add elements to the scope of work, the completion date may be delayed. The more modest the changes, the shorter the delay. Despite this risk, our firm has an excellent track record of meeting tough schedule demands. Thus we feel most confident that should you choose to enlarge your scope, we will still meet the time demands of your committee." [85 words]

After editing, the Fog Index drops to a more palatable 10.4. A swift scan reveals a long-word count of 9, and an average sentence length of $85 \div 5 = 17$ words. Thus $9 + 17 = 26$, and when multiplied by 0.4 yields a score of 10.4. Note that in the editing process the length of the original passage dropped from 103 to 85, which in itself helped to reduce the Index.

Building on this example, select a half-dozen samples from your arsenal of communications products. Consider an item of e-mail correspondence, the executive summary from a recent report or proposal, the text from a design award submittal, a memo to your staff, or a midproject letter to a client. Identify one or more 100-word passages in each item and compute the Fog Indexes. Next, take those same passages, edit them to replace the unnecessary long words, shorten the sentences, then recompute the Fog Index. Share the findings with your staff.

Editing a Text

You can usually make a silk purse out of a literary sow's ear by means of shrewd editing. The act of editing covers several levels of effort. It can begin and end with simple editing for punctuation, spelling, and factual accuracy. It can build up to major surgery when it entails replacing words, cutting sentences, and even rearranging entire paragraphs.

Supervisors in many professions are required to edit subordinates' writing, including design firms; public, institutional, or corporate facilities agencies; design schools; and magazines. Newcomers to editing should heed the following editing pointers:

Identify the text's precise intent.

Read the text through once; avoid getting bogged down in detail.

Reread the text and make any major changes of structure, such as moving paragraphs or cutting out chunks of text that detract from the desired effect.

Edit in detail, changing the order of sentences, replacing needlessly long words, and clarifying jargon. Check for spelling and correct usage (every firm or organization should have a style guide on hand; see the Resources). Verify factual accuracy.

Reread what you have, and make final corrections. Check especially the opening paragraph (does it sing?) and the closing paragraph (does the text take its leave on the right note?).

Note that any tinkering with someone else's text can ruffle their ego. Be gentle with the author, but not with the text.

The editing process varies according to whether you do it on paper or on a computer screen. On paper you can leave an editing trail for the author by using a colored pen or pencil and writing editorial queries in the margins. The author or publisher then inputs the changes on screen, perhaps after arguing over the changes.

If you edit directly on screen, the trail is lost (unless you have access to publishing software that lets you color-code outtake material). If you are pressed for time, and don't intend to stand on ceremony with the author, you can edit the text faster by working directly on screen.

Much editing is still done on paper using traditional editing. See the following example of pre- and post-editing.

Before

"The undersigned and her collaborating team members undertake to implement the necessary contract documents for your secondary level educational facility in the requested time frame of 35 workweeks, with the understanding that in the eventuality of your adding programmatic elements to the scope of work, the completion date will be subject to postponement commensurate with the extent of the aforementioned scope increase. Nevertheless our firm has achieved an excellent level of accomplishment in its confrontations with difficult schedule requirements, and we feel to the highest degree confident that should this eventuality occur we will satisfy the demands of your committee to its satisfaction."

Example	Mark	Meaning
Choose paper with imagination.	ℰ	take out
Choose paper with imagination.	⌒	close up
Choose paper with imagination.	○⩚	insert letter
Choose paper with imagination.	#⩚	insert space
Choose paper with imagination.	h⩚	change letter
Choose paper with imagination.	STET	keep as is
Choose paper with imagination.	∿	reverse letters
Choose with paper imagination.	⌒⬭	transpose word
Choose paper with imagination.	]	move in, align
Choose paper with imagination.	[	move out, align
Choose paper with imagination.	⑂	start paragraph
Choose paper with imagination.	/l.c.	lower case
choose paper with imagination.	≡u.c.	upper case
Choose paper with imagination.	ITAL	italicize
Choose paper with imagination.	══	set in small capitals
Choose paper with imagination.	≡	set all in capitals
Choose paper with imagination.	∼∼∼	set all in bold
Choose paper with imagination.	⌐⌐⌐	align, raise and lower
Choose paper with imagination.	⩚	use a ∧ to add a ,
Choose paper with imagination.	⊙	use a ○ to add a .
Choose paper with imagination.	⊙	use a ○ to add a ; or :
Choose paper with imagination!/	!/	use a / to add a ! or ?
Choose paper with imagination.	-/	use a / to add a -
Choose paper (with imagination.)	(/)	use a / to add ( )
Choose paper [with imagination.]	[/]	use a / to add [ ]
Choose paper with imagination.	⩔	use a ∨ to add ' and ""
Choose paper with imagination.	▢	Em quad space or indent

Common proofreading marks.

The undersigned and her collaborating team members undertake to implement the necessary contract documents for your secondary level educational facility in the requested time frame of 35 workweeks, with the understanding that in the eventuality of your adding programmatic elements to the scope of work, the completion date will be subject to postponement commensurate with the extent of the aforementioned scope increase. Nevertheless our firm has achieved an excellent level of accomplishment in its confrontations with difficult schedule requirements, and we feel to the highest degree confident that should this eventuality occur we will satisfy the demands of your committee to its satisfaction.

The edited copy.

After

"Our project team commits to completing required contract documents for your high school within the stipulated 35 workweeks. Please realize that should you choose to add elements to the scope of work, the completion date may be delayed. The more modest the changes, the shorter the delay. Despite this risk, our firm has an excellent track record of meeting tough schedule demands. Thus we feel most confident that should you choose to enlarge your scope, we will still meet the time demands of your committee."

Conclusion

The format of the written word will continue to change, with the ascendancy of the nontraditional formats of video, on-line, and multimedia. Design firms that today rely mainly on paper for producing brochures, proposals, correspondence, and reports will increasingly offer them in electronic formats, such as on a Web site or a CD-ROM.

Good writing is not obsolete. As suggested in chapter 12, good writing will become even more important, because the conciseness of the on-line medium demands a higher focus on economy of words and the arrangement of words for maximum impact. We see in some ways a throwback to the age of the telegram; when using more words than you need, the cost is on you.

A Selective Listing of Design Media

Addresses and names are omitted due to frequent changes. For current information, consult directories and Websites at the end of this list. (N) denotes a newsletter.

Professional Journals
@issue:, the journal of business and design, Boston, MA
AIArchitect, Washington, DC (N)
ANY, New York, NY
Architectural Record, New York, NY
Architecture, New York, NY
BSA, newsletter of Boston Society of Architects, Boston, MA (N)
Builder, Washington, DC
Building Design & Construction, Des Plaines, IL
Civil Engineering, New York, NY
Construction Specifier, Alexandria, VA
Design Intelligence, Reston, VA (N)
Engineering News-Record, New York, NY
Harvard Design Magazine, Cambridge, MA
ID, New York, NY
Interior Design, New York, NY
Interiors, New York, NY
Interiors and Sources, North Palm Beach, FL
International periodicals—see *Ulrich's*
Journal of Architectural Education, Washington, DC
Journal of Architectural Historians, Cambridge, MA
Landscape Architecture, Washington, DC
Metropolis, New York, NY
OCULUS, New York Chapter AIA newsletter, New York, NY (N)
Places, Pratt Institute School of Architecture, Brooklyn, NY
Planning, Chicago, IL 60603
Regional architectural publications (including *Texas Architect,* Austin; *ArchitectureBoston, Architecture Minnesota,* Minneapolis; *Architecture South,* Franklin, TN; *Wisconsin Architect,* Madison; *Florida Architect,* Tallahassee)
Residential Architect, Washington, DC
The Zweig Letter, A/E/P management newsletter, Natick, MA (N)

Client Journals
American School & University Magazine, Overland Park, KS
American School Board Journal, Alexandria, VA

Facilities Design & Management, New York, NY
Health Facilities, Chicago, IL
Hospitality Design, New York, NY

Special-interest Journals
Architectural Digest, Los Angeles, CA
Garden Design, New York, NY
House & Garden, New York, NY
Preservation, Washington, DC

Student Journals
Crit, Washington, DC (published by the American Institute of Architecture Students)

Periodicals and Directories
Burrell's Media Directory of Magazines and Newspapers
Publicity Directory for the Design, Engineering, and Building Industries, by the Fuessler Group, Boston, MA
Ulrich's International Periodicals Directory (R. R. Bowker)
Standard Rate and Data Services (SRDS) (Business Edition), Des Plaines, IL. Lists all audited business and trade periodicals.

On-line Journals and Indexes
www.saed.kent.edu (on-line architectural magazine)
www.archindex.com (digital version of the annual printed index. Includes back indexes to 1982)
www.cornishproductions.com (on-line magazine for design and architecture)

Resources

Writing

Bambery, Jane Brown; Jones, Paul Davis; Raymond, Cary G. *Insider's Guide to Getting into Print*. Natick, MA: Mark Zweig & Associates, 1994. Solid guide to publicity for A/E/P and environmental consulting firms.

Branwyn, Gareth (overheard by). Jargon Watch: *A Pocket Dictionary for the Jitterati*. San Francisco, CA: HardWired, 1997. A lively, five-by-three-and-a-half-inch nano-lexicon of the latest cool jargon. My favorites are *domainism* ("Internet prejudice. Judging others on the basis of how cool/uncool their email address is. See also Domain Dropping."), and *Ohnosecond* ("that minuscule fraction of time in which you realize you've just made a BIG mistake").

Brereton, John C., and Mansfield, Margaret A. *Writing on the Job*. New York: W. W. Norton, 1997. Practical writing guide in publisher's "pocket guide" series is for all occupations and professions. Amply equipped with examples that cover both format and content. Chapters include these themes: letters and memos; news and feature stories; interviews; press releases and kits; flyers and brochures; reports and proposals; manuals, agendas, and minutes; resumes and cover letters. Includes a useful chapter on editing a text. The slim format fits handily into a pocket.

Chappell, David. *Report Writing for Architects*. London: Architectural Press, 1984. Sample reports and guidelines, geared mainly to U.K. practices.

Clinton, Patrick. *Guide to Writing for the Business Press*. New York: The Business Press Foundation, and Lincolnwood, IL: NTC Business Books, 1996. Not, as you might think, a treatise on getting published, but rather a practical handbook for writers and editors.

Gunning, R., and Kallan, R. A. *How to Take the Fog Out of Business Writing*. Chicago: Dartnell Corp., 1994. Includes a neat, easy-to-compute formula that determines the amount of "fog" in your firm's written output.

Hale, Constance, ed. *WIRED Style: Principles of English Usage in the Digital Age*. San Francisco, CA: HardWired, 1996. Funky work that tells you where it's all at as you, in Hale's words, "constantly [navigate] the shifting verbal currents of the post-Gutenberg era." A tidal wave of new words, new meanings, and acronyms has hit the English language since the onset of the Internet. This coolly designed, boxed book—prevailing colors are salmon, lime green, and black—shows how style is being shaped by modern digital custom. Includes breathless listings of digital jargon (*Easter* egg, a "small cartoon, animation, or other feature hidden by a programmer in the code of a game or application to show off programming skill"); capitalized names (*Deep Blue,* for IBM's chess grandmaster); and acronyms. *WIRED'*s dictum: "Write the way people talk. Don't insist on 'standard' English. Use the vernacular, especially of the world you're writing about [with care—Ed.]. Avoid lowest-common-denominator editing: don't sanitize and don't homogenize."

Interstate Transportation Trainers. *Truck Drivers Dictionary.* Jamaica, NY: Interstate Transportation Trainers, Inc., P.O. Box 229, Jamaica, NY 11431, nd. Catchy insights into the way truck drivers talk to each other.

Johnson, Steven. *Interface Culture: How New technology Transforms the Way We Create and Communicate.* San Francisco, CA: Harper, 1997. Software designers as creators and manipulators.

Kliment, Stephen A. "But What Do You *Mean?" Architecture,* November 1996. A fruitless search for clarity in contemporary writing.

——."Eschewing Obfuscation: Ideas for Cleaning Up Our Language Act." *Architectural Record,* April 1992. Nuf said.

Minto, Barbara. *The Pyramid Principle: Logic in Writing and Thinking.* London: Minto International Inc., 1981. A basic exposé on how to organize your thoughts to build a clear, logical message. A classic.

Padjen, Elizabeth. "Writing a Winning Proposal," *Architecture,* February 1998. Practical common sense.

Strunk, W., Jr., and White, E. B. *The Elements of Style,* 3rd ed. Boston: Allyn & Bacon, 1979. Classic, no-nonsense, 72-page book has fed the principles of good writing to generations of American college students (first edition: 1935). Focus is on good usage of the English language, putting you on a fast-track to clear writing. Celebrated rules include: "write in a way that comes naturally"; "write with nouns and verbs"; "do not overstate"; "do not explain too much"; "avoid fancy words."

The Associated Press. *The Associated Press Stylebook and Libel Manual.* New York: The Associated Press, 1998. Complete guide to newspaper journalism.

——. *The Word: An Associated Press Guide to Good Newswriting.* New York: The Associated Press, 1997.

University of Chicago Press. *The Chicago Manual of Style: The Essential Guide for Writers, Editors, and Publishers,* 14th ed. University of Chicago Press, 1993. Someone said it matters less how you spell and punctuate than to be consistent. This bible of writers and editors tells you one way to go about it.

Graphics

Linton, Harold. *Portfolio Design.* New York: W. W. Norton, 1996. Practical, down-to-earth handbook on the design of portfolios and the underlying marketing, or self-marketing, objectives. Covers such topics as graphic concept, page layout, and image selection.

Wurman, Richard Saul. *Information Architects.* New York: Graphis, Inc./Watson Guptill Publications, 1997. Lavish, high-style graphics demonstrate architect Wurman's viewpoint that a disciplined process of logic and common sense are at the heart of any good explanation. Includes some 100 examples of information design, using examples of graphic design by the world's top graphic designers—all accompanied by Wurman's good, clear text. Wurman coined the term "Information Architect" to describe those—not necessarily architects—who work with words and pictures. His rules for understanding include: it's more important to get your point across than to be beautiful; edit drastically—don't include more information than the situation requires; try to gear new information to information the reader already has.

On-line

Charles, Curtis B., and Brown, Karen M. *Multimedia Marketing for Design Firms.* New York: John Wiley, 1996. Computers are the great equalizers. They allow small design firms to compete with large firms in many ways. One example is marketing. This book describes computer-aided or "desktop" publishing, then shows how to use it to develop such marketing tools as promotional diskettes, CD-ROMs, Web sites, and interactive multimedia. Book comes with a CD-ROM with multimedia software and demos.

Doherty, Paul. *Cyberplaces: The Internet Guide for Architects, Engineers, and Contractors.* Kingston, MA: R. S. Means, 1997. Accompanied by a CD-ROM and Web access. Guide to training, applications, sites.

Frost, Susan, ed. "Netspeak: a Glossary of Internet Terms," *SMPS Marketer,* February 1996. Two pages of the most common terms.

Novitski, B. J. "The Architecture of Cyberspace," *Architectural Record,* November 1997. The Web as a medium of expression by design professionals.

Padjen, Elizabeth. "Spinning Your Web Page," *Architecture,* May 1997. Nice, snappy, five-page overview of several architects' Web sites and interviews with the partners.

Robbins, Alan. "E-Mail: Lean, Mean and Making Its Mark." *New York Times,* 11 May 1997. Shows the impact of e-mail on style, grammar, and, yes, etiquette.

Scharf, Dean. *HTML: Visual Quick Reference,* 2d ed. QUE, 1996. You need HyperText Markup Language (HTML) to mark up your text files so they can be read from your Web site. If you decide to "do it yourself" to create your Web site, this little book is a good guide to handling the text.

Siegel, David. *Creating Killer Web Sites: The Art of Third-Generation Site Design.* Indianapolis: Hayden Books, 1997. On the Web: www.killersites.com. Designing Web sites that work. To quote the author: "Third-generation sites use metaphor and visual theme to entice and guide. They strive to make a site feel familiar and easy to navigate, with clear typography and high production values." The third generation supersedes first-generation sites, which were mostly type only, with slow modems and monochrome monitors. Second-generation sites had icons replacing words, tile images replacing a gray background, colored borders around images, and headlines replaced by banners. The book covers both the psychology and techniques for designers. Pretty technical, but useful as an in-depth gauge of advances in the Web site design field.

CD-ROM

ClipWORDS. Peoria, Illinois: Dynamic Graphics, 1997. Includes 20K selections of snappy headlines and phrases. For writers, designers, and marketing people. PC and Macintosh compatible.

Broadcast

The Associated Press Broadcast News Handbook. New York: The Associated Press, 1998. Tips for writing for the air.

Web Sites: A Selective Guide

www.acsa-arch.org (activities in U.S. architectural education)
www.aecnet.com (Internet access for building industry)
www.aiaonline.com (includes listing of AIA member firms' Web sites)
www.arch.buffalo.edu/pairc/ (general planning and architectural sources)
www.architectsusa.com (listings of architects; added features pending)

www.careermosaic.com/cm/crc/crc15.html (one of several resume-writing
    guides)

www.cornishproductions.com (on-line magazine Design /Architecture)

www.enr.com (publication listings)

www.epa.gov (sources on environmental issues)

www.gsa.gov/pbs/pc/hw-files/254-255.htm (all you need to know about
    SF254 and 255 files)

www.ld.com/cbd.shtml (Commerce Business Daily on-line)

www.nscee.edu/unlv/Libraries/arch/rsrce/webrsrce/index.html (publications,
    directory listings on architecture and design)

www.resumix.com/resume/resumeindex.html (one of several resume-writing
    guides)

www.yahoo.com (good search machine)

Credits

Color photos by Patricia Lambert.

Page 25. Top left: © 1995 SMMA. Top right, bottom left and right: © Walker Group/CNI 1997.

Page 26. Top left and right: © Walker Group/CNI 1997. Below: © Flack+Kurtz Consulting Engineers, LLP 1997.

Page 27. Top: Moore/Andersson Architects; photo,Timothy Hursley. Bottom, clockwise from center: William Rawn Associates, architects; photo, Steve Rosenthal. Buttrick White & Burtis, architects; photo, Matt Wargo. Bohlin Cywinski Jackson, architects; photo, Matt Wargo. Hardy Holzman Pfeiffer Associates, architects; photo, Elliott Kaufman.

Page 28. Top: Thomson and Rose house: Peter Vanderwarker. Bottom: Childs Bertman Tseckares, Inc., architects; clockwise from top in photo: Peter Vanderwarker, Edward Jacoby, Peter Vanderwarker, Edward Jacoby; center in photo: Ronnette Riley Architect/Dub Rogers. Center: © Venturi, Scott Brown and Associates, Inc. 1997, 1996.

Page 29. Center: © 1974 Cahners Books, a division of Cahners Publishing Co., Inc. Top and bottom: © The Ove Arup Partnership, 1997.

Page 30. Top: © 1996 The Potlatch Corporation. From vol. 2, no. 2 of *@issue: The Journal of Business and Design,* published by Corporate Design Foundation and sponsored by Potlatch Corporation's Northwest Paper Division. Design by Pentagram Design, Inc. Bottom left: Reprinted from *Engineering News-Record,* January 19, 1998, copyright The McGraw-Hill Companies, Inc. All rights reserved. Photo: © Texas Department of Transportation, 1998. Bottom right: Reproduced from *Architecture* magazine, January 1998, page 132. © 1998 BPI Communications, Inc.

Page 31. © Emap Construct 1998.

Page 32. Top: ©1997 Primavera Systems, Inc.

Index